An Introduction to Military Ethics

An Introduction to Military Ethics

A Reference Handbook

Bill Rhodes

Contemporary Military, Strategic, and Security Issues

PRAEGER SECURITY INTERNATIONAL
An Imprint of ABC-CLIO, LLC

A B C CLIO

Santa Barbara, California • Denver, Colorado • Oxford, England

Copyright 2009 by Bill Rhodes

Library of Congress Cataloging-in-Publication Data

Rhodes, Bill, 1959–
    An introduction to military ethics : a reference handbook / Bill Rhodes.
        p. cm. — (Contemporary military, strategic, and security issues)
    Includes bibliographical references and index.
    ISBN 978-0-313-35046-7 (hardcover : acid-free paper) — ISBN 978-0-313-35047-4 (ebook)   1. Military ethics—Handbooks, manuals, etc.   2. War—Moral and ethical aspects.   3. Just war doctrine.   I. Title.
    U22.R46   2009
    172'.42—dc22   2009022274

13   12   11   10   9   1   2   3   4   5

This book is also available on the World Wide Web as an eBook.
Visit www.abc-clio.com for details.

ABC-CLIO, LLC
130 Cremona Drive, P.O. Box 1911
Santa Barbara, California 93116-1911

This book is printed on acid-free paper ∞

Manufactured in the United States of America

The opinions in this book are those of the author and do not necessarily reflect those of the U.S. Air Force, the Department of Defense, or any other component of the United States government.

Contents

Preface

This work surveys some of the most basic and enduring problems of military ethics. The first chapter outlines some of the fundamental concepts of applied ethics and is intended to provide the philosophical groundwork for framing practical issues. The second chapter offers a historical overview of the Western Just War Tradition from the ancients to the 20th century. Chapter 3 takes on the unique aspects of military life, military members, and the use of military force in the name of a political community. Chapter 4 examines the ethical aspects of the resort to armed force in the contemporary arena. The fifth chapter surveys the conduct of armed hostilities and the ethical underpinnings of the rules of warfare. Chapter 6 is concerned with emerging controversies and challenges faced by modern militaries, such as humanitarian intervention and dealing with nonstate actors, including terrorism. Chapter 7 is devoted to cultural issues in the modern military, including controversies over the full integration of women into the services. The final chapter addresses professional identity for the modern military.

The issues this book addresses are complex, and reasonable people can disagree over many of them. Such disagreement offers fertile intellectual ground for learning more about the issues themselves, as well as for making progress in terms of policy choices. If this book stimulates thoughtful discussion among practitioners, it will have accomplished its purpose.

Acknowledgments

Although I had enjoyed academic engagement with the field of practical military ethics in college, my interest was stimulated by my experiences as a young military officer working in the Pentagon in the early 1980s. What I experienced there deserves acknowledgment as a spur to a lifelong interest in military ethics that has made this book possible.

I was fortunate to be sponsored by the United States Air Force for both an MA and a PhD in Philosophy, and I wish to express my gratitude for the opportunity. Few militaries would devote such resources to the academic study of ethics.

With those thoughts in place, I wish to acknowledge gratefully the contributions of many who have helped me with information, criticisms, and advice. These include Aaron Belkin, Jesse Carter, Jim Cook, Martin Cook, Edie Disler, Carl Ficarrotta, Shawn Gibson, Charley Hudlin, Jim Lauerman, Ann Rhodes, Kelly Shaw, Rhonda Smith, Kathy Thomas, Cynthia Wright, and Dan Zupan. As important as these people have been to the completion of this book, the errors in it are my own.

Ethics in the Real World

This book is an introduction to the study of military ethics. Unlike many books in the field, it does not seek to stake out particular positions or to make advances in problematic conceptual areas. Instead, it provides an overview of the moral challenges faced by military members and the methods and insights that ethics provides in reply. The problems are daunting, the responses imperfect, and the stakes high. Indeed, it is likely that the consequences of incompetence or bad luck in military pursuits are more devastating than in any other except, perhaps, statecraft. This suggests that studying military ethics can be depressing, even seemingly futile, but most who specialize in the field suggest otherwise. Military ethics can generate optimism by providing organizing principles for understanding the nature of military conflict and for developing approaches to help minimize war's evils. Applying the rigorous methods that characterize serious philosophy enables military ethicists to perform systematic analyses of challenges and to formulate policy responses to improve the lot of all. That military ethics is philosophically rigorous does not imply that it belongs only in the classroom or graduate seminar. To be sure, some of the theoretical underpinnings for the field involve intricacies in metaphysics and epistemology, but as a whole, military ethics is directed toward understanding and resolving real-world problems that demand decisive responses. Accordingly, the concepts and methods in this book are intended for application in the real world in which actions have consequences, some of which may be of historical magnitude. Indeed, it is there that an understanding of applied ethics actually matters the most. In the practical world of military life, there is no adequate substitute for honest assessments, wise judgments, and committed, competent, action.

Even when faced with the ill will, prideful ignorance, and organized destruction that characterize international conflict, some decisions are demonstrably better than others. Wars, as awful as they are, would be worse in the absence of military ethics.

CHAPTER 1

An Overview of Applied Ethics for the Military

Like much of applied philosophy, military ethics rests somewhat uneasily on a complex array of ambiguities and tensions. This is due in part to the nature of the challenges that face the military and in part because the term *ethics* means different things to different people. To get a stake in the ground, it is sensible to examine the nature of ethics itself to see just what it means in this book.

Defining Ethics

Making choices is at the heart of ethics. People do not think of the weather as being "ethical" or "unethical" because they do not think of the earth as an agent. That is, it does not exercise any sort of freedom of choice, and so it is not considered to be accountable for what happens. Weather, like other phenomena in the physical world, is determined by natural forces; it does not occur because someone chose to make it occur. Ordinary language reflects this fact: it would be strange to say that something in nature "ought" to be otherwise, but it is common to say that persons "ought" to have behaved differently than they did. Likewise, no one speaks of trees or rocks as deserving ethical praise or blame, but those sorts of judgments are used frequently in reference to people. In short, ethics presupposes choice, and choice presupposes at least some measure of freedom.

As an organized discipline, ethics emphasizes systematically finding the best reasons for making particular choices or crafting particular policies. It can be thought of as a guide to using one's freedom to choose. Studying ethics helps people distinguish between better and worse reasons behind particular courses of action and to choose the most reasonable path in light of values such as political freedom and facts such as the uneven distribution of military power. Military ethics applies to a specialized realm and has developed principles appropriate to it over time to help guide future practices. Although there are conceptual rough edges, overall these principles make good practical sense to experienced military professionals and statesmen, and they also make good theoretical sense to academic philosophers.

Critical thinking is the coin of the ethicist's realm. Although the real world of making choices is the touchstone of ethics, the study of ethics is often "idealized" in theoretical terms in much the same way that Newtonian thinking idealizes the physical world through mathematics. No thoughtful professional ethicist would suggest that the real world actually looks exactly like the theories and principles covered in this book. Instead, ethics helps to *illuminate* the real world and provide organized, reliable tools that have proven useful in handling problems the real world presents. In the field of military ethics in particular, clean and tidy solutions to problems are sometimes at hand, but often all options have some regrettable aspects. Military ethicists are quite familiar with the fact that life is not fair. Sadly, and too frequently, the best choice for a military member is still a bad one. Careful readers will sense a note of tragedy in much of the writing in military ethics; romantic delusions about military glory or windy political rhetoric have little place in a mature approach to the issues.

It is important to understand that ethics is a normative discipline. It deals in values and how to choose among them. It does not aim to *describe* the world of human conduct as it is, but rather to *prescribe* how things ought to be, providing a roadmap for informing decisions and improving the reality of life. Ethics is by nature about aspirations for humanity at both individual and communal levels. If "life is what you make it," studying ethics helps provide the blueprint. Ethicists acknowledge that humans and their institutions are flawed, but they also suppose that they can improve if decisions follow careful ethical analysis. Indeed, if it were not for recognition of those flaws, there would be little point in worrying over ethics.

An imperfect world does not constitute a reason to ignore ethics. Particularly in discussions of war, some are prone to dismissing ethics as irrelevant. "This is war" they'll say, and [quoting General Sherman] "war is hell." But the fact that people treat one another badly in war tells us absolutely nothing about whether they *ought* to do so. It is also the case that, as this is being written, some adults are abusing children and someone else is driving drunk. The fact that unethical behavior goes on and is likely to continue does not count against the study of ethics any more than the fact of terminal illness suggests that the study of medicine is pointless. Quite the contrary—the facts of suffering and evil make the study of ethics, and military ethics in particular, all the more worthwhile.

Obstacles

Students of military ethics often struggle with its supposedly universal nature. Many seem to think that what is ethical depends on what community or environment one is in at the time. For example, the military community has practices that civilians do not use such as saluting or requiring men to keep their hair short. And even the same communities change their practices over time. In the late

1970s, women over the rank of captain were extremely rare in the United States military. Today there are many women in the senior officer ranks. So it looks like ethics are relative both to one's community and to history. Moreover, warfare is an extraordinary condition even for communities that anticipate combat and train extensively for it. So in extreme conditions such as war, actions like killing become appropriate while they would never be appropriate over most of one's military career or indeed over the totality of most careers. Sometimes claims like these are deployed against the very idea of ethics itself. One argument runs something like this: "They send little kids against us with grenades in their pockets. If we follow the rules of war, we end up getting our soldiers killed. Therefore, the rules should bind us only if they bind them. And since the rules do not seem to bind our adversary, we would be silly to follow them."

Universal Moral Standards

Military ethicists encounter a more general version of this obstacle when people approach all ethical issues by replying "Who's to say?" This seems to be a good point. After all, who *is* to say what distinguishes right conduct from wrong conduct, or at least better conduct from worse conduct? What gives the ethicist the right to suggest that some practices are morally preferable to others? Who put *them* in charge? Aren't claims about ethics just opinions after all? And, since ethics are relative, isn't any one opinion as good as any other?

The field of military ethics denies this kind of thinking: it is said to apply to all communities, and all persons in them, all the time. In other words, there is nothing relative about what justifies the use of violence—it is universal. Whether a war is justified does not depend on which states are involved, but rather what ethical offenses have been committed and in what manner.

Military ethics exists because some choices really are better than others, even in international relations and war. Much of military ethics concentrates on understanding what makes one policy or choice superior to others. Put another way, military ethics seeks to understand what sorts of good reasons can be offered to support one course of action as being preferable to another. Generally, the reasons offered will be in support of some value—something worth defending.

To start, ethicists often appeal to some facts about the human condition. These facts are referred to in terms of natural laws.[1] These natural laws are not customs, politics, or popular opinion. Natural laws are *natural*—they cannot be changed by humans. One can be ignorant of the natural processes of the weather or biology, but that ignorance does nothing to change the facts. If one is to live well in accordance with nature's laws, one must adapt one's beliefs and activities to those facts. The facts are unlikely to change to accommodate the opinions of persons—no matter how insistent those persons may be. The laws of nature are not matters of opinion, although the opinions about what is true in nature certainly do vary—between cultures, individuals in those cultures, and across time. Many people in the modern United States believe in astrology, but such beliefs do nothing to establish the truth of astrological predictions. One is certainly free to use astrology as a source of insight for preventing and treating disease, but the utility of this approach is questionable at best. Others rely on the laws of biology, chemistry, and physiology to make decisions about health. A good understanding of these laws helps bring about better health in the near-term and also provides a firm basis for research that can provide even more understanding.

This is easy to see in the cases of physical science, but it seems less clear in matters of ethics. Many people grant that there are indeed natural laws in the hard sciences and even in social science, but they remain dubious about universal ethical standards. This skepticism about the universal nature of ethics is often called relativism.

Relativists, as the name suggests, hold that what is ethical is relative to what culture one finds oneself in. For example, in Britain it is proper to drive on the left side of the road, but in the United States it is proper to drive on the right side. The relativist points out that the drivers in each case simply adapt to local customs. Neither custom is better than the other—they are simply different. There are thousands of such differences for the relativist to name. If one crosses state lines in the United States, one will discover that the rules on taxation vary. Some states do not have an income tax, but others do. And there's no need to travel across state lines to find different practices. In most neighborhoods in the United States, there are some people who eat meat while others are vegetarians.

Ethical philosophers have a reply to this line of reasoning. They note that pointing out differences among practices does nothing to suggest that the practices are morally equivalent. All it shows is that different cultures do indeed have different practices. It provides no moral information at all because it is not an ethical or normative claim. It is merely descriptive.

Ethics, by contrast, is a normative discipline. It deals in what *ought* to be. And while the fact that opinions or cultures differ is true, it is merely descriptive. Customs or practices do not provide any information about what *ought* to be; they show what is. The fact that different cultures have different practices contains no normative information. It is merely an accurate description.

Ignorance or disagreement does nothing to establish the absence of a truth of the matter. For example, cigarette smoking kills many people. That one is more likely to die of cancer or emphysema if one smokes than if one does not is evidence of a natural law. People may be ignorant of the relationship and deny it. People may note that smoking is prevalent in some cultures and less so in others. Or they may acknowledge the relationship and decide for themselves whether to smoke. But the law itself is not affected either by ignorance or individual choices. Those who value their health are well advised not to smoke, regardless of their preferences about the matter.

Having shown that the fact of disagreement does not imply that there is no truth, it is easier to understand why the precepts of military ethics are said to bind universally. Some practices inhibit the flourishing of human life, whereas others promote it. Certainly, all things being equal, war is a detriment to humanity. It may not be as great a detriment as some other evils (genocide for example), but it is nonetheless evil. Hence, limiting its frequency and its destructiveness is in the interest of every human being, just as limiting the frequency and severity of disease is in everyone's long-term interest. And just as following certain laws helps to limit illness (avoid smoking and dig the latrine downstream from the drinking water), following the precepts of just war helps to limit war's evils.

Now some may be ignorant of these facts about war. Indeed, there may be political motives to foster ignorance. But this does nothing to alter the facts of the matter.

On Tolerance

Relativists, believing that all moral codes are equal, often move on to suggest that, as no code is any better than another, everyone ought to be tolerant. Of course this is true in the case of most cultural practices. There is no natural reason while driving on the left ought to be preferred over driving on the right. But just because people can give examples showing that some variances in practices ought properly to be tolerated, it does not follow that *all* practices ought to be tolerated. Indeed, suggesting that one ought to tolerate everything leads to a number of problems for relativism.

First, there is something odd about the logic. It has already been shown that one can't conclude that there is no standard of right and wrong from the mere fact that people disagree over what it might be. But there is more. The argument seems to run like this: First it is noted that practices vary among cultures and across history. Then it is concluded that no one set of cultural practices is superior to any other. From this conclusion it is deduced that no one ought to judge another culture's practices as inferior or superior to any other culture's. But this is peculiar, because that last step puts forth a standard that everyone ought to avoid judging cultures as morally superior or inferior. If this standard is no better than any other standard, why should one respect it? If it is better then it contradicts the claim that no one standard is better than another. If it is not better, why should anyone bother to follow it? The conclusions undermine the reasoning that led to them.

Put another way, to suggest that the absence of a universal standard implies that everyone ought to be tolerant is to supply a universal standard after denying that any such thing exists! Suddenly the relativist has provided a universal standard—everyone ought to be tolerant. Put yet another way, if there were nothing wrong with intolerance, why would anyone bother suggesting that everyone ought to be tolerant? To say that intolerance is wrong is to appeal to a moral standard. It makes no sense to say that people "ought" to behave in a tolerant fashion if the very idea of "ought" is denied in the first place? The argument frustrates itself.

Suppose, however, that the relativist's logic is accepted and accordingly any and all practices are to be tolerated. Unhappy results follow on the heels of this deduction, one of which is that everyone would be obligated to tolerate intolerance. Suppose a culture advocated the oppression of women or imprisoning peaceful dissenters. An obligation to tolerate oppression of this sort would permit violations of human rights. Indeed, if tolerance is the ethical standard, then it would be impossible to argue that the genocidal acts committed by Nazi Germany were immoral. Results like these seem seriously counterintuitive, yet they are logical consequences of requiring universal toleration.

Despite the popularity of relativism, few if any military ethicists subscribe to it. Military ethics holds that there are at least some universal standards that ought to be respected even in time of war.

This is not to suggest that military ethics views tolerance as a bad thing, but it is to suggest that putting forth a universal obligation to tolerate any and all practices is self-undermining. Most military ethicists would suggest that different practices ought to be tolerated generally, but some practices or activities ought to be condemned and actively resisted. For example, violent aggression against an unoffending nation should not be tolerated and may constitute a justified cause for resorting to war. At the level of individuals in war, no soldier should deliberately target a noncombatant. Military ethics offers thoughtful arguments for the obligation *not* to tolerate certain behaviors; indeed, it offers reasons to use violence against them and specifies how much violence is appropriate against which sorts of targets.

Universal Standards of Ethics: Three Families of Theories

Tolerance fails as a universal standard for ethics, but there other possibilities worth examining. Most military ethicists would propose at least one of three general avenues of approach to the question of what a universal "good" really is. The first of these, virtue theory, plays an especially important role in defining what sort of person a military member ought to be. The second, consequentialism, also seeks to inform decision making, but in this case the emphasis is on bringing about results that help to increase happiness, or, when that is impossible, at least to decrease unhappiness. The third, deontological theory, serves to inform decisions, especially those affecting fundamental human rights. Military ethics draws on all three of these ethical traditions, as each tradition yields important insights into the practical problems the military life entails.

Virtue Theory

The essential aspects of virtue theory are familiar to most adults, even though they may never have been formally introduced to it as a theory. It relies on each person forthrightly facing a question that is so obviously driven by common sense that it seems easy to overlook: what is the life most worth living?

Although this question is usually associated with the ancient Greek philosopher, Socrates (469–399 BC), it has a distinguished history in Western thought. It occupied much of the work of Plato (429–347 BC), who happened to be one of Socrates's students, and likewise the work of Aristotle (384–322 BC), who can be considered an intellectual successor to Plato. Modern writers such as Alasdair MacIntyre, Alexander Nehemas, and Robert Nozik continue to contribute to the tradition.[2]

This ancient problem of how best to spend one's life generates a variety of complex replies, but certain themes stood out 2,500 years ago as they do today. Among these is a requirement that one must consciously seek the good life—it is unlikely to happen without effort—and that the life sought out must be characterized by excellence, or virtue. In other words, if one is to live well, one ought to think deeply and live fully. This involves making one's talents as perfectly useful as possible and avoiding mistakes that adversely affect one's chosen endeavors.

The ancient Greeks did not use terms like *virtue* as narrowly as moderns might suppose. By a life of excellence or virtue, they simply meant a well-lived life. The specific life most worth living for one individual will vary in some ways from that appropriate to another person. For some, working with their hands is deeply satisfying, whereas others may be better suited to intellectual, political, or even military pursuits. In this sense virtue theory may sound like relativism, but it is not ultimately a relativist theory because it holds one value to be universally good: the well-lived or flourishing life. Individuals may pursue different sorts of careers that are appropriate to their individual talents and so engage in different pursuits, but all agree that they wish to live well. Doing so requires people to develop and use their talents to the fullest, to enjoy their communities, and to be fulfilled.

People tend to overlook what is probably the most important fact of anyone's existence—its finitude. Everyone's lifespan is limited. Individuals may not know when they will die, but they can be certain that they *will* die. This means that every life lasts for a finite quantity of hours. As a practical matter, people have choices to make as to how to spend these hours. These choices are shaped by individual characteristics; each individual has certain gifts and limitations provided by nature. If one is short the choice of professional basketball player may not be the best, but if one also has a facility with languages and an interest in international relations, a career in the foreign service might be appropriate. Although people are not entirely free to live any life they may wish, they can, as a practical matter, usually create lives for themselves that will be very much worth living. But they can also fail to do so.

One way to think about virtue theory is by analogy to buying a car. They buyer knows that he will have the car for a limited time, that buying one car means that he will not be owning a different car than the one he bought and that not all cars are equally suited to his particular needs and desires. What many consumers do in the face of these facts is research the options. They look at magazines or consumer reviews and seek to compare one car to another before they commit. Then, they must also execute the wise decision. They have to buy the car and care for it consistently if they are to get the value desired and expected. Virtue theorists suggest doing something similar regarding living lives. No one can avoid the continuous drawdown of the remaining hours of living. People live out their lives whether or not they take an active role in shaping them. Just as one ought to research the experiences others have had with various makes of cars, so one would be well advised to research just what life seems most worth living. That way, one may make educated decisions about how to live.

Some, sadly, do not live well. Often this is due to lacking the preconditions necessary to a flourishing life. Most modern readers can only imagine what it must have been like to be persecuted because of ethnicity or to face starvation daily. Many people have been born into conditions of such oppression or poverty or both that their chances to live a genuinely good life are constrained. For some who have had the bad luck to be born into such conditions, the first step is to free themselves from that oppression. This is difficult or impossible for all too many, at least without help. But if sufficient freedom is presupposed, then the cause of the failure lies elsewhere—it lies in persons themselves. And the cause is identifiable—flawed character.

To live well, one must embody at least two skills: the ability to choose well and then the ability to act on those choices. These are the two critical components of character and as such a weakness in either can compromise character. This is one reason why virtue theory concentrates on who a person ought to *be* in contrast to other theories that concentrate more on what people ought to *do*.

All of the public military academies, as well as many other schools in the United States, devote at least some of their resources to character development. To appreciate why, it is helpful to understand the interplay of virtue theory and modern life in a democracy.

Generally speaking, it is sometime during the teenage years that people's choices begin to have long-lasting effects on the rest of their lives. For many, decisions made in the teens or twenties have determined much of the subsequent 20, 30, or 60 years. And yet, given the perspective of middle or advanced age, it is clear to many that people tend to grow much wiser with time. Many of the most consequential decisions, such as choosing a career or a spouse, are made in young adult life when people are usually least wise. As a consequence it is no surprise that failing to live as well as possible is sometimes the result of bad decisions.

Avoiding bad decisions, of course, is the primary value of getting an education, and a liberal education at that. The term *liberal* means "free." A liberal education is simply an education appropriate to a free person. It is an education in the "whys" of life in contrast to just the "hows." In historical use, a liberal education was reserved for free people, and instruction on technique was appropriate for slaves or servants. Those oppressed people were denied a liberal education because it was considered dangerous for them. Today, in liberal democracies an education is almost universally available. And this makes perfect sense from the point of view of virtue ethics. Each person must make her own choices about how to live, and the chances of living well are tightly linked to how wise those choices are. Hence, any community that wishes to foster good living among its constituents will place a high value on education.

But wisdom is not enough. One can know what is best and fail to do it. Hence, it is important for the virtue theorist that people develop a certain self-mastery if they are to live well. This self-mastery enables people to do what is best even if they have impulses to do otherwise. Eating a balanced diet is best even if one wishes to eat a candy bar. It is self-mastery or moral virtue that turns the best choice into the actual choice. And although the example of resisting the temptations of a candy bar is trivial, many of the desires and fears faced by military members are not. The self-mastery required to face the possibility of imminent physical harm is substantial.

For the virtue theorist, then, there is a universal standard of good and evil. It is being happy where happiness is understood as living a flourishing life. The life most worth living is the life of virtue. One ought to be both wise and able to act reliably on that wisdom. Naturally social conditions that foster the discovery of the good life and living it are preferable to those conditions that inhibit it. Most liberal democracies are conceived with these sorts of goals in mind. A relatively free and secure community is more likely to have happy residents than one that is less free and less secure. Hence for many military ethicists, some social arrangements are more worth defending than others. And some characters are better formed than others for conducting that defense.

Consequentialist (Utilitarian) Theory

There is a second approach to what is universally good and, although it is consistent with virtue theory, it adds another important perspective to ethical thinking. This approach does not concentrate so much on the sort of person one ought to be but rather on how one ought to choose how to act. These options may amount to the same thing in some ways, but the emphasis in this approach, as well as the next, is on how to make decisions rather than on how to live well.

It is possible to find these sorts of themes as far back as the ancient Greek philosopher Democritus (born about 460 BC), but consequentialist thinking in its modern form is closely associated with two British philosophers of the 18th and 19th centuries: Jeremy Bentham (1748–1832) and John S. Mill (1806–1873). Bentham and Mill produced a systematic theory that has widely influenced modern liberal societies; in its essence it is concerned with creating policies and making decisions that bring about the greatest good for the greatest number of people affected.

The utilitarian's suggestions are very simple at base. First, moral value is to be found in the consequences of actions. The consequence people should seek to maximize, that is, *the* universal good, is happiness. The value of any act is in direct proportion to how much happiness it brings about. A good act is good because it helps to advance happiness, and an evil act is evil because it causes unhappiness. Happiness is not a finite quantity and accordingly the utilitarian scheme is an optimization scheme. One does not expect to attain a certain plateau of happiness in a community and then "call it done." There is always room for growth. It may be helpful to think of utilitarianism from the perspective of economics. Theoretically, at least, there is no end to the growth potential of a given economy. Growth is driven by how skilled the community is at exploiting resources, developing and deploying labor, and establishing intelligent policies. Something similar is true for utilitarian ethics. Given the right circumstances, each individual can "produce" ever more happiness, both for themselves and for others.

Second, everyone counts the same. That is, people are equal. No one person's happiness or unhappiness counts any more than any other person's. Social status, wealth, gender, and race are all irrelevant. All that matters is the ability to be happy or unhappy. Thus, given certain important qualifications that are addressed later, an act that renders one person unhappy but 100 happy is preferred over an act that makes 100 people unhappy and only one person happy. That means that if it is necessary for some to suffer so that many others become happy (or at least become less unhappy), then ethically speaking some ought to suffer for the good of the many. This concept plays a large role in modern thinking about military activities, where it is commonplace to require the subordination of individual interests for the good of a given group.

Third, happiness is reducible to pleasure and unhappiness is nothing more than suffering. A caution is in order, however, for not all pleasures are of equal moral worth. There is a clear difference in quality that makes some pleasures better, and therefore preferable over others, even if their quantity is smaller.

To illustrate this point one can simply go to the grocery store and compare the available chocolate bars. For the same amount of money, one can buy a 16-ounce bar of brand X chocolate or a much smaller bar of brand Y. If all pleasures that result from eating chocolate were the same, few people would ever buy the smaller bar. Yet the smaller bar sells well. For utilitarians the reason is obvious: both quantity and quality matter, and people often are willing to sacrifice quantity for quality. This is not true for everyone, however. Those who have no idea of the pleasures that higher quality chocolate may bring may opt continually for the lower quality brand. One must have experience with both sorts of chocolate to recognize the difference in quality. Once a person has sampled both, however, the higher quality becomes clear, and the choice for the higher quality becomes more likely.

If it is apparent that quality matters with chocolate, it only makes sense that it would matter as well with other sorts of pleasures. Utilitarians suggest that many of the highest quality pleasures have more to do with the mind than the body. But again there is a catch. One's mind must be developed in a way that enables it to appreciate the higher pleasures. Again, an education is crucial to achieving the good, and utilitarianism makes it explicit that education is good for everyone. The more educated any one person is, the higher qualities of happiness he can enjoy. This is true for everyone so it follows that education itself should be made widely available. All ships rise on the tides of refined tastes.

To gain a better understanding of this concept, think about the ability to read. Clearly, anyone reading this book has learned to read, but all readers were illiterate as children. Learning to read is just the sort of mental development that utilitarians value, for it opens up whole new realms of higher quality pleasures. It is one thing to be able to appreciate good chocolate; the ability to read is on an entirely different, infinitely more rewarding, plane.

Now the idea that everyone counts the same resurfaces. It is one thing to read a book to a child and so provide a bit of fleeting pleasure for her. Hence, reading to a child who enjoys hearing stories is clearly a good. But if one were to teach that child to read, much more happiness will likely result. As everyone counts the same, devoting time to educating others is a far greater good than merely reading to them. The effect of good acts multiplies, as more and more people learn to read and are therefore able to teach others to read. Each reader can educate herself in various crafts and services to the community, thereby raising the happiness of all. Being able to educate oneself means that some people can learn how to cure diseases or develop new technologies, again, with all things being equal, increasing the happiness of all.

Utilitarian thinking helped to inspire many reform movements, most notably in the Western world, where child-labor laws, for example, were enacted to remove impediments to children's education. Thoughtful citizens pay taxes to support schools, whether or not they have children, because they are aware that education pays off in terms of utility.

Notice, however, that sometimes the best one can do is to try to diminish suffering. For most, this obligation is so easily accepted that they never think much about it. If beloved Rover becomes old and lame to the point that he no longer seems able to enjoy living, and it seems that there is no hope for recovery, his family sadly but dutifully takes him to the vet to "be put out of his misery." They accept doing some harm (euthanizing Rover) so as not to allow even more harm (Rover's prolonged suffering). The end quite literally justifies the means.

A dog's suffering counts, but the suffering of an oppressed or threatened community counts for much more in both quality and quantity, so much so that a resort to war may be justified to alleviate it. Wars always involve suffering, and that naturally causes a decrease in utility, but war may bring about an increase in utility that would justify the cost. Mill himself authored a quote widely known in military circles: "War is an ugly thing, but not the ugliest of things. The decayed and degraded state of moral and patriotic feeling which thinks nothing worth war is much worse."[3]

Utilitarians recommend seeking the *optimal* outcome. Although some suffering might be inevitable, it is possible to make choices that tend to increase that suffering or decrease it. Even in circumstances where there is no perfect choice, some answers are still better than others. That said, no one ought to suffer or die in vain. It is one thing if one suffers for the good of others; it is an entirely different thing if one suffers with no positive result in terms of increased happiness or at least decreased unhappiness. One ought to pick one's fights.

Seeking the optimal outcome from every action seems like an almost impossible task. This is hard enough to do with financial investments, where the investment itself and any gain or loss can be reasonably closely understood just by looking at dollar figures. Even with all of the energy and research that people put into investing, it is still the hard truth that many people lose money in their investments. Given this fact, some may suggest that trying to put utilitarian ethical theory into practical use is hopelessly optimistic.

Utilitarians are aware of this problem and have a ready response that goes under the name of *rule utilitarianism*. Following well-thought-out rules simplifies life in lots of ways, and if the rules are formulated with the greatest good for the greatest number in mind, then following them should result in increased happiness overall.

For example, one might spend a long time calculating fuel burn, drive time, and crash risk for any given trip by car to come to the optimized speed for the trip. Or, one could simply decide to obey the speed limit and adjust speeds downward if conditions require. The speed limit may not be the precisely optimal speed, especially given differences in driver skills, automobile type and condition, and trip time, but it is generally adequate to serve the general utility. So, most drivers just naturally adopt the speed limit as a good reference speed and worry about optimizing no further. And they might say to themselves that obeying the speed limit is the ethical thing to do, whereas violating it is unethical. If there is a general consensus on that point, a community might adopt more rules designed to enforce the speed limit, such as taxing fuel to pay for the highway patrol. Drivers expect each other to follow the rule and the patrol to enforce it and will not generally accept justifications for breaking the rule. But if the rule itself were to fail to serve the general utility, then they could change the rule. What makes a rule good or bad is nothing more than the consequences of adopting it as understood in terms of happiness. As the design of roadways becomes better and the crashworthiness of autos improves, a community might decide that a higher speed limit is appropriate. On the other hand, the community may view saving petroleum to be more important for the general utility and so reduce the limit. The policy choices are just that—choices—and the better the choices, the greater the overall happiness. Throughout the process of making rules, however, the fundamentals of utilitarianism remain firmly in place: everyone has the right to be treated as equally important; happiness is the universal moral standard, and a policy's moral quality is dependent on the results it brings about.

Thinking back to the application of utilitarianism to the problems of warfare, the goal is often to reduce unhappiness to the greatest extent possible. A brief account of reactions to a bayonet may help point this out. During the First World War, some German soldiers were issued saw-back bayonets with large teeth on the top edge. The intention was innocent—to provide the soldiers with a tool that would cut wood effectively while still serving as a bayonet. But the large saw-tooth edges would obviously cause more severe wounds than ordinary bayonets. This fact was exploited by Allied propagandists and the Germans recalled the bayonets, reissuing them after filing off the saw-teeth on the back side of the blade.[4]

Sawback bayonets are by no means the only example of a weapon that is out of favor on at least partially utilitarian grounds. Most militaries, at least since the end of the First World War, have shunned the use of poison gases. Nuclear weapons have been detonated in war only twice, and biological weapons have not been used on a large scale for at least 100 years.

Deontological Theory (Rights Theory)

In complement to the focus on consequences stressed by utilitarian theory, rights theorists tend to focus on how people ought to be treated. If a given person deserves a certain sort of treatment, others, including states, have an obligation to treat her in that way. This approach to explaining a universal standard for ethical conduct is often called deontology, a word derived from the Greek term for duty. Rights to be treated in a certain way (or, perhaps more accurately, not to be treated in certain ways) impose duties on others. Hence, this theory is also sometimes called duty ethics. The different names should not cause worry. All of them describe a family of approaches that share certain commonalities. Although rights theorists certainly agree that everyone counts equally, they focus on how acts treat people as individuals rather than on the collective sum of happiness or unhappiness.

Utilitarian thinking, especially of the rule utilitarian variety, is generally consistent with rights theory, although the theoretical foundations of human rights are different under each approach. Rule utilitarians, at base, argue that respecting and defending human rights leads to the greatest good for the greatest number. A simple thought experiment will reveal that none of us could genuinely be happy if we were to live in a community in which human rights are overridden in the name of the collective good.

Imagine that the some very clever students at a college created a system to tap into the electronic communications of the student body. This small ring of students monitored the cell phone calls of their classmates and sorted them automatically by student. Members of the ring would be able to view the transcript of the conversation and add comments to be enjoyed by the other members of the ring. The ring would enjoy their access to the students' private communication, which would increase their happiness, in however crude a fashion. Meanwhile, the other students would have no idea that their communications were being monitored, so they suffered no degradation in their happiness. It would seem that there is a good thing going—a net increase in utility at virtually no cost.

Ordinary moral intuitions, however, say otherwise. There is something obviously unethical in this setup, even though the net quotient of happiness seems to be increased. It seems that somehow people should not be used merely as a means to accomplish other people's purposes, at least not without their consent.

Rights theory illuminates this intuition. It suggests that every human, no matter his status, is surrounded by a little envelope of rights just by virtue of being human. And although the metaphysical explanations for this envelope vary among different theories, the importance of the envelope does not. Indeed, one individual's envelope of rights entails moral duties that bind everyone.

By way of example, suppose for now that Ann has the right to the money she has earned by working as a nurse. She accepted the employment terms that were offered, performs her tasks conscientiously, and receives a paycheck every two weeks. One payday she goes to the bank, deposits her paycheck, and takes $100 back in cash. After she leaves the bank, she is confronted by a man who threatens her with a knife and steals the $100. Clearly a crime has taken place. And one can understand that crime in terms of a rights violation. Ann earned that money—she deserves it, but the robber denied her what she deserves.

This example illustrates one of the most powerful aspects of rights theory. It seems clear that the robber who stole the money did something wrong. But the same would be true for anyone who took the money from Ann by force. Ann's right to her money imposes a duty on the robber not to steal it. When he stole the money, he failed in his duty to respect Ann's right, but the same would be true for anyone who stole the money. Ann's right to her funds binds *everyone* else. In other words, one individual's right places an ethical obligation on everybody to respect that individual's right. Put differently, the rights of one impose duties on all.

This sort of relationship between rights and duties is sometimes much more narrow. Ann's right to the money that she earned imposed a duty on her employer to give her a paycheck, but not on anyone else. Similarly, the employer has a right to Ann's performing her duties as assigned. When she took the job, she promised to do the work in return for the pay. The contract between employer and employee imposes moral duties on each.

Imagine Ann in another scenario. This time she makes it to the store with her $100. She wishes to buy some clothes for a camping trip. She selects a denim shirt, heads to the cash register, and pays for the shirt. In this case, Ann's money is taken from her, but it is taken from her with her *consent*. She freely chooses to exchange her money for the shirt—no compulsion is involved. The cashier respects Ann's right to her own money, and takes it only after it is freely given to her. Ann respects the right of the storekeeper to retain the shirt until it is paid for, and the storekeeper freely allows Ann to take it in exchange for the payment. In thinking about how Ann earned the money, it is easy to see that the employment contract was based on the consent of each party.

There is something mightily important for military ethics in the background here. Most people readily appreciate the idea of consent and rely on it almost unconsciously. But consent itself relies on a precondition: freedom. The very concept of consent is unintelligible without a foregoing assumption of freedom. Compulsory consent is oxymoronic.

Freedom is at the heart of rights theory. The little stories here help to illustrate why. Ann does not consent to being robbed. The robber interfered with Ann's freedom to use her money as she deemed fit. That is crucial to understanding what makes something unethical under rights theory. It is not merely that fact that losing $100 renders Ann unhappy that explains the immorality. Rather, it is that Ann's freedom to choose what to do with *her* money was taken from her. It was not merely her money that was taken; it was her *right* to her money that was violated. Ann suffered aggression; she was treated merely as a means to accomplishing someone else's purposes. Ann therefore has a claim against the robber to restore her $100. This would not be the case if she simply lost the $100. In that case, she still would be out the $100, but her rights would not have been violated, and she would not have a valid claim against anyone. In the cases of theft and of losing the money, Ann is poorer by $100. But one sort of loss is immeasurably worse from an ethical point of view. Theft violates rights; misplacing money, although unfortunate, does not.

It is evident now that the robber has a duty to respect Ann's right to her money, but it is less evident whether a third party has any obligation to help her recover her $100. One might suggest that if Ann is robbed of her money, something unjust has occurred. But if she simply loses it and no one recovers it for her, nothing unjust has happened. Still, a kind stranger may choose to help her by giving her some money. One might think of the gift as an act of charity. There would be no injustice in ignoring Ann's plight, but an act of charity is done by helping her. Ann has no claim against the stranger to give her some money, but she is rightfully grateful if the stranger helps her. In other words, the stranger has no strict duty to help, but helping her is nonetheless a good thing in that, at a minimum, it serves to reduce Ann's unhappiness. Ordinary intuitions reflect this; the tug to alleviate the suffering of others, or to aid them in accomplishing their goals, is sometimes referred to as the obligation of benevolence.

Consider a variation on the case in which the stranger had been present during the robbery. One might be tempted to say that the stranger should have intervened to help Ann keep her money. Many would disagree, suggesting that although the stranger is obligated not to violate Ann's right to her money, there is no obligation to help Ann keep it, especially if doing so would expose the stranger to a risk of violent harm. The stranger has a strict duty not to harm Ann, but there is no such strict duty to prevent Ann's being harmed.

This distinction between not doing any harm and not doing anything *about* harm is important in ethical thinking. Here, it will be referred to as the "do/allow" distinction. Rights theorists do differ on just how much a human has a "right to," but all agree that humans should not be actively harmed unless there is some compelling justification for doing the harm. Some theorists suggest that human rights include, for example, the right to basic subsistence or healthcare, which suggests a right to be helped. Others are more minimalist, suggesting that the only uncontroversial right is the right to be free from uninvited interference.

People use the do/allow distinction so often that they sometimes overlook it. Virtually everyone agrees that it would be immoral to shoot children, but there is much less agreement on whether there is a moral obligation to prevent a child's dying even when the means to do so are available. Millions of children die every year from malnutrition and disease, yet most people, most of the time, do little or nothing about it. The fact of inaction in the face of suffering does nothing to establish an ethical claim, but it is a striking empirical fact that people who would never think of harming a child do in fact routinely allow harm to millions of children. Although harm is frequently allowed against thousands without much moral outrage, however, even one murder mobilizes law-enforcement efforts that may cost millions of dollars over time. Whether the child dies of malnutrition or gunshot, the result is the same for the child, but ordinary intuitions suggest that the moral natures of the deaths are distinct.

Many utilitarians and rights theorists suggest that this intuition is flawed, and it may well be. Exactly where to draw the line between the unjust and the uncharitable is controversial, but that discussion, which is relevant in many ways to military ethics, will have to wait until later. It is enough for now to note that people do make a distinction between doing and allowing harm, judging the former much more harshly than the latter.

Immanuel Kant (1724–1804), a foundational figure in the development of deontological theory during the Enlightenment, made a similar distinction between the sorts of duties human have. He assigned the unfortunate names of "perfect and "imperfect" to the two categories of duties. Generally, perfect duties are duties not to violate rights. Imperfect duties, however, are duties to help. They are still duties, but they bind only under certain conditions. Of importance, rights theorists generally agree that it is improper to override a perfect duty in the name of an imperfect duty. Whether it would *always* be unjustifiable is controversial, as will become apparent soon in the discussion of war's conduct. For now, it is enough to illustrate the point with a simple example. Say that John is a millionaire and Jack is poverty-stricken. Jack becomes ill and needs a drug that costs $50 to save his eyesight. The $50 would make a tremendous difference to Jack's well-being, and its loss would hardly be noticed by John. Nonetheless, it would be wrong to steal the $50 from John and to give it to Jack because the duty to respect what John deserves binds more stringently than does Jack's need for help. The first is a perfect duty, and the second imperfect.

Note that in cases like this one there are other choices. One could simply ask that John donate the needed $50 and then give it to Jack to save his eyes. To respect John and to help Jack are both moral obligations. The key point is that an obligation to help cannot justify overriding the rights of others. If John donates the money, no rights are violated and the desired end result is achieved with no one's rights having been overridden.

These obligations can be modified by agreement, however, as some members of a community freely take on obligations that they otherwise would not have. No one is forced to take on the role of police officer. But should Henry agree to become a policeman, he takes on obligations that he did not have before. Henry the officer does have a perfect duty to help defend Ann's $100 because to do otherwise would be to break the promise he made when taking on a law-enforcement role. To understand this more clearly, think back to Ann's fundamental right to be free from unwanted interference. Like all other thoughtful people, she understands that there are times in real life when this right will likely not be respected. In other words, some people do immoral things to others—rights violations are a fact whether or not they ought to be a fact. Appreciating this reality, Ann is glad that her community has made arrangements to protect her rights. She agrees to be subject to the laws of the community herself and to pay taxes to support law enforcement. It would be unreasonable to enter into such agreements unless she had a belief that those in law-enforcement roles actually would do what they are hired to do: deter crime and prosecute criminals in order to defend Ann and everyone else. Ann relies on the promise that Henry makes when he becomes a policeman and lives her life in accordance with those expectations. She exercises her freedoms with the assurance that they will be defended by those who have promised to do so. And Henry has a corresponding duty to do his part—to patrol the streets and to respond to Ann's call when she makes it. Henry would have only an imperfect duty to help Ann if he were an ordinary citizen, but Henry has a perfect duty to perform the role because he has promised to do so. Doing what one says one will do is a perfect duty because others have the right to rely on one's promises. Otherwise, Ann would be relying on a false promise that she had believed to be true. Thus, although Ann does not have a right to the help of ordinary citizens, she does have a right to Henry's help. She has freely paid for that help; he has freely taken on the role.

Volumes have been written about this approach to rights theory, and any account here will necessarily be rough and incomplete. For present purposes it should be clear that deontologists care a lot about human beings as human beings. Their capacity to feel pleasure or pain matters, of course, as does their ability to contribute to the general well-being of a community, but what is really special about people is their freedom to consent. This freedom plays a major role in modern thinking about armed conflict. In liberal democracies that consent is embodied in legal codes and contracts. Most people consent to the rules of their society without even thinking about them. But it is an interesting characteristic of liberal democracies that they rely on the consent of the governed for their political authority. If people do not consent, they are free to argue for a change in the codes or to leave the community. If they do consent, it is clear that they value their community, perhaps even to the point of being willing to defend it during a conflict.

Consider aggressive war as a rights theorist might. Aggressive war is waged against a victim without the victim's consent just as the robber took Ann's money without her consent. Whatever else it is, aggressive war is an offense against freedom. Just war thinking holds that defense against aggression is morally justified. It also holds that there is an important difference between those who consent to engage in war (combatants) and those who do not (noncombatants).

States Rights

Modern thinking links the notion of states rights closely to individual rights. In brief, the rights of states derive from the rights of their citizens.[5] A state that respects and fosters the rights of its members enjoys rights itself. In such states, the members of the state generally consent to their government. Accordingly, that state has the moral right to be free from interference. The consent of the citizenry is, as a practical matter, generally contingent on the state's fostering the free exercise of human rights within its territory. It is also dependent on the international community's recognition of the state as enjoying the support of its population.

The right of people to participate in their own governance and to determine the direction of their state, both domestically and internationally, is central to this conception of a state's rights. If the members are happy with their government, endorsing its policies and decisions as representing their preferences, their rights extend, in a fashion, to protect their government.

No government is perfect. The idealized conception of states rights as deriving from those of its inhabitants is never fully realized in reality. Governments always fail in some regard, and some members of every political community are unhappy with at least some aspects of their state. Hence, the idea of a legitimate rights-bearing state does not have mathematical exactitude. Still, the general conception is clear enough. Attributes such as generally open government, a reliable mechanism for peaceful transfer of political power, the respect of the international community, and the rule of law characterize states that enjoy rights. On the other hand, states that oppress their own citizens or portions of them, make policy and decisions secretly, severely restrict emigration, muzzle the press, or fail to tolerate political opposition generally invite skepticism about their own legitimacy.[6]

Likewise, the government's right to defend itself is contingent on its defense of the rights of its constituents. Interference from a foreign power obviously impedes the rights of a community to determine its own future. It is in this sense that citizens have a right to expect their government to defend them, and their government, accordingly, has an obligation to do so.

Tying the Three Aspects Together in Applied Settings

The foregoing overview of different approaches to universal moral values may leave one perplexed. All three theoretical accounts claim to ground morality for all, yet they offer different sorts of grounds.

Philosophers specializing in theoretical ethics spend much effort debating the matter of which approach is most adequate, but controversies at the level of theory need not concern the military ethicist too much. Military ethics is an applied science, and the test of adequacy is in individual conscience. For that reason, most military ethicists consider all three approaches when considering an applied issue.

Charles Myers (PhD, colonel, USAF, retired) has offered a tidy rubric for exploiting the three approaches by noting that each exploits a distinct aspect of any one real-life moral problem. He notes that any morally laden decision involves three aspects: the agent making the decision, the action taken, and the resulting outcome. Thus any comprehensive moral consideration ought to encompass all three: the person responsible, the act, and the outcome. Evaluations about the person might be approached most powerfully from the perspective of virtue ethics. Deontology provides insight into the moral character of individual acts. Consequentialism's vantage point is most helpful in evaluating outcomes.[7] Professionally minded military members care about all three aspects and, therefore, would be well advised to take all three perspectives into account.

The Context of Military Ethics

Military members rarely enjoy the clarity and logical consistency for which ethical theory strives. Their world is often one of limited choices and divergent values. Thoughtful military ethicists appreciate these constraints and tensions, realizing that what works well in theory may sometimes fall short in practice, even with the best of intentions.

This problem is due, at least in part, to the problems that military ethics addresses. Political and military decisions are often constrained by circumstances that leave people with no genuinely *good* choices. For this reason, it may be appropriate to think of these difficult decisions in terms of "better and worse" instead of "right or wrong." Moreover, the choices often involve divergent tugs on a thoughtful person's conscience. That is, competing values may be in play and the choice of one course of action, which would serve one value, might be at the cost to a second, competing value. A few of these limitations and tensions are mentioned here for introductory purposes; they are discussed in depth in later chapters.

Freedom and Necessity

Ethics presupposes freedom, but people may not be as free as they would like. Much of military ethical thinking takes place in the context that offers only limited choices. Military ethics reflects this fact with frequent reference to "necessity." For example, although a nation may cherish its independence, other nations may threaten that very independence through physical aggression. The victim of aggression may have only limited choices—active defense or loss of the very freedom that makes choice possible. Likewise, an individual may find himself in a situation that quite literally demands "kill or be killed!" Or, an air force may be faced with the question of how to handle a hijacked airliner that is likely to be flown into an occupied building. If the air force shoots the airliner down, the citizens in the building will be saved, but only at the cost of hundreds of innocent passengers who had the misfortune to be on the hijacked airplane. If the plane is not shot down, then the hijackers will use it to kill both the occupants of the building and the passengers.

Different Roles

The military member's role as state-actor may conflict with other roles she has as a human being. Military endeavors may require substantial risk to life and limb or extended deployments away from home, yet the member's role as, say, a parent conflicts seriously with the military demand. Militaries do their best to motivate their members to resolve this tension in favor of the state's interest, and some go so far as to suggest that dying in the defense of the state is in the interest of the human who is also a soldier.

The military member's role may also be in tension with his role as a citizen. Most persons in the military service of a state are first citizens of that state. As *military members* they are, of course, obligated to uphold the policies of their state and to obey lawful orders. *As citizens,* they are free to disagree with their state's policies. History teaches that more than a few soldiers have died fighting wars that they believed were mistaken.

Winning and Conduct in War

Winning a just war may require using unjust means. As will become evident soon, traditional thinking about war has two major divisions: *jus ad bellum,* or the justice of going to war, and *jus in bello*, or justice within war. Generally speaking, going to war is a decision made by political figures, whereas decisions regarding how to fight are made by militaries themselves. The division is not nearly as clean in the real world as it is in the tradition. For example, it may be the case that one cannot win a just war except by fighting unjustly.

Conscience and Policy

Ethical imperatives in the military may conflict with the realities of life in a bureaucratic world. Initiative and good moral character are said to be military virtues, yet they sometimes lead a military member to question "the rules." A small example will suffice to illustrate the tension. It sometimes occurs that a military member will face discharge for being overweight, at least in the U.S. military. The rules specify a maximum weight, but it could be the case that an overweight individual may be extremely valuable to the military. Can such a problem be solved without sacrificing something valuable? Another much more serious issue arises when a military leader's considered professional judgment contradicts the wishes of civilian leadership. Can a general in good conscience lead troops in a history-making expedition that his judgment tells him is almost certainly doomed to fail, and in the process weaken the national security he is supposed to provide?

The tensions that permeate military ethics are tough to resolve fully. This book is meant to introduce the ethical problems facing military members and their political bosses, including the citizens of Western liberal democracies. It also presents what the best minds working on these problems and tensions have handed down to the present day. It must be admitted at the outset, however, that these real-world issues are tough to describe accurately, let alone address successfully. Anyone working in military ethics would do well to acknowledge that humans, and especially states, are better at creating problems than they are at solving them. Good judgment is always required. The best we can do is to do our best.

Notes

1. The term *natural law* is used in several ways by philosophers. The first meaning, which is seen in many of the historical figures, refers to a theological view that God created an ordered universe, and this universe consistently operates according to laws. These natural laws can be apprehended through reason, but many are revealed through scripture. Therefore faith and reason yield the same sorts of ethical guidance. The Bible counsels against theft for example; reason and experience by themselves also reveal that stealing is a bad idea. In this sense of natural law, emphasis is often placed on purposes as an ethical guide. It is considered unethical to interfere with something's natural end and morally appropriate to facilitate progress toward that end. Infanticide is accordingly prohibited, as it precludes a baby's living its life, whereas curing a disease is morally laudable because it helps a being live and fulfill its goals.

Other philosophers usually mean something less restrictive by the term. Here there is no necessary theological connection. Natural laws are simply descriptions of the patterns by which the world works. The laws of physics, biology, and ethics are all discoverable through reason. There is an observable pattern that some diets are more likely to lead to obesity than others. It is likewise a natural law that people prefer health over disease. Thus it is an imperative of both biology and ethics that one choose to avoid a diet of nothing but sugar and fat. Most parents understand this regardless of their religious convictions, and so they teach their children to eat a balanced diet.

2. See Alisdair MacIntyre, *After Virtue* (Notre Dame, IN: University of Notre Dame Press, 1981); Alexander Nehemas, *The Art of Living* (Berkeley: University of California Press, 1998), and Robert Nozik, *The Examined Life* (New York: Simon and Schuster, 1989).

3. United States Air Force Academy, *Contrails* (USAF Academy, CO: Association of Graduates, 2008), 92.

4. Shawn Gibson, "The Bayonet Connection," e-mail message to author, December 22, 2008.

5. There is some controversy over this way of deriving states rights. The controversy is addressed in chapters 4 and 6.

6. Brian Orend has contributed to the modern understanding of states rights by proposing three criteria he argues must be met for a society to be regarded as "minimally just" and therefore to be accorded rights. Orend's first criterion requires that the minimally just society be "generally recognized as such by their own people and the international community." He suggests that such states are recognizable, for example, by holding periodic elections and being permitted to participate in international associations and diplomatic relations. His second criterion requires that the society "avoid violating the rights of other countries," in particular by refraining from violent aggression. His third criterion requires them to "make every reasonable effort to satisfy the human rights of their own citizens." Brian Orend, *The Morality of War* (Peterborough, Ontario: Broadview Press, 2006), 35–36.

7. Charles R. Myers, "The Core Values: Framing and Resolving Ethical Issues for the Air Force," *Airpower Journal* 11, no. 1 (1997): 38–53.

CHAPTER 2

Just War Thinking (JWT) in Historical Perspective

This chapter introduces the major themes of thinking about justifying the use of armed force on behalf of a political community from a historical perspective. The next chapter examines the major philosophical streams of thought that have been brought to bear on the problem and shows how they are in play today.

To avoid misunderstanding, it is worth mentioning at the outset that numerous terms are in play in the contemporary vocabulary of just war. They all refer to the same body of thought. Sometimes, especially in religious contexts, one hears the term *just war doctrine*. In other contexts it is sometimes called *just war theory*; some writers refer to the *just war tradition*. Here it is called *just war thinking*, or JWT for short.

The word *thinking* is used for a number of reasons. First, the development of JWT has taken more than 20 centuries, and it has evolved substantially over time. Second, modern specialists in the field do not quite agree on the criteria for a just war. Although there is widespread general agreement on major themes, certain important differences are in evidence. So the thinking about just war is ongoing in part because the ethical challenges presented by the use of force have not yet been adequately met. It is also ongoing because the challenges presented by armed conflict themselves evolve, and these challenges together constitute a third reason for emphasizing thinking. Whatever else is clear, it is obvious that JWT addresses a moving target and will likely continue to develop.

The historical contributions of JWT's major figures fall more easily into place if one starts with a general understanding of its present form. Considerable controversy continues over many aspects of JWT today, but there is general agreement regarding its two major divisions and the major themes within each. The first division, *jus ad bellum,* has to do with justifying going to war. It is generally but not exclusively thought to be the domain of political, as opposed to military, figures. The second division, *jus in bello,* refers to the moral conduct of war and is generally considered to be in the purview of military members, as they are empowered to wage war and are accordingly responsible for its conduct. It follows that military members are generally not held to account for the justice of the wars they wage.

Generally Accepted *Jus Ad Bellum* Criteria

Legitimate Authority

This criterion requires that any commitment to engage in warfare must be made by a state's lawful representatives. Political factions, businesses, and private individuals do not have the authority to declare war; governments do. The legitimate authority in a liberal democracy represents the will of its citizens.

Just Cause

War invariably involves doing and suffering harm. Accordingly, the *casus belli,* or reason for going to war, must be sufficiently serious and morally warranted. Defense against unwarranted physical aggression is widely accepted as a just cause. Domestic political needs, ethnic or religious hatred, and economic aspirations are not considered just causes.

Declaration of Cause

Those initiating a war are required to make their reasons clear to all. This not only allows the adversary a clear view of the ends for which the war is fought, but also helps to ensure that wars are started only for just reasons.

Right Intention

This criterion requires that war be waged with regret. To enjoy doing harm is to violate the criterion. The intention should be to bring about as just a stable equilibrium internationally as is practical. A good analogy might be the intention a good surgeon has when performing an operation. Surgery itself is always harmful, but the intention is to effect an enduring cure, not to cut or otherwise harm the patient.

Proportionality

This criterion is included to help ensure that a war prevents more harm than it causes. To go to war over a trivial matter is to violate the criterion. This criterion, like others that require the prediction of outcomes, can be especially challenging to apply. Hindsight may be 20/20, but political judgment about the future is rarely as accurate.

Reasonable Hope of Success

A state should avoid engaging in a war unless thoughtful people believe on good evidence that there is a decent chance of achieving the goals of the war. Difficult to apply as it is, the criterion suggests that if defeat is inevitable, avenues other than war should be pursued.

Last Resort

War should not be considered as the first option to obtain international political goals. Diplomatic negotiation, appeal to public opinion, or seeking relief from the United Nations are all better options and should be attempted before one commits to violence.

End of Peace

Wars should be fought with the goal of a just peace. This criterion is sometimes omitted, as much of its content may be subsumed under right intention.

Generally Accepted *Jus in Bello* Criteria

There are two central criteria for the conduct of war, although their application can be quite complex. Responsible adherence to these *jus in bello* criteria is a military responsibility, as the military conducts hostile operations as opposed to deciding whether to resort to them, which is a responsibility of statesmen. Some writers include respecting *jus in bello* criteria as one of the *jus ad bellum* criteria.

Discrimination

Those fighting are required to target only combatants and other military targets. That is, they are to discriminate between legitimate and illegitimate objects of harm, targeting only the former.

Proportionality

Military operations should cause death and destruction only in proportion to the military goals they are intended to achieve. Meeting this criterion within a war is required for meeting the *jus ad bellum* requirement of proportionality.

Subsequent chapters examine these criteria and their application in substantial depth. For now, however, it is convenient to have these in mind for a survey of how these criteria came to the contemporary world through history.

Foundational Christian Contributions

St. Augustine (AD 354–431) and His Predecessors in the Ancient World

The most substantive history of JWT begins with St. Augustine, but thinking about the ethics of war is evident in the Western tradition well before his time. Plato offers some recognizable themes for just war in his *Republic*.[1] Aristotle mentions in his *Politics* that war can be justly waged against men who, "though intended by nature to be governed, will not submit."[2] Cicero, writing in the first century BC, suggests legal criteria for resort to war that continue in use today.[3] It is Augustine, however, who serves as the best introduction to the tradition in ethical terms. His thinking reflects both the sense of tragedy and the aspirations to limit it that have accompanied JWT through the ages since. It is helpful to approach Augustine's thinking in light of a tension between two competing tugs—the hope for peace and the need for security.

The Tugs of Pacifism and Realism. Augustine was a Christian, and Christian thinking up to that time had been, generally speaking, pacifist thinking. Christ's Sermon on the Mount famously includes "if someone slaps you on the right cheek, turn and offer him your left."[4] The preponderance of the available evidence suggests that for early Christians, this pacifism precluded entry into the military. Other aspects of military service, such as submission to temporal authority, offended Christians as well. Roland Bainton, in his *Christian Attitudes toward War and Peace,* notes that there is no indication at all of Christians in military service until AD 170–180.[5] The history of JWT, however, is a history of working to resolve tensions, and the extant historical record suggests that thoroughgoing Christian pacifism was relatively short-lived.

During the 10 years of AD 170–180, things began to change regarding Christian attitudes toward military service. The tug opposing pacifism is summed up neatly in Bainton's quote from the critic of Christianity, Celsus (ca. AD 178): "If all men were to do the same as you, there would be nothing to prevent the king from being left in utter solitude and desertion and the forces of the empire would fall into the hands of the wildest and most lawless barbarians."[6] Notice that the appeal here is to the good of the empire—a public good that Celsus took to be threatened by pacifism. Order and security, even though imperfect, do have substantial value. And indeed, Bainton notes, the first evidence of Christian service in the military is found in AD 173.[7] By the time of Constantine (ca. AD 274–337), such service was evidently commonplace. It is this juxtaposition of a Christian conscience in a public role that constitutes one of the foundational tensions for the development of JWT.

It is helpful to keep these developments in mind when considering Augustine's famous work, *The City of God.* There, Augustine contrasts two realms—earthly and holy. These realms do not refer to geographical or political boundaries. Instead, they refer to abstract conceptions of life after the biblical fall from grace and after redemption. The first is the earthly city and the second the heavenly. All

Christians hope for the City of God to be made manifest, but so far it has not been made so. The "real world" is filled with corruption and evil. Indeed, the earthly realm consists of states that are morally little different than bands of robbers.[8] Nonetheless, although all communities are imperfect, some are more imperfect than others. And within a given community, policy choices can work to improve life, or, for that matter, to do the opposite. In any event, the governing authorities are necessary to make decently secure life possible given humanity's fallen condition. Conflict and threat of harm are real and cannot in good conscience be ignored by a public official. Bainton describes Augustine's position clearly: "When all was said and done, the empire stood for order against barbarian chaos. The empire was Christian. The Church was able to give guidance. Some semblance of justice might be realized. Therefore, the empire was to be defended and Christians might fight."[9]

As Paul Christopher has pointed out, Augustine has laid here another enduring philosophical foundation for thinking about just war. His two cities apply regardless of where the lines appear on maps. The theory of just war, then, is a theory for all.[10]

Attitudes toward War. Another distinction is important here and will make its way into much of the later just war tradition. The same action can be accompanied by many different attitudes. One can do violence with glee or regret. For Augustine's Christian worldview, the attitude regarding the violent act is a key determinant of its moral quality. One's attitude is an aspect of the self that is at least somewhat under one's control in a way that facts about the world are not. People, therefore, are responsible for their attitudes in a way they are not for events that are out of their control. This fact is central for Augustine's work in resolving the tension between Christian pacifism and earthly conflict. One can wish that violence were not required even as one does it. Moreover, there are differences in the motives one might offer for doing violence. For Augustine, the Christian is part of an historical process that would eventually bring the City of God into being. Any violence deliberately committed, therefore, ought to be committed in a way that is consistent with the end of Christian order on earth. "For even they who make war desire nothing but victory—desire, that is to say, to attain peace with glory . . . It is therefore with the desire for peace that wars are waged."[11]

Augustine's office—he served as a church official in Hippo, in North Africa, which was threatened with Vandal invasion—caused him to worry about the interests of those living within his domain. He realized that they needed protection from people who might seek to harm them, and that protecting them might require violent means. In the city of God, of course, no coercion would be necessary, but this was not true in the earthly city, where order and safety sometimes required coercion internally and defense externally. For a private person, pacifism might still be an adequate response to a corrupt world; after all, on the Christian worldview, it is better to suffer evil than to do it. But for a public official to decide on pacifism would potentially put others, not just the self, on an altar of sacrifice.

Given the opportunity, most private persons would not hesitate to call on state officials (in the form of police or other protective services) when they felt threatened. Hence, with regret and with the proper motives, armed violence might justifiably come into play on behalf of the citizenry. This justified response is rendered necessary by the immoral actions of others.[12] Moreover, this violence is in some ways not the individual's own, but rather the responsibility of the state. "[T]hey who have waged war in obedience to the divine command, or in conformity with His laws have represented in their persons the public justice or the wisdom of government . . . have by no means violated the commandment 'Thou shalt not kill.'"[13] For Augustine, it was public office in the service of the state (or, in obedience to God's command—discussed later) that justified violence on behalf of the state and its inhabitants.[14] This idea of doing violence as an aspect of official public duty has important repercussions for others. Members of the community are obligated to follow the community's appointed authorities. Wars are properly the responsibility of public officials; obedience is the lot of the ordinary soldier. Obedient service is accordingly justified even in an unjust war. Augustine makes this point clearly in "Reply to Faustus the Manichean 22." "[A] righteous man . . . under an ungodly king, may do the duty belonging to his position in the state in fighting by the order of his sovereign—for in some cases it is plainly the will of God that he should fight, and in others, where this is not so plain, it may be an unrighteous command on the part of the king, while the soldier is innocent, because his position makes obedience a duty"[15]

This important concept has, with some controversy, lasted until today in JWT. Some call the idea the "moral equality of soldiers."[16] The philosophical basis for this concept is explored and critiqued at some length later. For now, it is important to understand that Augustine drew a distinction between the soldier and his sovereign that relied on the obedience the former owes to the latter. If a soldier does violence on behalf of his sovereign, even in an unjust war, he is not guilty of murder, although if the same soldier were to kill on his own behalf as a private citizen, he would be guilty.

Augustine's approach to distinguishing justifiable killing from morally culpable murder does not appeal to the idea of self-defense. It relies instead on the defense of the community, obedience, and the hope for a just, heavenly future. Doing violence on behalf of others, then, can be viewed as an act of charity because the violent act ought to be committed with a proper attitude of love for all involved. Augustine is not relying on a rights-oriented view of JWT, as most modern thinkers do. Rather, his is a Christian conception of love and salvation. This conception can be a two-edged sword. Augustine believed that one could kill justly, not only in service to one's citizens, but also in obedience to God's command. It is not hard to see how this view would later be used to justify religious wars—something that modern JWT does not countenance.

Whereas Augustine's thinking about war reflects the tensions felt by a faithful person in an unjust world, it also reflects an appreciation of an obligation to do something about that injustice. Some modern pacifists would take issue with

Augustine's fulfilling that obligation by violent means, as, they argue, evil may be resisted successfully without resort to physical violence. This approach is explored later. For present purposes, it is important to keep Augustine's historical significance in mind. Much in his version of JWT is no longer fashionable, but the problem he was trying to address is essentially the same now as it was more than 1,500 years ago. Some of the distinctions he made between justified and unjustified violence remain recognizable and in active use today.

St. Thomas Aquinas (1225–1274)

Thomas Aquinas is probably best known as a great theological and philosophical systematizer. His influence on Catholicism, which incubated much of JWT historically, is profound and enduring.

Aquinas explicated and organized the JWT of Augustine. He put forth three criteria for judging whether to resort to war that are both reminiscent of Augustine's thought and a part of *jus ad bellum* today.

The first, proper [legitimate] authority, limits the right to wage wars to sovereign rulers. Private individuals, or even coalitions or parties within a community, are to resolve their disputes short of war. The second, just cause, requires that those who are to be attacked must be attacked only because they have done something to deserve it. The third, right intention, requires that wars be waged with the intention of avoiding evil and promoting good.[17] All three criteria must be met.[18]

Aquinas also writes of certain aspects of *conducting* a just war—what today is understood as *jus in bello*. For example, he considers whether ambushes can be justified. Laying an ambush for an adversary might be considered unjust, as the very nature of an ambush relies on a certain kind of deception. For an ambush to succeed, the adversary must believe that no enemies are nearby—otherwise they would not walk into the ambush. Aquinas concludes that ambushes can be justified, as they do not actively deceive the enemy but rather rely on concealment.[19]

Double Effect. Aquinas noted that one act can have two effects, and that the moral quality of the act is then affected by which effect was intended. This idea of "double effect" is still in use today, especially when the issue of harm to noncombatants is in play.[20]

Aquinas uses the idea in his discussion of killing in self-defense. The act of killing in this case has two effects—one good and one bad. The good effect is the saving of a life that otherwise would have been lost to the attacker. But the bad effect is the death of the attacker. Notice, however, that the defender *intended* only to save his life. The bad effect is foreseen, perhaps, but not intended. Like Augustine, for Aquinas, the intention of the actor makes a great deal of difference for moral evaluation. But Aquinas is much more systematic than Augustine on this point. An example will help make this clear.

Suppose that Rover becomes afflicted with a swollen paw. The veterinarian determines that surgery is necessary to restore the function of the paw. The act of cutting the paw open has two effects, only one of which is intended—curing Rover. The second effect, causing Rover discomfort, is the evil one, but it is not intended. The moral quality of the intention can be determined by the veterinarian's asking herself a simple question—would I be satisfied if I could cure Rover without doing the harm that surgery entails? If the answer is sincerely yes, and there is no self-deception in play, the veterinarian can say that her intention was only to bring about the good effect. The suffering caused by surgery is foreseen, but not intended.

There is more to double effect. Aquinas adds that the bad effect must not be out of proportion to the good effect. If the cure could have been accomplished short of performing surgery, but the veterinarian performed it anyway, her doing of excessive harm is to be morally condemned.

Moving back to the killing of human beings, there are some for whom an intention to kill can be justified—those acting on public authority in defense of their community. "[I]t is not lawful for a man to intend killing a man in self-defense, except for such as have public authority, who while intending to kill a man in self-defense refer this to the public good, as in the case of a soldier . . . although even they sin if they be moved by private animosity."[21] This statement seems to suggest that intending to kill in self-defense is justified only insofar as doing so is "referred to" the good of the citizenry. In other words, intending to kill in defense of the self would not be justified unless intending to kill while defending the self was a kind of public good. If so, then it is the soldier's acting on behalf of the community that justifies the intent to kill. His own well-being does not justify the intent to kill, but the well-being of others does. And in any case, one is never justified in killing from hatred or animosity. The justification for the killing lies in its detachment from private conscience and its attachment to the public good.

Still, certain persons should not engage in violence, even on behalf of the state. The clergy are forbidden from doing violence because it is inconsistent with their identity as clergy.

> Now warlike pursuits are altogether incompatible with the duties of . . . a cleric, for two reasons. The first reason is . . . [that they] are full of unrest, so that they hinder the mind very much from the contemplation of Divine things, the praise of God, and prayers . . . [Second] . . . those who shed blood, even without sin, become irregular. Now no man who has a certain duty to perform, can lawfully do that which renders him unfit for that duty. Wherefore it is altogether unlawful for clerics to fight, because war is directed to the shedding of blood.[22]

The second reason is worth a bit of pondering, as it reinforces the idea that even justified killing is evil. It leaves a moral mark on the person doing the killing, and this mark is incompatible with the idea of clerical purity.

It is hard to overestimate the importance of Aquinas, and especially Augustine, in the development of JWT. Many of their contributions remain recognizable in the 21st century. The conceptual foundations they established made their way into the secular world of international law.

The New World and the Secularization of JWT: Vitoria (1492–1546) and Suarez (1548–1617)

The Spanish exploration of the New World brought more than geographic discoveries; it generated moral controversy at home. Many Spaniards objected to their government's ill treatment of indigenous Americans.[23] Although one could attempt to justify the enslavement of Native Americans using the old Aristotelian arguments for "natural slavery,"[24] such claims were difficult to maintain in the face of discoveries of great civilizations in Central and South America.[25] And even if the Americans were somehow less intelligent, the Aristotelian conception would suggest only that it would be proper for them to be subordinate to others in the way that children are subordinate to their parents. It would not justify the massacre and pillage that were being wreaked on the New World.[26]

Francisco Vitoria

Francisco Vitoria held a chair in theology at the University of Salamanaca. His work is significant for JWT on a number of fronts. One can discern important notions of impartiality and reciprocity in it. First, he rejected religiously based justifications for violence. He also explicitly rejected imperialistic motives and glory-seeking as just causes.[27] Instead, "[t]here is a single and only just cause for commencing a war, namely, a wrong received."[28] And even then, not all wrongs received would constitute a just cause.

Spain's exploration and subsequent dominion over parts of the new world introduced intriguing problems. Before the Spanish arrived, the Americans were living in reasonable harmony and ruling over themselves successfully. Spanish law or Church law had no jurisdiction over these previously autonomous cultures.

Now of course one can think of the members of other cultures as inferior in some way to one's own. This was the sort of reasoning found in Aristotle's idea of natural slaves. But Vitoria discounted such an idea as contrary to the evidence. Instead, he thought in terms of the universal natural law. In brief, the idea is that there are natural laws that should be evident to anyone, regardless of their cultural background, given ordinary reason and experience. Any adequately organized and harmonious community had to be following certain natural laws regarding interpersonal relations, otherwise their community would cease to exist. Just as reason could discern a pattern among the seasons and exploit that knowledge to conform agricultural endeavors to those patterns, one could also discern natural facts and laws about the relationship of humans and their cultures. One such fact is that there is a difference between innocent people and those who are guilty of something. In the latter case, the idea of guilt usually relies on the individual in question having behaved in some way that wronged another. Thus in the domestic arena, it is common to distinguish those who have committed some sort of offense from those who have simply been minding their own business. Just communities seek to take action against the former because of their precedent actions, not because of who they are or their cultural identity. And the action taken should be proportionate to the offense. Not every offense deserves the death penalty. Such a model is appropriate for handling conflicts among different cultures, according to Vitoria. The assumption he relies on is a modern one—that people and their communities are innocent unless facts surface to the contrary. It takes a wrong action on someone's part to invite violent retaliation. Accordingly, for Vitoria and many subsequent just war thinkers, the only just cause for war is as a response to aggression.

Vitoria's contribution to *jus ad bellum* does not stop with his more precisely restricted notion of just cause. He refines his predecessors' insights and anticipates several modern criteria including proportionality and the end of peace. Given a just cause, the war ought not to aim at destroying people, but rather it should be fought "only so as to obtain one's rights and the defense of one's country and in order that from that war peace and security may in time result."[29] A just war cannot be a war of annihilation.

War, Vitoria emphasizes, is the business of political leadership. What has come to be called the criterion of "legitimate authority" restricts the ability to start wars to sovereign rulers. And even a legitimate authority needs to be very careful in starting a war. Of particular interest is Vitoria's recognition that, even if one is clear on the criteria for a just war, one may still be unclear or wrong regarding whether real-world circumstances satisfy those criteria. For this reason, the ruler is advised to consult with wise men regarding matters as grave as going to war. And even then, there is the possibility of error. Vitoria recognizes here again that the real world of statecraft in general and conflict in particular may limit one's assessments and one's options. An adversary or a third-party state may seek actively to deceive, or one's view of a particular situation may be plagued with inconsistent information. Vitoria does not require rulers to be all-knowing, but he does require them to be diligent in seeking the best possible information. He extends this requirement to others holding public office or advising rulers on questions of resort to war.[30]

It is important to note here that Vitoria is consistent with earlier thinkers in holding rulers responsible for determining the justice of their wars, but he does not generally require the ordinary soldier to make any such determination. Vitoria maintains that the ordinary soldier typically is in no position to determine whether a war is just. That is, he cannot be expected to understand the business of his superiors, but he can be expected to have faith in their decisions.[31] In the case where the soldier is not ignorant, however, that is, when he knows that the war is unjust, he cannot justifiably fight in it, even if he is required to do so by political authorities. "This is obvious, since one may not lawfully kill an innocent man on any authority, and in the case we are speaking of the enemy must be innocent."[32]

This distinction in the scope of responsibility is in active use in modern JWT, although it does stimulate controversy. The nuance in Vitoria's thinking deserves notice. He understands that states of mind are difficult to determine, but he seems clear-eyed regarding the human capacity for self-deception or willful ignorance. Such mental frailties are to be guarded against vigilantly, as the business of war is such a serious one.

Vitoria extends his natural law reasoning to distinguish among members of communities engaged in war. Just as there is a difference between innocent and guilty in the domestic arena, so there is in warfare. This crucial distinction remains in the JWT today as the *jus in bello* principle of discrimination. Interestingly, Vitoria links his *jus ad bellum* arguments for just cause to his *jus in bello* requirement for discrimination. As just wars are fought to defeat wrongdoing, and innocent people, by definition, do not do wrongs, they are not to be the objects of violence.[33] Modern JWT figures would have a lot to say about this perhaps overly simplistic moral prescription. But the important point here is that even though a community may be justly attacked, for Vitoria that does not imply that every member of that community is a legitimate target. Vitoria denies the idea of collective responsibility. This very modern-sounding thinking is consistent with Vitoria's universalism. He refuses to allow that any individual may be attacked unless that individual has done something to deserve it. Membership in a community, even if that community has committed wrongs, is not a sufficient reason for that member deliberately to be harmed. The ordinary person is assumed to be innocent unless shown to be otherwise.[34] Children are probably the best example of those who ought to enjoy immunity, but many—indeed-most—others are usually blameless.

Of importance, Vitoria's respect for what has become known as the principle of discrimination extends to placing the burden of proof on those who would inflict violence. It is not up to the innocent to prove their innocence; rather the soldier's default is that a person is innocent unless compelling evidence suggests otherwise.

This assumption, however, does not guarantee immunity for the innocent. Vitoria realizes that attempts to wage war morally encounter practical impediments that may sometimes bring about evil results, even if no evil is desired. The inaccuracy of weapons or the co-location of the innocent with legitimate military targets may put the innocent at mortal peril. This unintended but foreseen killing of the innocent is an application of Aquinas's notion of double effect. The character of armed conflict itself and the weaponry used in it are part of the causal account Vitoria gives. The innocent deaths are in part due to the nature and tools of war. The just war can bring about tragedy without rendering its warriors unjust. But along with Aquinas, Vitoria limits the application of double effect to those instances in which the evil done is outweighed by the good achieved.[35] And regardless of proportion, the slaying of the innocent must be *necessary*. That is, there has to have been no other way to achieve victory.[36] Again, the idea of limit is explicit in Vitoria. Wishing for a war without innocent deaths is one thing; winning one without them is something else again. Vitoria tries to reconcile the competing tugs of winning war and respecting innocent lives. He insists, first of all, that the innocent deaths must not be the intended consequence of the military operation. They are the unintended, evil effect, whereas advancing toward victory in a just war is the good effect. Second, the evil effect must not be out of proportion to the good effect. Last, there must be no alternative to the killing of the innocent. For Vitoria, under these conditions, their deaths, although certainly evil, may be justifiable.

Francisco Suarez

Like Vitoria, Suarez approached the moral problems presented by war from a natural law perspective. His most significant contributions lie in two aspects of JWT: the distinction between offensive and defensive war and the nature of just cause.

Suarez permitted war on grounds of self-defense,[37] but he insisted that the proper attitude is necessary for a war to be honorable; it is behavior that is to be attacked, not individuals as such.[38] Offensive wars could be just as well, so long as they were waged to correct an injustice already committed.[39]

The concept of just cause is treated extensively. War's inherently evil, destructive nature always requires careful justification.[40] Like his predecessors, Suarez held that if there were avenues short of war available to correct wrongs, then a war could not be justified, but in the absence of such alternatives, warfare is permitted.[41] He emphasized that the cause for war must be serious, because war is itself serious. Wars are not to be waged over trivial matters, although Suarez is at pains to note that what may seem trivial to an offender may not seem so trivial to those suffering the offense.[42]

Just causes break into three general classes for Suarez. The first is the taking of property; the second, denial of commonly recognized activities such as trade or free passage; and the third is "any grave injury to one's reputation or honor."[43] The insult need not be a direct one; offenses suffered by one's subjects, friends, or allies may be sufficient cause. In the case of friends or allies, however, a just cause is evident only if they would be justified in defending themselves.[44] Moreover, Suarez explicitly endorses punishing wrongdoing as a just cause but only as a last resort, that is, after negotiations for other means of recompense have failed. This idea of last resort receives much attention today, although it is usually construed a bit more broadly than Suarez seems to have construed it. Suarez views punishing wrongs in the international realm to be analogous to punishing domestic crime. If one state is wronged by another, there is also an offense against international peace.[45]

Suarez surfaced the question of certain military members' responsibility for *jus ad bellum* issues. Rulers are encouraged to seek the counsel of their senior military officers. If such counsel is sought, then the senior officers are required to inquire carefully into the matter of just cause and to offer honest advice. If their advice is not sought, however, their role becomes like that of common soldiers; they bear no responsibility for the justice of the war outside of *jus in bello* concerns.[46]

Relations among states are fraught with complexity and uncertainty, as Vitoria noted. Suarez takes up the problem extensively. For him, the head of state, the military commanders, and the common soldiers must all enjoy as much certainty as is realistically possible in that their roles sometimes permit them to wage war. Naturally, the ruler is required to investigate carefully the purported just cause. A preponderance of the evidence is sufficient to make a decision, but in genuinely equivocal cases, just cause is called into doubt.[47] In cases like these, Suarez suggests that the contending parties ought to compromise, taking as objective an attitude regarding the matter as possible. He proposes selecting mediators acceptable to both sides, although he grants that such an event would be rare in actual practice, because one side or the other may not trust the mediators.[48]

Suarez considers whether a ruler ought to be certain of victory before initiating war. After all, one could think a ruler incompetent if he attempted to enforce domestic law without sufficient force to render successful arrests likely, but he rejects the requirement for certain victory on three grounds. First, certainty is impossible. Second, requiring certainty may necessitate undue delay in initiating a war. And third, such a requirement would prohibit the weaker from ever engaging the stronger in war. Instead, Suarez suggests that a sovereign contemplating war should have a reasonable expectation of victory or at least 50–50 odds.[49] This concept survives in modern JWT as the criterion of "reasonable hope of success."

In general, the idea that wars can be justified on religious grounds is rejected. Suarez explicitly discounts the idea of men seeking vengeance on God's behalf because God has more than adequate power to seek His own.[50] The only exception is the case in which a ruler opposes his subject's conversion to Christianity. In that case, those wishing to convert may be defended against their own ruler.[51] And the lack of religious belief itself is neither cause for war nor evidence of needing a European ruler, "for it is evident that there are many unbelievers more gifted by nature than are the faithful, and better adapted to political life."[52]

If a cause is honestly just, its justice ought to be discernible by the rulers of the opposing state. For this reason, Suarez requires a declaration of that just cause before initiating violence. This gives the opposition an opportunity to examine the cause and determine whether they agree that it is just. If they do, then war may be avoided by accommodating the requirements of justice. In other words, if the state that is about to be attacked sees the justice of the other side's cause, it can avoid war by satisfying its demands, thereby remedying the *casus belli* and settling the matter short of bloodshed.[53]

Suarez's natural law reasoning extends to the right to be educated in the natural law and in religion. In the event that a nation were to believe in false gods or practice irrationality, a Christian state that lived according to the natural law would be justified in sending missionaries to enlighten it. If the attempts to educate were to be met with armed hostility, then violence might justifiably be used to defeat it. It is interesting that Suarez defends this justification on the grounds of natural law. All human beings have a natural right to learn the natural laws, so, for Suarez, anyone who obstructs that learning is guilty of wrongdoing against the innocent, and as such warring against them is a form of defending the innocent.[54]

Ordinary military members are provided ethical guidelines as well. Pillaging and other unnecessary harm are forbidden, and commanders are required to ensure compliance with this prohibition.[55] Likewise, Suarez forbids intentionally harming innocent persons. He appreciates, however, that innocent people are sometime harmed unintentionally in war, and he appeals to double effect to justify their deaths. "[In] such a case the death of the innocent is not directly intended, it follows rather as an incidental consequence.[56] The key points here are necessity and intention. The deaths of the innocent are foreseen but not intended; those causing the innocent deaths are justified in doing so if there is no other way to achieve victory. This approach to justifying the death of innocent people in war remains in contention today, and is addressed in chapter 5.

Life and property are different things, and Suarez is much less restrictive concerning the latter. He permits pillaging under certain conditions, justifying it in terms of the equitable treatment of soldiers. Common soldiers are bound to follow the orders they are given. This requires a certain fortitude, which soldiers are obligated to demonstrate as required. And if, with the consent of their ruler, some soldiers happen to make off with loot, this may be regarded as compensation for the risks they bear.[57]

Like Aquinas, Suarez permits concealment of military plans and operations, although he insists that one must keep faith with one's enemy. This is true, of course, only if each side keeps faith with the other. If one state breaks faith, the second is not obligated to keep faith.[58]

It is clear that Vitoria and Suarez contributed many concepts that have a familiar ring today. Most important, they approached the problem impartially. What holds for one commonwealth holds for all like commonwealths because natural laws are universal laws: they apply equally regardless of one's political or geographic status.

Hugo Grotius (1583–1645) and the Roots of International Law

Grotius is famous for his comprehensive book, *The Law of War and Peace*, published in 1625. In it the natural law approach is both defended and applied. His systematic, common-sense approach yields a result that bears a striking resemblance to modern JWT.

Grotius lived during one of the most violent periods of European history—the Thirty Years War. This war of Christians against Christians made it clear that any appeal to religious hierarchies for solving disputes between states was doomed to fail. Grotius put it this way: "On trifling pretexts, or none at all, men rush to arms, and when once arms are taken up, all respect for law, whether human or divine, is lost."[59] Whatever appeal there may have been to ecclesiastical authority as a means of keeping a relatively just peace was clearly futile, as the war was fought over contending views of the Christian religion and its influence on the affairs of states and their populace.

A defense of international justice itself opens *The Law of War and Peace*. Grotius grants that, for many, "might makes right" is the only accurate description of relations between states. But, he rejects this view by deploying an analogy between life within states and life among states. Humans cannot live well without society, and societies therefore require law to maintain order among their members. The same is true among states. Grotius goes on to appeal to the Christian God as the source of all goods, but he does not believe that one has to acknowledge God's existence to understand the laws of nature. Anyone of reasonable intelligence can deduce that living in an orderly and just society is advantageous to every law-abiding member. And just as it is advantageous to live amicably with one's fellow citizens, it is advantageous for states to live amicably in the international arena.[60]

For Grotius, individuals arrange their societies by consent, and so the laws people invent for themselves (these are often called *positive* laws) are not natural laws. Unlike natural laws, which remain unchanged over time, positive laws may be changed. To use a modern example, individuals can agree to drive on the right side of the road, as in the United States, or on the left, as in Britain. Which side really is not important; either one is consistent with the nature of humans. But the failure to agree would be problematic indeed, and much mayhem and death would result if there was no agreement on *some* common side for each direction. Likewise, many other laws established for communities are human inventions. Because human beings are social beings, however, the requirement to live in a community in order to live well is a law of nature. Laws of nature are discovered rather than invented. It is impossible to legislate a well-lived life's dependence on an orderly and safe community out of existence; it is a natural fact. Moreover, all humans, even the most powerful rulers, are subject to natural law. The mighty may violate natural law, but they can never overturn it. Natural laws accordingly provide a firm foundation for relations among both individuals and states.

Following the law is in each citizen's interest. Indeed, the law protects each citizen from all the others, something no individual could ever do alone. And so, obeying the laws that the community has established is to a citizen's advantage, even though sometimes it may appear otherwise in the short term. Those who break the law undermine the very order on which their well-being, and indeed, their lives depend. So it is with the community of nations.[61] Grotius appeals to what seems to be a common sense appreciation of long-term, mutual self-interest. Although at any given time, some states will be much stronger than others, and it may therefore seem that they could act with impunity, in fact, the element of time is not on their side. The relative strength of states changes over the years. State A may be the strongest state today, but it cannot count on that being true 50, or even 20 years from today. If State A decides to violate international law by taking unfair advantage of other states because of their relative weakness, a precedent is set that the strong may oppress the weak, regardless of justice's demands. Eventually, that precedent may come to haunt State A, as history teaches that the power equation always shifts. Further, even the strongest of states may be confronted by a combined force of smaller states and may need assistance in defending itself.[62] Understanding these facts, State A should realize that respecting international law is in its long-term best interests. The rulers of today make decisions that will affect their grandchildren and later generations as well.

Grotius and Resort to War

Grotius did not restrict the right to wage war to heads of states. "Private" wars as well as "mixed" wars (wars that have both public and private aspects) are sometimes permissible.[63] The discussion of his work here considers public wars only.

Like his predecessors, Grotius holds that (public) wars require the authority of the state's ruler. But even rulers are not permitted to require their subjects to violate natural law. Should one receive an order to act contrary to natural law, one would be justified in disobeying it.[64]

Clear-headed sensitivity characterizes Grotius's treatment of just cause. Like Vitoria and Suarez, he excludes all causes except defending against or responding to harm.[65] In the case of defense, the injury need not have already been inflicted; imminent threat is sufficient for nations just as it is in cases of private self-defense.[66] Self-defense justifies violence not because of any misconduct of the aggressor; rather it derives from the common and natural urge to stay alive.[67] This distinction is familiar to modern just war thinkers. The right of self-defense does not depend on the moral guilt of the assailant. The assailant may be intoxicated or insane, but the person assaulted still has the right to defend himself against an immediate threat. Here, Grotius appeals to double effect—the preservation of one's life is the intended outcome; the death of the assailant is foreseeable but not intended. Indeed, for self-defense to operate as a just cause for doing violence, there must be no other option than violence.[68] If a better option (escape, say) were available but one still killed, claiming self defense, it would seem that the death *was* intended after all. Moreover, this right to protect oneself does not convey the right to do anything at all that might seem necessary. For example, innocent third parties may not be harmed even if doing so would contribute to one's protection.[69]

Defense justifies violence only in cases of imminent threat. A mere suspicion or fear that one may someday be attacked does not qualify as a just cause.[70] Grotius explicitly excludes what today is called "preventive war": "[T]he bare possibility that violence may be some day turned on us gives us the right to inflict violence on others is a doctrine repugnant to every principle of justice."[71]

For the sake of accuracy, it should be noted that much of the foregoing discussion of self-defense as a just cause regards what Grotius calls "private war," that is, war that is not conducted on a state's authority. But he says that the concepts apply equally to "public war," those wars declared by a government.

Another major category of just cause, punishment, is discussed in some depth as well. Here again his work laid foundations for principles in common use today.

For Grotius, natural law holds that those who violate the rights of others unfairly have willed the punishment that the rights violations entail. But another question remains—who has the right to inflict the punishment?[72] Given that in relations between nations no one ruler is superior to another, the right to punish belongs to the rulers of states. In a departure from earlier JWT, Grotius suggests that any ruler has the right to punish another state for transgressions.[73] The right to punish belongs to each member of the community of nations just because a violation of the law of nations is a crime against the community, not merely the victimized state. This insight substitutes an internationalized framework for thinking about justice for a particularized one. It favors no member of the international community over another. Within a state, the government assumes the right to prosecute crimes against citizens or their property on behalf of the well-being and security of all citizens. Grotius takes that same logic to the international level, where, in the absence of a global authority, each member has the right to punish violators. But, Grotius warns, to use punishment as a just cause is to require clear evidence that punishment is warranted in the first place.[74]

History, states, and governments being what they are, Grotius devotes himself extensively to distinguishing between genuinely just causes, dubious causes, and mere pretexts for war. Among the unjust causes he includes fear of other nations' power, desire for better lands, or a desire for emancipation on the part of those held in lawful slavery. It is equally unjust, however, to make war in order to enslave others.[75] He notes that "Expediency does not confer the same right as necessity."[76] By this he seems to rule out waging war for political ends that are not necessary for a state, but merely advantageous.

Doubtful causes require treatment as well, for ambiguity plagues relations among states and moral questions do not lend themselves to mathematical precision.[77] Here, Grotius echoes Suarez; in matters as important as war, doubts should cause rulers to refrain from war, and instead seek some other means of resolving their dispute, such as arbitration.[78] And, if a ruler contemplating initiating warfare himself believes it to be wrong, then that very belief is enough to render waging the war impermissible.[79] Grotius goes on to note, however, that the opposite is not true. Although objectively speaking, a war cannot be just on both sides, those waging it against each other may, nonetheless, both *believe* that they are fighting a just war. Many are ignorant of what an honestly objective view of political matters would reveal, even if such a view were possible. This means that unjust acts may be committed without unjust intentions. Having put this distinction between the objective justice of a war and how it is subjectively believed to be just in place, Grotius deduces the moral requirement that rulers ought to be transparent about their reasons for going to war. Restated, his argument takes this form: Ambiguity in international relations, coupled with the frailties of human beings, results in doubts about justice of some wars. But wars are grave matters, often involving the deaths of many innocent persons. Therefore, going to war requires clear and easily understood justification.

Moreover, even in a case where the justice of a war may be evident, Grotius counsels rulers to forebear. What is permitted is not always wise or charitable. If punishment is warranted, one ought to punish out of love, as good parents do. Hence, as a wise and thoughtful parent might exercise forbearance over a child's transgression, so a ruler might be wise to do so in international relations. The virtue of forbearance tempers the cold dictates of justice and renders those who forbear more virtuous than those who insist on demanding everything that is their due.[80]

One may be obligated to refrain from a just war on the grounds of justice, as well as forbearance. It is just to punish transgressors, but rulers are also obligated by justice to protect their subjects from unnecessary losses of life and property. Wars naturally risk those losses. Thus justice among states must be viewed in light of justice within one's state. Indeed, he points out that rulers are obligated to *all* of their subjects. This means that if some subjects have suffered at the hands of an adversary and are thus seemingly "owed" a war to redress the wrongdoing they have suffered, the ruler must nonetheless consider the effects of a subsequent just war on all of his subjects.[81] Indeed, Grotius goes so far as to say that a ruler may require one subject to suffer for the good of the others. This he explains as arising from the duty to love others in one's community.[82] To help understand this point, think of the modern policy of refusing to negotiate with those who take hostages. The hostages are in some sense being sacrificed for the good of the state, because giving in to such a demand would naturally encourage more hostage-taking.

Grotius is a keen student of human folly and the risks it poses to communities. This is particularly true in the case of rulers, whose decisions about warfare can affect the lives of many but who are nonetheless subject to the same human conditions that limit the rest of us.[83] Accordingly, Grotius advises statesmen to adopt a carefully critical skepticism regarding any eagerness to resort to warfare. This counsel to take a long-term, comprehensive look at the potential consequences of political decisions is captured further by Grotius's consideration of ends and means. He explicitly acknowledges that decisions to engage in warfare have consequences that may be understood in terms of good and evil and recommends that rulers seek to make decisions that would survive a critical analysis of cost (evil) and benefit (good).[84] Modern military ethicists understand this line of thinking as the *jus ad bellum* criterion of proportionality.

Grotius's treatment of proportionality, however, ought to be understood in light of his deep appreciation of the horrors of war. No doubt the Thirty Years War helped make the horrors vivid for him. Even if a war is deemed just, that does not make resorting to war something good. Rather, the evils of even a just war ought to be taken into account by just, practical rulers.[85] This insight anticipates the modern *jus ad bellum* criterion of last resort.

So far Grotius's work has been considered as it pertains to rulers. He also addressed the obligations of subjects. Not surprisingly for a natural law theorist, he appeals to an individual's reason to help illuminate the obligations that arise in the case of someone's being ordered to fight in a war. If it is clear that the war is unjust, the individual must refuse to fight in it, regardless of orders from human superiors. The case is more controversial if the justice or injustice of a particular war is in question in the person's mind. Grotius treats these cases of doubt judiciously. On the one hand, it might be suggested that disobedience is immoral and that it threatens the civil order. On the other, killing unjustly is a worse evil than is disobedience. Grotius settles on the ethically more conservative course, advocating disobedience in the case of doubt.[86]

These reflections on the doubts or concerns that ordinary people might face when confronted with war again lead Grotius to recommend transparency on the part of rulers. A wise ruler makes the reasons for war both public and compelling for his subjects. If the war is just, it ought to be seen as just through the lens of ordinary reason. Then, doubts will be removed. The very existence of these doubts, however, suggests that the war is unjust or that the rulers have not revealed all of the facts behind their decision to wage war.[87] In no case, however, do individuals lose the right of self-defense. That means that they may fight in an unjust war if the adversary is killing innocents.[88]

Grotius and Conduct in War

Unlike many later theorists, Grotius views the question of just conduct in war as being tightly linked to the justice of the war itself. Most of what follows, then, rests on the assumption that those doing violence in war are doing so in a war that is itself justified.[89] First, however, it is appropriate to highlight once again Grotius's remarkable sensitivity to the human condition. It is particularly evident regarding the mistakes that people engaged in a war tend to commit. He notes that people do violence out of varying mental states. Some kill in war out of deliberate intention, but many find themselves compelled or caught up in warlike enthusiasm. Not all are equally deserving of punishment. Moreover, many victims on each side are simply unfortunate. They become involved in war's harms merely by virtue of geography.

Grotius approaches the problem of killing by deploying concepts already familiar from his treatment of just cause. Killing must be limited to two classes of victims: those who deserve it as a just penalty and those who deserve no harm but are necessary to kill in order to protect life and property.[90]

Assuming that a just war is being waged against a wrongdoer, then, Grotius accepts that harm may be done unintentionally to innocent people, but, of course, he does not endorse it. Even in the case of "incidental" killing of the innocent, however, Grotius sets a high threshold; such killing must be the justified by its being the only means to keep many other innocent people safe.[91]

Grotius notes that justice may permit what love or virtue might prohibit.[92] Talk of chivalry, although largely limited to training environments today, echoes this insight in the modern military.

Although much of his discussion is focused on the treatment of captives, Grotius offers some general underlying considerations for evaluating the guilt of those who kill in war. He relies on Aristotle's distinctions between wrongdoing, error, and misfortune. Those guilty of wrongdoing have deliberated on the act before committing it. In the case of misfortune, the spur to the wrongdoing is external to the person committing the act, as in the case of coercion. The middle state is error, in which the harm is foreseen, but not intended. Each of these cases deserves a different sort of response if justice is to be served. In the case of premeditated wrongdoing, the wrongdoer is obligated to make reparations and is liable to punishment as well. In the case of misfortune, neither reparation nor punishment is required. In the case of error, reparation is required, but punishment is not.[93] Many cases of killing those who do not deserve to be killed fall into this middle class.[94] Killing that is done from "necessity" is to be judged more leniently than murder.

With the charitable tone that permeated Grotius's approach to the problems of *jus in bello* in mind, it is easy to appreciate his denomination of certain classes as innocent just by virtue of who they are. Children and women (unless they have committed crimes or are performing the duties of men) are excluded as targets.[95] More interestingly, those whose activities have nothing to do with violence in war are also excluded. On this ground he excludes scholars, farmers, merchants, and artisans.[96] These exclusions seem to anticipate a distinction commonly used by more modern military ethicists—one that differentiates activities that can serve only military purposes from those that serve everyone's. Notice that farmers, the clergy, merchants, and others serve the needs of human beings whether or not they are soldiers. Everyone needs to eat. But persons who deliberately engage in organized armed conflict engage in acts that can be coherently understood only as either war or crime. The fact that they, too, need to eat does not thereby make the farmer a legitimate military target.[97]

As suggested previously, Grotius appreciates that warfare is a temporary state and that those waging war do not on that account lose their humanity. Prisoners, even if they may have transgressed (by carrying arms against their future captor) before being captured, are therefore to be spared death, as they no longer pose any sort of threat.[98]

The forward-looking moderation that characterizes Grotius's treatment of *jus ad bellum* and *jus in bello* extends to conduct after victory is achieved, or *jus post bellum*. Wars are to be waged with the goal of a just peace in mind, and conquerors are obligated to make that just peace a reality. Once the adversary's ability to harm is obviated, the victor is well advised to exercise moderation both for virtue's sake and as a means to the end of a lasting peace. Grotius recommends that the vanquished be permitted to retain governing power as long as it does not threaten the security of the victors.[99] Indeed, he notes that it is often more difficult to maintain possession of a territory than it is to gain possession of it, noting with Florus that while "provinces . . . are taken by force, they are held by justice."[100] Even if security concerns render leaving government in the hands of the conquered unwise, one may still leave them partial power and their laws and customs. Grotius recommends that they be permitted to continue their religious practices as well, as this kindness costs the victors little but is cherished by the vanquished.[101]

It is hard to overstate Grotius's importance to JWT's evolution. His insights and careful appreciation of human and political conditions render a fair summary nearly impossible. He advanced JWT by translating it into a universal language that any reasonable person could both understand and apply to the real world. This laid the foundations for international law as we know it today.

Enlightenment Thinkers

The Enlightenment improved on the preceding JWT with an extremely influential underpinning for thinking about states and their citizens—the development of rights theory. Although the theory itself has already been introduced, at this point it is appropriate to discuss two major historical figures in the theory's development: John Locke (1632–1704) and Immanuel Kant (1724–1804).

Locke famously argued that the moral status of a state is dependent on its respect for the rights of its individual members. Typically, this respect is signified by the citizenry's agreeing to the state's exercise of power. The "consent of the governed" is the moral basis of the state's authority.

This means that individual rights are logically prior to the rights of governments. Accordingly, a government that rules without the consent of its citizens is not legitimate and may morally be cast off by the people themselves. This idea, central of course to both the American and French Revolutions of the late 18th century, is equally central to an understanding of modern politics and JWT.

Immanuel Kant, writing in the period of these revolutions, evolved an extraordinarily detailed analysis of morality itself that forms an important component of understanding rights. As outlined previously, the idealized notion of a right to noninterference is crucial to this theory (and to Locke's). The right to noninterference means that one has the fundamental right to be left alone and at liberty unless one consents to some restrictions on that right. Most citizens of liberal democracies give their consent to many restrictions almost without thinking and so willfully accept limits on their freedom in return for the security and other benefits their communities provide. It is important to note, however, that the very idea of consent presupposes freedom. It is often in this sense that modern just war thinkers refer to the value of freedom and the obligation to defend it.

Kant made another contribution to JWT that is of ongoing and arguably increasing influence. In an essay he called "Perpetual Peace," Kant outlined the idea of a federation among previously independent states. Kant granted, with earlier JWT, that violence is the only mechanism available to nations to defend their rights in the international arena insofar as no other means of defense was available; however, he did not take this state of affairs to be unsusceptible to improvement. Instead, Kant argued that it was possible to build a league of free states that would operate together to guarantee mutual safety over the long term. The federation would be composed only of those states having republican style governments. Such states, according to Kant, would be unable to resort to war in the absence of their population's consent. If consent were to be given, these states, recognizing that peaceful relations serve the interests of all in the long term, would act to defend the rights of individual members of the league, whether the threat came from within the league or from without. Other states would observe the success of the league, guaranteeing its expansion over time.[102]

Kant's thoughts are so obviously embodied in the modern day United Nations as to make the observation seem almost trivial. Like his essay, however, it must be observed, that the devil is in the details.

20th Century Development: Michael Walzer

Talk of human rights is pervasive in modern liberal democracies. The 1948 United Nations Declaration of Human Rights, inspired in part by the savagery of the Second World War and the Holocaust, has taken the discourse further into the international arena. As a matter of conceptual history, the overview of the history of JWT concludes with the 20th-century classic, *Just and Unjust Wars*. Most of those working in the field of military ethics today regard this book, which first appeared in 1977, as indispensable.

Walzer relies on the importance of freedom from interference as a crucial element in understanding the distinction between just and unjust wars. As a grossly oversimplified summary, those wars that are necessary to defend human rights against aggression are generally justified. Those that either fail to respect or actively seek to deny human rights are generally unjust wars. Walzer's evaluation, therefore, of the Allies engagement in the Second World War, shows it to be justified. Naturally, however, the Axis powers were unjustified, particularly in their genocidal respects. To test this claim, one might ask those under Nazi rule in Europe whether they consented to that rule. Plainly they did not, as they actively resisted the Nazi invasions and occupations. On the other hand, Allied forces were welcomed in Europe as liberators—quite literally setting occupied Europe free.

On the other hand, Walzer judges the United States's involvement in Vietnam as unjust. This judgment is based on the fact that the majority of Vietnamese did not express their consent to the regimes that the United States defended. Walzer takes the will of communities as compelling the respect of other communities unless that will gravely endangers human rights.

Walzer is probably most well known for his analysis of certain violations of traditional *jus in bello* criteria in the name of the defense of rights. This well-known contribution goes under the name of "supreme emergency" and is addressed at length in chapter 5.

Notes

1. Plato, *Republic,* 470e9, trans. G.M.A. Grube, rev. C.D.C. Reeve (Indianapolis: Hackett Publishing 1992), 146.

2. Aristotle, *Politics,* 1256b22–26. *The Basic Works of Aristotle,* trans. Benjamin Jowett, ed. Richard McKeon (New York: Random House, 1941), 1137.

3. Regarding the criteria for a just war: (1) It must be waged by the state, not an individual of party. (2) A formal declaration of war is required. (3) Good faith is to be observed with the enemy. And (4) magnanimity toward the defeated is to be observed. Roland Bainton, *Christian Attitudes Toward War and Peace: A Historical Survey and Critical Re-evaluation* (New York: Abingdon Press, 1960), 41–42.

4. Matt 5: 39–40. Also see, Matt 5:9; 5:21–22; 5:43–48; 26:52–53; Rom 12:17–21. *New English Bible: New Testament* (Cambridge: Cambridge University Press, 1972), 7.

5. Bainton, *Christian Attitudes Toward War and Peace: A Historical Survey and Critical Re-evaluation,* 67–68.

6. Ibid., 68.

7. Ibid.

8. St. Augustine, *The City of God.* trans. M. Dods (New York: Modern Library, 1950), 113.

9. Bainton, *Christian Attitudes Toward War and Peace: A Historical Survey and Critical Re-evaluation,* 95.

10. Paul Christopher, *The Ethics of War and Peace* (Englewood Cliffs, NJ: Prentice Hall, 1994), 35.

11. St. Augustine, *The City of God,* 687.

12. Ibid., 683.

13. Ibid., 27.

14. Augustine does, however, exclude monks and priests from shedding blood. Bainton, *Christian Attitudes Toward War and Peace: A Historical Survey and Critical Re-evaluation,* 14.

15. St. Augustine, "Act, Agent and Authority," in *War and Christian Ethics,* ed. Arthur F. Holmes (Grand Rapids, MI: Baker Book House, 1975), 65.

16. I believe Michael Walzer was the first to put the concept this way. See his *Just and Unjust Wars* (New York: Basic Books, 1977), 34.

17. Thomas Aquinas, "Summa Theologica," in *The Morality of War.* eds. Larry May, Eric Rovie, and Steve Viner (Upper Saddle River, NJ: Pearson Prentice Hall, 2006), 27–28.

18. Ibid., 28.

19. St. Thomas Aquinas, Summa Theologica: Second Part of the Second Part, Question 40, Article 3. Available at http://www.newadvent.org/summa/3040.htm#article3. Accessed July 8, 2009.

20. Modern versions of double effect typically require that only the good effect be intended, that the evil effect cannot be a means to the good effect, that the act itself not be intrinsically evil, and that the good effect be proportionally greater than the evil effect. Double effect is treated in detail in chapter 5.

21. St. Thomas Aquinas, "Summa Theologica," in *The Morality of War.* eds. Larry May, Eric Rovie, and Steve Viner, 32.

22. St. Thomas Aquinas, "Summa Theologica," in *War and the Christian Conscience: From Augustine to Martin Luther King, Jr.* ed. Albert Marrin (Chicago: Henry Regnery Co., 1971), 72–73.

23. Francisco de Vitoria, "On the American Indians," in *The Ethics of War: Classic and Contemporary Readings,* eds. Gregory M. Reichberg, Henrik Syse, and Endre Begby (Malden, MA: Blackwell Publishing, 2006), 291.

24. Aristotle, Politics, I, 4–7 (1253b23–1255b40) trans., Benjamin Jowett in *The Basic Works of Aristotle,* ed., Richard McKeon (New York: Random House, 1941).

25. Gregory M. Reichberg, Henrik Syse, and Endre Begby, eds., *The Ethics of War: Classic and Contemporary Readings,* 289.

26. de Vitoria, "On the American Indians," in *The Ethics of War: Classic and Contemporary Readings,* 293.

27. de Vitoria, "On the Law of War," in *The Morality of War.* eds. Larry May, Eric Rovie, and Steve Viner, 39.

28. Ibid.

29. Ibid., 48.

30. de Vitoria, "On the Law of War," *The Ethics of War: Classic and Contemporary Readings,* 319.

31. Ibid.

32. Ibid., 318.

33. de Vitoria, "On the Law of War," in *The Morality of War,* eds. Larry May, Eric Rovie, and Steve Viner, 41.

34. Ibid.

35. Ibid.

36. Ibid.

37. Francisco Suarez, "Justice, Charity, and War" *The Ethics of War: Classic and Contemporary Readings,* 341.

38. Ibid.

39. Ibid., 342.

40. Ibid., 348.

41. Ibid., 347.

42. Ibid., 348.

43. Ibid.

44. Ibid., 349.

45. Ibid., 349–350.

46. Ibid., 359.

47. Ibid., 357–358.

48. Ibid., 358–359.

49. Ibid., 352–353.

50. Ibid., 353.

51. Ibid., 355.

52. Ibid.

53. Ibid., 361.

54. Ibid., 356.

55. Ibid., 361.

56. Ibid., 365.

57. Ibid., 363.

58. Ibid., 367.

59. Grotius, *The Law of War and Peace.* trans. Louise R. Loomis (Roslyn, NY: Walter J. Black, 1949), 20–21.

60. Naturally, the analogy of an individual living among her fellows in a state to a nation living among its fellows in an international community is far from perfect. The dis-analogous elements are many, but at least two deserve mention here. First, an in-

dividual living in a nation is held accountable for her actions as an individual, but the actions of a ruler often bring consequences for entire communities or nations. Second, individuals are ordinarily subordinate to the authority of their communities, and that authority is backed by overwhelming force. The relative power of states, however, varies widely.

61. Grotius, *The Law of War and Peace*, 8.

62. Ibid., 9.

63. Ibid., 38.

64. Ibid., 59.

65. Ibid., 72.

66. Ordinary intuitions suggest that Sam is justified in defending himself against an assailant once it becomes obvious that the assailant is intent on doing physical violence to Sam and Sam has no other way to avoid the violence. Sam is morally permitted to block a punch and respond with one of his own even if the assailant's punch never lands on Sam.

67. Grotius, *The Law of War and Peace*, 72.

68. Grotius, "On the Law of War and Peace" in *The Ethics of War,* 402–403.

69. Grotius, *The Law of War and Peace,* 73.

70. Ibid.

71. Ibid., 77.

72. Ibid., 207.

73. Ibid., 226.

74. Ibid., 228.

75. Ibid., 245–247.

76. Ibid., 246.

77. Ibid., 250. Grotius alludes here to Aristotle's observation in the *Nichomachean Ethics* (1094b12–28) that "precision is not to be sought for alike in all discussions . . . it is the mark of an educated man to look for precision in each class of things just so far as the nature of the subject admits" Aristotle, "Nichomachean Ethics," trans W. D. Ross in *The Basic Works of Aristotle,* 936.

78. Grotius, *The Law of War and Peace*, 251–252.

79. Ibid., 250–251.

80. Ibid., 255–256.

81. Ibid., 260.

82. Ibid., 261.

83. Ibid., 256–257.

84. Ibid., 257.

85. Ibid., 259.

86. Ibid., 266–267. Grotius attributes this advice to Pope Adrian.

87. Ibid., 267.

88. Ibid., 267.

89. Ibid., 344.

90. Ibid., 347.

91. Ibid., 353.

92. Ibid., 347.

93. Ibid., 350.

94. Ibid., 348–350.

95. Ibid., 354.

96. Ibid., 355.

97. Ibid., 271–272. Grotius makes a related point in his discussion of an adversary's trading partners, distinguishing among the goods traded in terms of their usefulness for making war.

98. Ibid., 356–357.

99. Ibid., 376–377.

100. Ibid., 377.

101. Ibid., 378–379. Grotius qualifies this recommendation by permitting whatever measures are necessary "to protect the true faith".

102. Immanuel Kant, "On History" trans. Lewis White Beck in Kant, *On History,* ed. Lewis White Beck (Indianapolis: Bobbs-Merrill, 1963), 85–135.

CHAPTER 3

Philosophical Foundations of Military Ethics

Military ethics focuses on a relatively narrow but extremely consequential arena of human conduct. It is narrow in the sense that the problems it studies and the prescriptions it provides apply primarily only to state-actors: political leaders and the military forces that execute their decisions. Ordinary individuals are stakeholders in the decisions of state-actors, but most of them know little about international relations or military matters. They usually know even less about military ethics. Yet military ethics is profoundly significant because those state-actors may use violence that affects the course of global history. Lives may be enhanced, diminished, or ended by war's effects, regardless of the knowledge or preferences of those so affected. As Leon Trotsky supposedly noted: "You may not be interested in war, but war is interested in you."

Military ethics works in a specialized problem space tied tightly to political philosophy, history, and psychology. Influences from all of these characterize the field, helping to define its limits and contributing depth. Its jurisdiction is further characterized and enriched by the nature of military service itself and the functional requirements that nature imposes on military members.

Three interrelated aspects of this jurisdiction demand examination. The first has to do with structural and social characteristics that form the backdrop for understanding ethically significant aspects of military service. The second concerns some of the most fundamental normative aspects of military service, that is, the ethical obligations that come to an individual as a result of entering military service. This includes what are sometimes called the military virtues. The third is composed of competing philosophical perspectives regarding the use of force, and the creative tension that results both for military ethics as an academic endeavor and military persons as a practical part of the job.

The Nature of Military Service

Many civilians seem to regard the military community as akin to exotic folk living in a distant and isolated land. This sense of distance is created in part by geography. Most of the military community in many countries is centered on self-contained bases that are sometimes remote and often secure. Many military members not only work but also reside on the base, especially when deployed. Moreover, the military wears special dress and practices special customs. These include the willing surrender of certain freedoms, submission to a strict hierarchy, and, of course, engaging in deliberate acts of both killing others and risking violent death. Depending on the era, this social distance may magnify the general public's admiration for the military or diminish it.

The military's seemingly strange ways reflect an important and ethically salient fact about military members. Military people occupy a special place in society; in some ways their place is perhaps better described as being along society's borders. They enjoy privileges and bear burdens that, taken together, form a unique sociological landscape accompanied by equally unique ethical issues.

Two special qualities of military service are particularly relevant for military ethics. First, militaries act as agencies of their states or communities. Second, this agency includes the functions of dispensing and absorbing violence. These two aspects of military service are at the core of many of the seemingly odd aspects of the military community. Most military customs and policies are, at least in theory, functionally linked to them.

The first special quality has to do with the military's acting on behalf of a political community. Entry into the military renders an individual distinct from most others in that it constitutes entry into public office. When a person is acting as a military member, at least in a liberal democracy, she is acting as a representative of her state. Her actions are taken in the name of the community that she defends. Ordinary language, for example, referring to the military as *the service,* reflects this relationship—performing military functions is a service to the community. That service is performed on the community's authority and with the community's funding. Consequently, the moral quality of the service reflects on the community served. Many militaries are intensely image-conscious as a result. This consciousness is driven in part by the same sorts of public-relations needs that are common to many organizations, but it is also driven by special ethical concerns. The military is entrusted with violent power by the community it defends. The community, therefore, must be able to trust its military with its security. As the military acts on the authority of its community, the community's image also depends on the military's international reputation.

The military member enjoys support from the state, but that support varies in ethically important ways from the more ordinary relationships that form between corporations and their employees. The agreement to serve may include inducements that benefit the member, or it may result from conscription. In any case, the relationship is patently asymmetrical in that the needs of the state openly supersede the preferences of the member, and in many cases the member is legally committed to serve regardless of her inclinations. The military member frequently is unable to control her own occupational destiny, especially in those states that subordinate the military to civil control. Moreover, the soldier is legally bound to do the state's bidding even at substantial personal inconvenience or hardship. Indeed, a military member is expected to serve the state unto maiming, capture, or death.

This asymmetry is reflected in an individual's transition to military service. Unlike introductory training courses in corporate settings, basic military training seeks to create a thoroughgoing change in identity: it aims to change character in ethically meaningful, as well as militarily useful, ways. If successful, the training establishes certain commitments in the trainee that by their very nature trump ordinary contractual specifications. In most militaries the law makes it impossible or very hard to quit at will in the way that civilians may until one's term of service is completed, but the commitment that militaries seek goes well beyond the boundaries of written agreements. The desired commitment is at the level of deep personal values. Training seeks to change more than what trainees know or can do. It seeks to change what trainees *care* about. States expect their soldiers to do what they are told; the best way to ensure this is to create soldiers who *do not need* to be told. Compliance to the state's orders is best when it is most willing.

It is in part for these reasons that just war thinking (JWT) holds military members strictly responsible for adherence to *jus in bello* principles, but in general, it does not hold them responsible for determining the justice of a war itself. Militaries fight in wars that are not their own in much the same way that physicians treat diseases that are not their own. Both may hope that prevention will maintain health and security, but when it fails they have a duty to respond. Most military members can no more control which wars they will fight than can an emergency room physician what traffic wrecks will occur. For the soldier, to refuse to fight is to refuse to do the state's bidding, with attendant moral and legal peril.

Second, the military member's activities on behalf of the state are ethically remarkable. He is permitted, even required, to kill other human beings deliberately, perhaps many of them. He can do this without being considered guilty of murder if the appropriate conditions are met. Even if he never performs violent acts, it is ethically significant, particularly to deontological thinkers, that he must *intend* to do so. Indeed, much of a military member's time is spent in perfecting the expertise to harm others efficiently, or at least to facilitate that very end. He is expected to become the sort of person who willfully destroys others, often much like him, under certain circumstances.

This intention may present difficult moral problems in itself, regardless of whether the intention is ever carried out. For example, if an officer is assigned as a nuclear missile launch officer or to operate other weapons of mass destruction, then she is expected to form an intention to murder under at least some circumstances. The complex moral issues attendant to these intentions and the techniques military ethics has evolved to handle them are described in chapters 5 and 6.

She is also a legitimate target for adversaries to strike. Should they do so and kill her in conformity to *jus in bello* principles, they are not guilty of murder, and her death, although tragic, is not a result of a crime. At least in liberal democracies, she supposedly understands that she can be a target and is willing to die for the sake of others. One famous military intellectual, Sir John Winthrop Hackett, referred to this aspect of a military member's life as "the unlimited liability clause."[1] The clause may not be executed, but the soldier knows that it could be. This knowledge, in turn, poses ethically laden issues regarding family life. The military member's relatives endure risks that ordinary families do not bear. Military families live with the possibility that the soldier may not come home from a deployment, or may come home but be horribly disabled. At least in theory, the member herself understands and accepts these risks, but her child may not, even as he bears them.[2]

Tradition has evolved to recognize these distinctive aspects of military life in multiple symbolic ways. Oaths are administered demanding obedience to lawful orders. Symbols of rank are mandatory wear and make one's position in the hierarchy explicit. The uniform itself has ethical import. Military members wear a uniform not merely to distinguish themselves from other nations' actors on a field of battle, but to distinguish themselves from the nonmilitary members of their own state. The wear of a uniform signifies that the person inside is a legitimate military target in times of conflict. This aids, of course, in the practical application of the *jus in bello* principle of discrimination. A uniform, or other visibly identifiable sign, helps keep the noncombatant free from harm. The uniformed combatant draws fire away from noncombatants. And if there is anything noble about military service, surely some of that nobility is found in this very concept. The combatant takes on a role of target to spare others. He designates himself as a legitimate target by wearing special clothing and carrying out special activities that noncombatants do not.

Military Training and Socialization

As a matter of sociological fact, most civilians are probably less distinct from the military than many of them think. After all, the military is a social construction, as is the role of soldier. Militaries across the world have adopted generally similar means to transform civilians into soldiers with remarkable efficiency. This observation entails another: military training's effectiveness does not rely on the purposes that a given military serves. The sociology of the training's effects is independent of the moral status of the state providing the training. The Nazis were able to train their soldiers effectively despite serving an obviously immoral political cause.

Basic training in most militaries takes only a matter of weeks, and overall the attrition rate is quite low, in part because most of basic training is not terribly hard to accomplish. Militaries design the training to look difficult and perhaps even dangerous, but it is not so rigorous that most trainees cannot succeed. As Gwynne Dyer has pointed out, "anybody's son will do."[3] Training techniques have been perfected over thousands of years, and military trainers have much professional advice and empirical data to draw on. The recruit, usually in her teens or early twenties, has experienced most of those years as a child and is often still seeking an adult identity. The question of whether military training will "work" is so easily answered on the vast empirical grounds of military history as to be pointless. Despite authority's dependence on consent, resistance is futile, at least in the aggregate.

A deeper question has to do with determining what sort of personal characteristics military people *ought* to have. It is clear that military training can change people. The relevant ethical question asks what they should change into.

Military Virtues

Many military organizations have evolved descriptions of the sort of person they wish their members to be. Typically, values like courage, respect, and excellence are named, but most such lists are underspecified aspirations. They do point to something serious about moral psychology and military ethics, but as yet there is neither an adequate theoretical framework nor an organized empirical data set to support a genuinely rigorous account. Still, it seems safe to say that military members are ethically obligated to serve others, to obey lawful orders, and to exercise the self-mastery their specialties require within the ethical guidelines of JWT.

Plato, in the *Republic,* spends a good deal of time considering military virtues.[4] That work remains in common use in military ethics circles. Of relevance here is Plato's comparison of the military virtues to virtue in a dog. Both soldiers and dogs require courage, which is said to be a sort of wisdom in knowing what to fear and what to love. A good dog knows its own family, but is suspicious of what it does not know, ready to take defensive action should the family be threatened. The good dog is ready and able to do and to suffer harm in defense of its family. More, while their material demands are few, properly trained dogs are very responsive to praise, often seeming to value it above satisfying their physical appetites. A loyal dog earns a family's appreciation and esteem in a way analogous to that earned by loyal soldiers.

Dogs can be vicious as well as courageous. If a dog is mistaken about what to love and what to fear, it may harm its family rather than defending it. The dog that turns on its own family is still ready to suffer harm and endure pain, but it is not a good dog. This means that the virtues of a good dog require directing toward a good, moral end. The good dog expects to receive direction, and is obedient.

Bringing up a puppy requires a certain amount of thought and care if a good dog is to be the result. This where thoughtfully crafted training is required, for dogs, although capable of becoming good, do not do so by accident. A domesticated family dog is the product of careful human intervention based on time-tested results.

It seems doubtful whether dogs can appreciate the idea of developing and directing their virtues in the service of morally worthy ends, but soldiers can.

For good soldiers, education is required in addition to training. Virtuous soldiers understand both how to be and what to be for.

Subordination of Self

Military operations are almost always team efforts, requiring the coordination of multiple interlocking individual efforts. At the level of warfare itself, the numbers participating may reach into the millions. This reality drives a need to organize individuals into groups that can reliably function together to accomplish tasks. Add the arduous and potentially lethal conditions under which these operations take place and the crucial importance of effective command and control, including harmonious obedience down to the level of the individual, becomes more obvious.

The need for organization exists in most business endeavors and even in recreational sports. In this respect, the military is similar to any large corporation or even a local amateur baseball team. But there is a stark distinction. The interdependence that business life embodies may determine whether the business flourishes or withers, but even in the worst case of bankruptcy or dissolution, the unemployed will still be alive. A failure in business operations may destroy a business, but it likely will not cost anyone's freedom or life. In cases where lives are at stake, as in a surgical theater or an airplane, the requirements for good organization and teamwork become more stringent, but even then failure will not risk a state's sovereignty. But a failure to work well as a military setting may end up destroying the military itself and put at peril the nation it was supposed to defend. For this reason, militaries put tremendous emphasis on an ethical requirement to value the needs of one's group above personal desires. Sometimes this is referred to, as in military "core values" statements, as the virtue of selflessness. In its highest manifestation, an individual's identification with his unit is so thoroughgoing that he sees little distinction between the unit's well-being and his own. Indeed, the psychic well-being of virtuous persons in positions of authority depends on the well-being of their subordinates and their units as functioning organic entities. Fear of failing one's subordinates or failing to accomplish the mission that others are depending on become predominant ethical worries.

The virtue of selflessness creates salutary effects. One of the most enjoyable aspects of military living is the camaraderie that well-functioning units enjoy. Many other virtues flow from and enhance this enjoyment. Mutual honesty, promise-keeping, and respectful treatment all tend to help the members enjoy each other's company and to work well together. On the other hand, lying, infidelity, or disrespect tend to make life miserable by creating schisms in the group and inhibiting accomplishment. Wholehearted trust in each other is a functional requirement for successful combat operations. In a world where people coexist in sometimes cramped quarters under hostile conditions, the ordinary virtues of civilian life take on what is sometimes literally a vital importance. And even under less trying circumstances, there is usually noticeably more kindness and willingness to help one another in such units than is found in civilian life, even among close business colleagues. Selfishness in military life is shameful; selflessness creates greater enjoyment and productivity for everyone.

Effective commanders know the value of harmonious interpersonal relationships and actively seek to foster them. The sociological results are often remarkable. Camaraderie easily overcomes artificial barriers like socioeconomic distinctions or ethnic differences. Such tangential matters pale in the face of accomplishing a high-stakes task together. The military's history of racial relations, for example, although imperfect, has been far happier than the civilian arena. Members of racial minorities commonly supervise whites in the U.S. military. This is not to suggest that equitable treatment has extended across all communities. Some groups continue to suffer overt discrimination that is often said to be justified by the value of unit cohesion. Later chapters examine the ethical dimensions of integrating women and homosexuals into the military.

Subordination in the Service of Principles. From the start of basic training, new recruits are taught to subordinate themselves to the needs of their units. This subordination is, at least in theory, replicated at each organizational level. That is, each small unit is a part of a larger organization to which it is both ethically and legally required to subordinate itself. This relationship continues all the way "up the chain" to the civilian authority over the military. At the national level, the military's subordination means that it both suffers and creates violence on behalf of the nation. Ethically speaking, this violence should be directed in a fashion guided by JWT, that is, in the service of moral principles.

Keeping centered on the ultimate moral obligation to serve others is imperative for military members and leaders. Should that principled purpose be forgotten, the virtue of selflessness can become a vice. If the subordination to the good of the group results in that group's becoming the ultimate locus of obligation, then the military unit can degenerate into something much like a criminal gang. Lawbreaking, cover-ups, and vows of silence can occur if loyalty to one another supersedes the moral obligation to serve others. Tribalism of this sort poses challenges to military ethics and hazards to noncombatants.

Key to overcoming this challenge is a clear understanding that the group does not constitute its own purpose. Under JWT, military organizations exist to defend some greater good. To put the concept under brighter light, compare a criminal gang to a military organization. Both the gang and the military unit have special rituals, a code of honor, and requirements for selfless service or devotion. The gang, however, exists to secure and perhaps enrich itself and its leaders, whereas the military exists for the good of others. That is not to say that the good of a nation's citizenry is somehow logically inconsistent with the good of the military, but it is to say that the moral salience of the former is greater than the latter's. The good of the nation is both logically and morally distinguishable from the well-being of the military unit in the same way that the good of a patient is logically and morally distinguishable from the good of a physician. Appreciating this distinction makes it ethically possible for commanders to bring grave but necessary risks on their units even though doing so is emotionally difficult.

This distinction between the military and its purpose is foundational for military ethics for at least two interrelated reasons. First, it offers a justification for sacrificing the group in the service of a morally weighty cause such as the defense of freedom. Defending freedom, on this line of thinking, is worth the harm the group suffers. To sacrifice freedom to ensure the survival of a military group would be to fail in the military's very purpose.

Second, the distinction is logically required by *jus ad bellum*. In the absence of such a distinction, it would be possible to equate the moral good with one's tribe. Indeed, the well-being of one's military community (however it is defined) would be as morally weighty as anything could be. This would mean that two armies fighting against one another could rightfully claim equal moral justification. The cause that justifies Nation A's military killing their adversary, Nation B's military, would be offset by Nation B's just cause to defend itself against Nation A. Now although the adversaries may *believe* that they both have equally just causes, as an objective moral fact this is likely to be false.[5] In moral terms, some causes do trump others. In JWT, this is seen most starkly in the moral condemnation of aggressive war and the moral acceptance of fighting in response to aggression. An aggressive war remains an immoral war, regardless of how unselfish the soldiers waging it might be. On the other hand, defending the right to be free from aggression is at least morally acceptable and more likely morally praiseworthy. Given the pivotal importance of the concept, JWT has evolved a nuanced treatment of just what constitutes aggression (see chapter 4).

Group Dynamics and Violence

Killing another human, especially for impersonal motives conveyed by an authority, is a morally remarkable act indeed. Virtually everyone except the sociopath has a deeply held belief that killing is an awful thing to do, even if it is justified. Most religious traditions explicitly condemn it, as does domestic law. Social coexistence requires that individuals refrain from deliberately harming one another, let alone killing one another.

Militaries transform the pacifism that characterizes civilized life into a willingness to kill under tightly controlled circumstances. Historical accounts and social science have revealed that the effectiveness of this sort of transformation varies. Perhaps counterintuitively, the evidence suggests that it is a mistake to suppose that most soldiers will kill, even if they believe they are at risk of being killed. On the contrary, it seems that soldiers usually neither run away nor kill.

More than 27,000 muskets were recovered after the Battle of Gettysburg during the American Civil War. Most of these, it is logical to assume, were left behind by casualties. Of the 27,000-plus muskets, almost 90 percent were loaded. About 45 percent had been loaded more than once; one had been loaded 23 times.[6] Especially given the amount of time that it takes to prepare a muzzle-loading long arm for firing, one would predict that the majority of weapons collected from soldiers who were killed or wounded at Gettysburg would have been unloaded. Similar findings emerged from a somewhat controversial survey of American rifle companies conducted during the Second World War. General S.L.A. Marshall studied units that had recently been engaged in combat in both the Pacific and European theaters and determined that the proportion of infantrymen who actually fired their weapons fell on average in a range of 15–20 percent, with especially effective units firing at a rate of 25 percent.[7] He published this finding in *Men Against Fire,* which became required reading in American military schools soon after it was published in 1947. Marshall's methodology has come under some scrutiny of late; the criticisms center on Marshall's lack of quantitative rigor. Still, there is widespread agreement that a large portion of U.S. combat soldiers during the Second World War did not fire.[8] And there is no doubt that the U.S. military took the findings seriously. Since the book's publication, training techniques and socialization processes have changed, and firing rates have increased substantially.

Dave Grossman (Lt. Col., USA, ret.), in his excellent book *On Killing,* has offered an interesting analysis of the phenomenon that Marshall and others noted. With Marshall, Grossman points out that even if they do not actively seek to kill their adversary, very few soldiers run away from combat. Instead, most remain with their comrades and "posture." That is, they stand their ground and perhaps go through the motions of killing, but in fact seek to avoid doing so unless other factors are brought into play.[9]

Killing rates rise with the proximity of comrades. Crew-served weapons, such as heavy machine guns and artillery, are almost always fired.[10] Especially in cases where the killing is done at a distance, say by a crew in a bomber, refusal to participate is quite low.[11]

These findings explain much about the nature of military service. The individual is reluctant to kill, even when threatened, but comrades in close proximity seem to exert mutual influences that overcome their reluctance. It is no accident that military culture emphasizes the well-being of the group over the individual.

Obedience

The moral obligation to obey orders pervades military life. This obligation, joined with that of selflessness, makes excellent functional sense in the practical world of applied military ethics. Like the obligation of selflessness, it stems in part from the fact that militaries do not exist for themselves but rather are formed to serve political bodies. The moral authority on which a military operates has its roots outside of the military. In Western liberal democracies, military members acting in their official capacity do so in the name of the citizenry.

As with selflessness, the obligation to obey also stems from the teamwork that many military operations demand. Efforts need to be coordinated and unified, and all the players need to know what to do and where to turn for guidance.

Especially in fast-paced operations, there is little time to make decisions. Following orders is a way to help get things done and to preclude confusion that may become fatal. Loss of effective command and control makes defeat likely.

Habitual obedience is accordingly considered a military virtue that military training strives mightily to instill and generally succeeds in doing. It has been a long time since there was any battlefield utility in marching large masses of soldiers in complex formations, but training environments still feature close-order drill, as it fosters the inculcation of rapid and unified obedience. As with subordination of the self, however, the moral status of obedience is dependent on context. If members are not mindful of the principles their virtue is intended to serve, disaster looms. Unthinking obedience among military members can produce atrocities.

Social scientists have studied obedience extensively. They have found that the presence of an authority can go a long way toward motivating violent acts. One of the best known investigations was conducted by Stanley Milgram at Yale. The Milgram experiments showed that roughly two-thirds of his subjects were willing to give painful, and even potentially lethal (450 volt), electric shocks to another person if a seemingly legitimate authority asked them to do so.

Ordinary New Haven residents recruited by Milgram were told that they would be assisting in his experiments on learning. The experiment required the "assistant" to read lists of words for the "subject," who was actually a confederate, to memorize. Should the learner make a mistake, the assistant was told to administer an electric shock. A dial before the assistant was marked with intensities ranging from 15 volts to 450 volts. Each subsequent mistake required the subject to turn the dial to the next higher intensity.

In fact, the "assistants" were themselves the unknowing subject of the experiments. No actual shocks were administered, but the learner acted as though he was getting shocked. At the first few mistakes, when supposedly mild shocks were administered, the learner would feign receiving an unpleasant but tolerable jolt. As the voltages increased, however, the confederate began to show signs of distress, asking to stop the experiment and even warning of heart trouble or pretending to lapse into unconsciousness. If the subject asked to stop, the scientist would insist that he continue.[12]

Milgram and his colleagues were astonished to discover that compliance with a perceived authority could result in such ill treatment of an innocent victim. It is perhaps less astonishing to those with military experience. Anyone who has experienced basic training, and especially the trainers themselves, is aware that a disposition to obedience can elicit surprising behaviors. As with the virtue of selflessness, it is of vital moral importance to remember what one should be obedient *to*. The very real danger that obedience and social conformity will compel what conscience would otherwise forbid, made manifest by events such as the Holocaust or the My Lai massacre, is of profound significance for military ethics. Military authority is a form of power, and the use of power entails ethical responsibility. That is one reason why recruits are instructed that they must obey only *lawful* orders. It is also why well-functioning militaries are careful to educate their members in what both legal dictates and military ethics require. If this is done properly, those in a position to issue orders will understand that their authority is not unlimited. The same legal system that grants them the authority to give orders also limits what the orders may contain. The same thinking that describes obedience as a virtue requires that the orders to be followed themselves follow the guidelines of military ethics. The absence of such limits would constitute an abuse of authority.

Educated subordinates enhance the safeguard. In the event that the superior issues an illegal order, the subordinate should know that it is not binding and seek to assist the superior in finding another course of action. Military ethicists are clear about this. All members, regardless of rank, retain their own consciences and responsibility. To attempt to shield unethical actions behind the virtue of obedience is to get things backwards. "Just following orders" may provide some shallow sense of psychic comfort to those with a stricken conscience, but it does nothing to change the moral quality of an act.

Self-Mastery

Any organization that involves itself in complex, team-oriented operations using sophisticated equipment requires skilled and self-disciplined personnel. This requirement is particularly stringent in the military. The military member must have the courage to stay focused on the job at hand under hostile, life-threatening conditions. The stakes riding on the team's operational success, which in turn depends on every individual's self-possession, can be very high.

Gaining and maintaining the skills imperative for effective functioning requires self-mastery. Understanding that one ought to develop a certain skill is one thing; getting up and doing it is another. This is true whether the individual skill involved is simple or complex. Becoming and staying physically fit may be fairly straightforward, but the self-discipline it requires is substantial. Remaining focused on mission accomplishment when one's life is at risk is simple in theory, but it requires self-mastery beyond the requirements of ordinary life. Similarly, becoming adept in geopolitical strategy requires more than good cognitive abilities; it requires devoting the self to becoming an effective strategic thinker.

Many military practices reflect this need to gain and maintain skills. A substantial portion of military life is devoted to education and training. Basic training is only the tip of the iceberg. Technical schools help members gain an initial competence in a given field, but it is every supervisor's task to help subordinates become ever more capable. Formal professional schools, appropriate to military grade and experience, punctuate a military career. At least in the U.S. military, 10 percent or more of one's career may be spent undergoing formal schooling. Success in these schools is a strong predictor of future promotion.

The emphasis on education and training through formal schooling and individual mentoring is a reflection of the value militaries place on individual competence, but achieving an acceptable level of competence remains the individual's ethical obligation. Others' well-being, and perhaps her own, may depend on how well this obligation if fulfilled. The same is true, of course, for any team, but the high stakes in military operations do serve to elevate incompetence toward immorality. At senior levels, incompetence is commonly a precursor to moral disaster.

This increase in ethical obligation that accompanies increased seniority has interesting corollaries. There is an implicit obligation to know oneself. All things being equal, there is no strong moral obligation to advance in rank, but there is a moral obligation to exercise competently the authority that increased rank brings. Hence, seeking and accepting promotion obligate a military member to gain the competence that the new position requires.

It is a sad fact that not everyone in any given position has, or is even capable of gaining, the competence that ethical obligation requires. Well-functioning military organizations therefore work hard to "promote well," although success is mixed. In some cases, military policy and culture send mixed messages. The U.S. military has practiced an "up-or-out" policy in its officer corps that requires promotion for retention. Other militaries allow officers to remain at a relatively junior grade for their entire careers if they so desire. Regardless of the policy, however, the individual member is morally obligated to make himself good at his job. The obligation exists in itself as a part of military identity and function. Promotion may hinge on competence, but that is not what renders self-mastery obligatory. Rather, it is the military function itself that demands the virtue.

Use of Force

As noted in the historical overview, JWT attempts to reconcile the tension between pacifism and the often harsh realities of political life in the international arena. For purposes of introduction, realism and pacifism can be thought of as opposite ends of a spectrum. Generally speaking, the realist holds the state's well-being as superseding other values. If the territorial integrity, sovereignty, or perhaps even the prosperity of a state seems to require killing, the realist is willing to accept that. The pacifist, by contrast, views nonviolence as morally binding. If that commitment entails that a state suffer, the pacifist is willing to make that concession. Just war theorists are found between the two, seeking to balance the most compelling claims of each extreme while avoiding extremism themselves.

There are many subtle variations of each position, and this account can provide only a general outline of the logic behind each. In the detailed exploration of JWT that follows, the themes of both realism and pacifism resurface in more moderate form.

Realism

Realists come in many strains, but they are united by agreeing that states' interests are of paramount importance. That is, the well-being of one's state requires certain actions that trump all others, including the interests of other states or individuals, even the lives of at least some of the individuals of one's own state. For purposes of this introduction to the concept, varieties of realism can be conceived as clustered around one end of a continuum that has pacifism at its other end and JWT toward the center. At the extreme realist end, there are those who discount entirely the idea of moral considerations coming into any play in international relations. Other realists are more moderate, suggesting that moral considerations matter, but to a lesser degree in international relations than they do within a community. These positions acknowledge some just war considerations, but still consider the needs of the state to be supreme if the demands of JWT conflict with state interests.

Necessity. Realists remind military ethicists of a counterbalance to freedom—namely, necessity. They often note that much of human life in the political sphere is determined, rather than free, and that none of us is free in many of the domains that are most important to us. This determinism is a fact of nature and applies both at the level of individuals and at the level of international relations. Humans, like all animals, are subject to certain desires and fears. One may not wish to become hungry, but hunger presents itself regardless. People *need* to eat. Similarly, they dislike pain. Regardless of one's moral commitments or philosophical orientation, pain is aversive. These facts of nature limit freedom at the level of individuals. All things being equal, people will eventually act to satisfy their desires and to avoid what hurts.

It takes resources to stay alive and to avoid the pains that life may present. As all humans seek to satisfy more or less the same basic needs, competition for resources comes to characterize human existence. Communities may form to allocate resources and burdens among their members in a reasonably peaceable fashion, but no such community exists internationally. Worse, humans, being subject to the laws of biology, will tend to grow the populations of their communities to the boundaries of what their resources will support. This often leads to competition for territory. Those enjoying a particular territory need it to maintain their very lives and so will defend it violently if necessary. War is therefore an inevitable consequence of nature given a lack of an organized global community. It is true that war is terrible—indeed, it is composed of deliberately creating aversive experiences for the competitors. But preferences for peace instead of war do little to alter or ameliorate the deterministic forces of nature. That competition for resources is unfortunate does not make it less real.

This determinism does not demand a detailed metaphysical justification for the realists' purposes. Simple experience is adequate to give the claim persuasive weight. The realist therefore counsels that moral considerations are either misplaced or relatively unimportant in international relations. The important thing is to gather sufficient power to guarantee survival. Any worries over ethics, at least to the extent that they do not serve to increase power, are quaint at best and threats to survival at worst.

Realist talk is common but by no means uncontested in military circles. There are military members who hold that military ethics is an impediment to the only goal that counts: victory. It is not unusual to hear tough-sounding talk that tries, for example, to justify killing noncombatants on the grounds that it will save military lives on one's own side. This talk, however, almost always appeals to necessity. "You have to do these things in order to survive," suggests that there is no choice in the matter, and, by extension, that moral judgments of military activities are as misplaced as moral judgments about the weather. But for the military ethicist, that appeal to necessity can be interpreted as a signal of moral judgment itself. The military member who is appealing to necessity does it in an attempt to *justify* what her intuitions tell her is evil. This attempt to evade responsibility, far from providing an excuse, actually ends up making the point that ethics applies to acts of violence and to the people who conduct them.

All human beings are subject to the ravages of violence in much the way they are subject to disease. People do not wish to become ill, but despite their wishes to the contrary, they sometimes do fall sick. Likewise, people do not wish to become involved in wars, but sometimes they are forced into them. The history of political interaction offers plenty of examples where rational discourse gives way to armed conflict. In those cases, the conflict is often resolved according to the deterministic laws of physics. The truth of this is especially apparent at the level of the individual combatant. Bullets and shrapnel obey the laws of physics, and so do human bodies. Applying the proper amount of force to a human will kill, regardless of the justice of one's cause. Just as sickness can strike the noblest person, people with ethical commitments stop bullets just as well as those lacking them. And, like an epidemic or natural disaster, war can come to the state regardless of its moral character. In both cases, it is well to be prepared.

Power Relations. Being prepared often involves having sufficient power to maintain or perhaps advance the interests of one's state. It requires an unromanticized appreciation of the patterns that characterize international relationships. For many realists, this involves appreciating the supposed fact that all states will seek to serve their own interests before serving any moral principles. Generally, serving states' interests is said to reduce to the acquisition and maintenance of power relative to other states. Competition is inevitable in the long run, although there may be cooperative arrangements in the short term if they are seen to serve individual state's interests.

The power required is not limited to amassing lethal military forces. Any sort of capability to influence other international actors is valuable, including economic wealth. The power to induce fear or respect in others is valuable as well. If one appears sufficiently strong, with the political credibility to wield that strength, one may never have to devote resources to actual fighting. Intimidation will do the job. It is perhaps useful to illustrate this point with the example of nuclear deterrence. Given the context of 20th-century history with its two world wars, the cold war was relatively peaceful. That relative peace depended on the belief that immoral levels of violence would be deliberately unleashed given certain provocations. Nuclear armed nations continue to deter aggression by creating a belief that at least certain sorts of actions on the global stage will spark such levels of retaliatory destruction that no rational calculation of a competing state's interests would suggest taking those sorts of actions.

The Melian Dialogue. One of the best historical introductions to realist thinking is provided by Thucydides in his account of the Peloponnesian War (431–404 BC) between Athens and Sparta. Part of his history is a report of the Athenian expedition to Melos, a colony of Sparta, in 416 BC. The Athenians arrived with a substantial military force and offered the Melians a stark choice— either surrender or fight against near-impossible odds.

It is difficult to improve on this part of Thucydides's account of the negotiations:

> Athenians: . . . [Y]ou know as well as we do that right, as the world goes, is only in question between equals in power, while the strong do what they can and the weak suffer what they must.
>
> Melians: . . . [S]ince you enjoin us to let right alone and talk only of interest . . . [we believe] that you should not destroy what is our common protection, namely, the privilege of being allowed in danger to invoke what is fair and right.[13]

The Athenians, like many after them, are not impressed by this appeal to moral concepts. Asserting that it is a natural law that whoever has the power to govern others must use that power to do so, they insist that it is in both the Melian and the Athenian interest that Melos submit to avoid bloodshed.[14]

The Athenians eloquently articulate the central elements of realism. The laws of international relations are not ethical in nature; rather they are laws about power relationships. Realists do not make these laws, but all are necessarily bound by them. Sufficient strength may free a people from submission to another state, but it can never free them from the laws of power relationships. Whatever freedom a state enjoys is a product of the power it can wield. This does not suggest, however, that just any act of violence makes as much sense as any other. Rather, the waging of war ought to be directed by a clear-eyed understanding of whether it is in a state's interest.

Ironically, perhaps, this notion of a state's interest opens into an ethically rich domain: how ought a state to determine what is in its interests? History teaches that many decisions statesmen make thinking to serve their state's interests turn out instead to harm them. It may be suggested that adopting realism as a guide to policy, especially realism in its most extreme forms, actually works against a state's interests. This line of argument appeals to the difficulty strong states have in maintaining their strength over time. Certainly, the strong "do as they will," but it is the rare state that stays stronger than others for long. Should a strong state act without restraint in the international arena and subsequently weaken, it may well come to regret the realist precedent that it set when it was strong. This suggests that applying moral restraint to a state's activities serves that state's interests over the long run, as the Melians proposed. The present generation in any strong state may prevail by discounting the relevance of moral considerations, but their grandchildren may regret their grandparents' realist thinking, as emerging powerful states follow the precedent set generations earlier.

Moreover, the citizens of a state may be offended by the harsh actions of their own government. Should this occur, maintaining military prowess becomes difficult as the population's support for the actions of their government withers. The same effect may occur internationally, especially given the technological realities of the 21st-century's media. To maintain strong international influence in the face of widespread public opprobrium is difficult, and good public relations are a form of power. Consequently, it is likely in even the strongest state's interests to reject at least the most extreme forms of realism.

A weightier criticism of realism notes that its central propositions about morality's irrelevance or relative unimportance are, ironically enough, unrealistic. Almost everyone *does* make moral judgments about how states conduct themselves. Modern readers can empathize with the Melians and render judgments about the Athenian generals. It is common to judge the justice of wars as well as conduct within them. The Nazi aggression in the Second World War is widely regarded as immoral, as is the Battan death march. Ordinary people, let alone philosophers, do critically evaluate statecraft and military operations. These judgments deny that the necessity that is said to render moral considerations inapplicable is as thoroughgoing as the realists maintain.

In defending realism, some suggest that ethical judgments are appropriate within states because there is a common community standard within a given culture, but in the absence of any well-defined international ethical standards, power becomes the only relevant measure. In international relations, "might makes right" becomes literally true because there is no demonstrable "right" beyond power. Although *within* well-functioning states there is a commonly accepted power sufficient to compel compliance with that state's laws, there is no analogous power *among* states. Thomas Hobbes (1588–1679) puts the case eloquently:

> [I]t is manifest that during the time men live without a common power to keep them all in awe, they are in that condition which is called war; and such a war as is of every man against every man. . . . To this war of every man against every man, this also is consequent; that nothing can be unjust. The notions of right and wrong, justice and injustice, have there no place. Where there is no common power there is no law; where no law, no injustice. Force and fraud are in war the two cardinal virtues.[15]

This line of argument, as it regards international relations, is subject to criticism on a number of counts. First, the argument relies on the sort of relativistic claims that were shown to fail in chapter 1. The fact of disagreement internationally does nothing to prove that there is no moral standard. Neither does the fact that some actors behave as though fraud were a virtue. Second, to say that there is no common power is different from saying there is no ethical standard of conduct. Likewise, to say that there is no law is not to establish that there is no right and wrong.[16] Military ethics, at least insofar as it pertains to the use of force between nations, would be pointless if the extreme realist's claims were accepted. Indeed, it might be pointed out that the necessity that some realists argue makes conflict inevitable does not entail war. One can point, for example, to most communities who, most of the time, settle their internal differences short of armed conflict. Further, one can accept that necessity bounds choices without choosing to be an extreme realist.

Military ethics is nonetheless informed by realist thinking. The interest of states in their own well-being forms a cornerstone for military ethics. JWT is meant to serve the interests of all states and all persons over time. In this sense, it is compatible with at least some more moderate forms of realism.

As noted in the previous chapter, early Christian pacifism, arrayed against this general theme of power and necessity, helped form the creative tensions that spawned the JWT.

Pacifism

It is worth noting that virtually everyone in settled communities today is a practicing pacifist, at least in private life. If one has a dispute with a neighbor, the community expects that it will be resolved short of violence, and in almost every case that expectation is met. Should violence occur, the authorities may be called to "keep the peace." Indeed, part of being civilized is routinely to refrain from "disturbing the peace." And, perhaps ironically, military installations are often some of the most peaceful places in the United States, with low speed limits, polite—even decorous—manners, and careful attention to appearances.

Still, many people think of pacifism as an outlier's position. They have in mind here pacifism as a position that rejects not only personal violence but also violence on behalf of one's state. In response, advocates of pacifism can deploy powerful, practically oriented arguments that surprise those who have dismissed the position out of hand.

Pacifism is grounded philosophically in various ways. At the level of concept, arguments for pacifism break into two general types: secular and religious. The first approaches pacifism as a method of achieving political ends that is both empirically and morally preferable to violence. This defense of pacifism appeals to both deontological and consequentialist ethical theory, as well as the psychology of conflict, to suggest that nonviolent methods are as effective, if not more effective than violence at settling disputes, and much less costly in moral terms. Other pacifists base their commitment on theological grounds. This approach does not deny the secular grounds of the first approach, but it is not motivated by them. Rather, the commitment to nonviolence, or even nonresistance, is a form of religious faith-in-action that bears important similarities to virtue theory.

Pacifism—Secular Ethical Grounding

Much of the secular pacifist's persuasiveness hinges on the effectiveness of using nonviolent means to achieve political ends. Many believe that pacifism is hopelessly idealistic and that pacifists will always need militaries to defend them, as they are helpless in the face of violent aggression. It is important to understand, however, that pacifism does not necessarily equate to allowing evil people to do harm. Some pacifists, especially those who adopt the position on religious grounds, do advocate nonresistance, but others view nonviolence as a strategically viable method of opposing evil. There is nothing about a *pacifist* ethic that suggests being *passive* in the face of moral wrongdoing. Most pacifists grant that one is morally obligated to resist evil; it is the means of resistance that is of concern. For pacifists of this sort, developing the military virtues discussed previously is, perhaps ironically, just as important as it is for military members themselves.

To better appreciate how the pacifist might effectively resist evil, it is worthwhile to remember the nature of war. Conflict between states is, as Carl von Clausewitz noted in *On War,* ultimately a battle of wills. *"War is thus an act of violence intended to compel our opponent to fulfill our will."*[17] Today, Brian Orend makes a similar point in noting that wars are always about how a particular community is to be governed. If war is ultimately about gaining political objectives, there is nothing about conflict between states that logically requires physical violence. The political objectives for which wars are waged are in essence psychological objectives, having to do with what an adversary *wills*. For the pacifist, political bodies in the international arena may necessarily come into conflict, but it is not at all necessary that the conflict be resolved violently because it is strength of will that prevails in conflicts. Physical violence is a means to influence will, but other means may be equally or more effective at substantially less cost.

One can point today, for example, to the practice of nuclear deterrence as creating an international mindset conducive to avoiding physically violent conflict. If that example is rejected because it threatens violence, the pacifist can point out well-known pacific political movements such as Gandhi's, which led to India's independence from Great Britain, or Martin Luther King's success in the U.S. civil rights movement. These movements changed the minds of their opponents without resort to coercive violent force. Pacifists use examples like these to suggest that whereas effective resistance to evil may be morally compulsory, violence is not.

Gene Sharp is probably the most far-reaching and systematic writer on the concepts and methods of organized nonviolent resistance. He developed a comprehensive and fascinating theory of nonviolent action based on a few simple concepts pioneered by Gandhi and others. In brief, Sharp argues that nonviolent resistance succeeds because of a few simple facts about authority and governance. Those who would rule cannot do so alone; they require the cooperation of others to govern. Rulers induce others to cooperate, and usually people do. But nonviolent action is possible because people *can* refuse to cooperate. If they do so as a group, with determination and steadfast will, they may effectively oppose political power.

For Sharp, nonviolent action is a "means of combat"[18] that requires many of the traditional military virtues in its practitioners. Among these are a subordination of the self to the good of the cause, teamwork, and self-discipline. Given these characteristics and a unified determination, nonviolent resistance can succeed. Sharp cites numerous examples of successful nonviolent action in his three-volume work. Only one example, known as the Rosenstrasse protest, is used here, but it is illustrative of the success nonviolent methods can enjoy, even against a brutal regime like Nazi Germany.

In Berlin, in February and March 1943, the Nazis arrested hundreds of Jewish males who were married to non-Jews. These men were imprisoned together. Before long, their wives began to assemble outside of the building where the men were being held. According to one report, 6,000 protestors arrived. Authorities tried to disperse the demonstrators, including by threatening gunfire, but the women remained. As one of the prisoners recounted the incident, the SS, "[s]cared by an incident which had no equal in the history of the Third Reich, headquarters consented to negotiate. They spoke soothingly, gave assurances, and finally released the prisoners."[19]

Deontological Approaches to Pacifism. Secular pacifists deploying deontological arguments for their position note that rights are inevitably violated in war. Among other reasons, they point out that it is almost impossible to conduct warfare in the modern arena without harming noncombatants and thus necessarily violating the *jus in bello* principle of discrimination. Therefore, because war always entails killing noncombatants, war itself must be rejected. Moreover, even if war killed only combatants, it would still be wrong to deliberately take human life when the same political objectives might be achieved without that evil. The international arena usually offers alternatives other than "kill or be killed" if one is sufficiently creative to find them.

Some respond to this argument by noting that it is based on faulty assumptions. One can grant that many wars involve the death of noncombatants without saying that wars necessarily kill noncombatants. By way of example, naval warfare traditionally involves only combatants. Moreover, the evil that the deontologist points out is not a product of war itself but rather of statesmen and soldiers who fail to respect the just war requirement for discrimination. Put differently, the limits that discrimination places on war would, if respected, meet the objection that the deontologist puts forth. A prohibition against murder is both logically and morally distinct from prohibiting war, and JWT details that distinction in a way to meet the deontological worry.

The pacifist might point out that the JWT principle of discrimination only prohibits the deliberate targeting of noncombatants. Accidental death is foreseeable, and, given the nature of some modern weaponry, noncombatant deaths may well number in the millions should a war break out. These noncombatants have a right to life that war would be likely to violate, and therefore, war ought to be prohibited. But again, the premises of this argument can be granted without having to grant the conclusion. Just because some wars violate the rights of noncombatants does not entail that all war should be prohibited, especially when one considers that waging war might save innocent lives.

The combatant/noncombatant distinction is critical to the just war theorists' responses to the pacifist in the arguments sketched here, but the distinction itself might be called into question by the pacifist. It is commonly suggested by just war theorists that a combatant, being engaged in doing harm on behalf of his community, therefore becomes a legitimate target of military force himself. Exactly why this is so, however, is not entirely clear. First, if a combatant is fighting justly in a just war, in what sense can harming him be morally justified? He is doing something good, not something evil. And his adversary, who presumably is fighting an unjust war, should not be fighting in the first place. Because a soldier fighting for justice should not be harmed, and one fighting against justice should not be fighting in the first place,[20] all war ought to be prohibited.

All killing is wrong also in that it violates persons' rights to their lives. A combatant is still a human being, no matter how her government sees fit to use her and regardless of how ignorant or self-deceived she may be. She may be acting against her own will, on the orders of a state that she detests, or out of wholehearted but misinformed fervor for the cause, but in any case she is not shown to deserve punishment, let alone capital punishment. She may be acting as an agent of another, but her right to her life is her own. If this is the case, all killing in war is unjustified, and consequently war ought to be prohibited.

Suppose that a teenager enters the military, successfully accomplishes the training that is required, and subsequently finds that he is ordered to do violence to others. In attempting to carry out these orders, he is killed. Some pacifists suggest that cases like this show war to be doubly evil. In the first place, many teenagers are incapable of genuinely informed consent because they are simply too young and inexperienced to understand just what the military is asking them to become. This is a form of victimization, akin to being abused by a person in a position of trust. The recruit is subsequently victimized again by being killed. He suffers harm that he cannot comprehend. Worse, in the case of conscripted soldiers, the ethically salient matter of an individual's consent is ignored by the conscripting government. Again, the pacifist argues, rights are violated by the very act of conscription and more severely so when the conscripted soldier is harmed or killed. These rights violations result from war and, therefore, war itself ought to be rejected.

In the logically possible but rare case that a pacifist rejects war but accepts violence in domestic affairs, a further avenue is available to the deontologist. In this case, the pacifist may grant that capital punishment might be justified after deliberate judicial processes and elaborate defenses for the criminal left no doubt that he was guilty of a capital crime. In other words, one may accept killing on the authority of a state in cases where guilt is demonstrated beyond a reasonable doubt, justifying this killing on the grounds that it defends the rights of crime-victims, gives the capital criminal deserved punishment, and sends a clear message about the value of peaceable domestic living. Even if one accepts this sort of justification for violence, however, killing in war is to be rejected, because the victims of war are legally innocent. Insofar as those waging war obey their lawful orders and the laws of warfare, they are guilty of no crime and so should not be harmed.

Note that these deontological arguments for pacifism do not require that rights be left undefended. Rather, they reject war as a means of defending rights. Indeed, the case for the deontologist against war can be made even more strongly, as it is war itself that constitutes a severe threat to human rights.

For deontological pacifists, then, any attempt to construct a theory of just war is doomed to fail because there is, in the end, no such thing as a moral justification for the deliberate taking of lives that war necessitates.

Consequentialist Approaches to Pacifism. From a consequentialist perspective, it may be argued that modern wars are almost never proportional. As wars are fought for political objectives, in theory anyway, a state's leaders ought to restrict the harm they cause in proportion to the political goals sought. As a matter of historical fact, however, this rational balancing of cost and benefit usually fails to occur. Wars tend to take on a logic of their own, frequently escalating well beyond the expectations of those who start them. Often, each side becomes focused on military victory and the political cause that was used to justify warfare in the first place falls into irrelevance as the violence expands. There is a morally regrettable tendency to magnify or widen the originally declared cause to explain why suffering that has already been endured was justified and to gain support for still more violent effort. Worse, a sense of vengefulness can come into play, with each side justifying its own escalation by reference to the precedent escalation of its opponent. If war is the cure, the consequentialist suggests, it is better to remain ill.

One can point to the First World War and ask what good from that war could offset the estimated 1.7 million French or 2 million Germans who died.[21] The same query might be directed toward the 1982 war between Great Britain and Argentina over the Falkland Islands that killed more than 900 combatants.[22] Although the casualty count is low as 20th-century wars go, it is hard to see what good was achieved at even that relatively low numerical cost, which was, it should be noted, infinitely costly to every individual killed.

Suffering the harm of capitulation is evil, but suffering the harm of modern war, with its tendency to feed ever more voraciously on itself, is worse, especially in a world of nuclear weaponry. And, in the end, one side will almost certainly conclude that the fighting is not worth continuing. Taking all of this into account, a thoughtful response ought to be a rule-utilitarian prohibition of war as a policy choice. Pacifism, in other words, becomes the least costly choice given the empirical information available.

Like all consequentialist reasoning, this argument is subject to criticism on empirical grounds. Although there seems to be little doubt that the suffering caused by the First World War, including its role in contributing to the causes of the even more calamitous Second World War, was disproportionate to the good it achieved, this is a backward-looking claim. Present concerns regarding whether to go to war involve the future. That one can cite instances of disproportionate suffering caused by violence does not establish that future wars necessarily will be disproportionate, especially as modern weapons become more precise and nonlethal techniques emerge. Moreover, as in the case of at least some deontological objections to war, the fault does not lie in the idea of just war but in the fault of statesmen to adhere to the *jus ad bellum* and *jus in bello* requirements for proportionality.

The pacifist arguing from consequentialist grounds can advance a further claim. Even if one grants that future wars would be fought in accordance with every just war criterion, resolving conflicts short of war is both feasible and far more proportional because it reduces the killing that war inevitably requires much more than violent means, however restricted, ever could.

Suppose that the average person killed in a modern war would have lived to be 75 years old had he not been killed. If one considers that each person killed is unable to seek his own happiness, let alone contribute to others, the disutility of even one 20-year-old's death would be substantial. Multiply this disutility by the sometimes large populations of killed and maimed that war produces and the disutility of warfare becomes much weightier. Then add in the capital and labor costs of preparing for and waging wars and consider what might have been achieved with them had they been put to peaceful purposes, and the case is seen to be even more compelling. Wars are waged at huge opportunity costs.

In summary, secular pacifists do not counsel against resistance, but rather against war. Given the alternatives available, such pacifists consider war to be an unethical policy choice in that it always violates rights and often does more harm than good.

Pacifism—Religious Grounding

Many religious traditions provide grounds for pacifism. Because of its importance to the Western tradition, however, only Christian thinking is elucidated here. There are variations among these thinkers, but most Christian pacifists appeal to a form of virtue theory to describe their position. The virtuous ideal is found in Jesus, who both preached and practiced nonviolence. The Sermon on the Mount is often cited: "Do not set yourself against the man who wrongs you. If someone slaps you on the right cheek, turn and offer him your left."

"Love your enemies and pray for your persecutors; only so can you be children of your heavenly Father, who makes his sun rise on good and bad alike, and sends the rain on the honest and the dishonest. If you love only those who love you, what reward can you expect?"[23]

Passages such as these, coupled with the example of Jesus's suffering harm while refusing to return it, are frequently taken by pacifists to suggest that using violence in the service of a temporal entity like a state is incompatible with a genuine commitment to Christian living. Indeed, some pacifists have suggested that if citizenship requires a willingness to kill on behalf of the state, such a state must have a Satanic nature.[24] A wholehearted commitment to a Christian identity would preclude taking the state's interests so seriously as to interfere with the pacific lifestyle, particularly when doing so would entail killing one's fellow creatures.

Many just war thinkers have objected to a religiously based refusal to do violence as irresponsible. It is one thing to allow oneself to suffer evil, but quite another to allow one's neighbor to be harmed when violent interference might save her from it. Just as one is obligated to love one's enemy, one is obligated to love one's neighbor. But advocates of this sort of pacifism can reply that one is still obligated to love one's enemy. The necessity to love everyone precludes doing violence against anyone.

This refusal to do violence may indeed allow harm that might have been prevented had violence been used, but the doing of any violence is always harmful, and worse, inconsistent with a commitment to Christianity. For modern Christian pacifists like Stanley Hauerwas, it is not at all clear that the use of violence to prevent harm is preferable to allowing harm in the first place.[25] Either path may bring tragic results; but more important, results are not the issue. Although they may be the keystone to moral decision making for a consequentialist, they are not so for the Christian pacifist. Living in faith is.

Concerns about Pacifism

Pacifism has been criticized widely as both ineffective and incoherent. Critics note that the historically successful nonviolent resistance efforts that are cited by pacifists usually fail to take into account other factors that helped change the adversary's will. For example, Gandhi's nonviolent resistance movement against British lasted for decades, but the British did not grant independence to India until they were recovering from the devastation of the Second World War. In the same vein, the Holocaust provides all too many examples of unresisting people being put to death, and it did not stop until violence compelled it to.

Now, of course, the pacifist can respond that nonviolent resistance requires many of the elements of military strategy and the inculcation of military virtues in its practitioners if it is to succeed. Accordingly, the pacifist's methodology may be no more at fault than the defeated militarist's. As many militaries fail, and yet military methods are still widely accepted, they argue, instances of pacifist resistance failures do not show that the method itself is at fault. If pacifist "armies" were effectively trained and disciplined, they might well succeed more frequently, and so the question of effectiveness remains largely unanswered.

Other critiques of pacifism are philosophical in nature and attempt to show that the position is dubious in its own right. For Elizabeth Anscombe, the case against pacifism is clear. Some people will pursue evil ends and will not stop pursuing them unless they are violently resisted unto their deaths.[26] Hence, for Anscombe, it is obvious that violence will sometimes be justified. Other philosophical attacks against pacifism are a bit more involved.

Perhaps the best known criticism has been formulated by Jan Narveson in his widely reproduced 1965 article "Pacifism, a Philosophical Analysis." Narveson's critique relies heavily on rights theory. As noted in chapter 1, to have a right, such as the right to life, imposes duties on others to respect that right. When one's property is stolen, one's rights are violated by a criminal act. In the world of applied ethics, having a right is useless if it is routinely violated. Hence, people expect that their rights will be defended. To that end, laws and law enforcement are established and, in a properly run community, these will guarantee the enjoyment of rights. This guarantee necessarily entails that sufficient force may be used to defend successfully against the violation of rights.

For Narveson, it is this guarantee of rights that does the heavy philosophical lifting. To have a right must entail that one is able to defend against its being violated. If someone is determined to use violent means to violate another's right to life, then, for Narveson, the means necessary to defend that right to life are justified. With luck, defending rights would never require violence, but if it does, then violence is not only morally justified but morally required. Narveson argues that the pacifist position is incoherent because it holds that all persons have a right not to be the victims of violence and yet denies the means necessary to defend that very right.[27]

Just War Thinking as a "Middle Position"

Appreciating the tension between realism's view of the state as vitally important and the pacifist's commitment to nonviolence is helpful in coming to understand JWT's philosophical evolution. Nonviolence characterizes relations between members within a state; indeed, it is one of the most important ways in which states benefit their citizens. Under JWT, violence is accepted, given certain conditions, to maintain the security the state provides for its members. The ethical justification for the violence rests on defense of the peaceable domestic life within the community. The character of modern military service reflects this distinction, holding the military member morally distinct in important ways from ordinary citizens. The same person may be a private pacifist and be willing to do violence on behalf of his state, but only under the conditions JWT requires.

Peace is presupposed as the desired condition for JWT. It holds from the outset that war is an evil, but it recognizes that nonpacifists, such as the Athenian generals, may threaten the peace. Aggression, like disease, exists regardless of the ideals or commitments one may hold. JWT's practical intent is to preclude war when possible and to lessen its evils when it is justified to go to war. The first is the objective of *jus ad bellum*—the second of *jus in bello*.

There is a logical difference between just methods and just purposes. The distinction between these two major branches of JWT rests in part on this logical difference. Although the moral distinction is becoming controversial among modern thinkers such as Jeff McMahan,[28] the central idea is that, descriptively speaking, one may engage in an unjust war but still use only just methods in that war. Likewise, one may engage in a just war but pursue victory using unjust means. The distinction between going to war and fighting in war is manifested in political custom and practice. Military members are required to obey lawful orders, ultimately originating in political circles, and, at least in the United States, are expected to refrain from political activity. One can easily see how a soldier may find herself engaged in a war that she may regard as unjust.

The distinction between purpose and method helps clarify the concept of what Michael Walzer has termed the "moral equality of soldiers." This notion insulates military members from accountability for their government's decisions to wage war. State leaders decide on waging wars; ordinary soldiers do not. This distinction is reflected in commonplace moral evaluations of soldiers. Consider Robert E. Lee or Erwin Rommel. Both engaged in wars defending political powers that systematically violated human rights. Yet both are commonly understood to have been icons of professional military ethics. One can find quite a few U.S. military bases named for officers who once actively engaged in rebellion against the United States itself during the American Civil War.[29] At least one U.S. service academy requires its freshmen to memorize quotes from both Lee and Rommel. Plainly, at least to ordinary ways of thinking, fighting on the wrong side does not signal that a person is of bad character.

On the other hand, one may think of waging unrestricted submarine warfare in the Second World War or the Tokyo fire-bombings and raise serious doubts about the morality of those actions, yet few would dispute that the Allies were fighting in a just war against the Axis. Examples like these show why the soldiers fighting against each other are said to be morally equal. Their moral praiseworthiness or blameworthiness does not arise from which "side" they are on (indeed, they have virtually no control over that in most cases), but rather from how they fight. Their wars are not personal; their actions in the context of war, however, are their own, even as they act on the authority of their state.

This distinction between a state's cause and an individual soldier's responsibilities serves many purposes. It acknowledges that most military individuals have little influence on the choice of their mortal adversaries. Accordingly, a professional detachment toward the enemy is appropriate. This detachment has salutary implications, not least of which is its role in tempering personal hatred for the opponent, which helps restrain violence against prisoners and enemy wounded, as well as smoothing new alliances with former adversaries. Likewise, limiting the soldier's obligations to the *jus in bello* grants a sort of moral shield to those who follow the laws and orders of their government. Militaries require obedience to their political superiors, and so soldiers are relieved of at least some of the responsibility for their participation in any given war. Although "just following orders" does not relieve the soldier of the requirements of *jus in bello,* it does, at least for most JWT, relieve him of responsibility for the war's purposes.

Tensions between **Jus in Bello** *and* **Jus ad Bellum.** Much has been written about the relationship of *jus in bello* criteria to *jus ad bellum.* Ideally, the tradition calls for fighting only just wars and fighting in those only by just means. In the real world, however, distinctions and ideals are frequently hard to realize. Especially from the perspective of realism, one can appreciate why achieving one's purposes might seem to require that one adopt unethical means. After all, one fights a war to win it. Depending on how the just cause criterion is met, the moral obligation to win may seem so overwhelming as to justify almost any means to that end. On the other hand, to say that one ought to win regardless of moral costs seems to undermine the very purpose of JWT.

This tension, and possible means of resolving it, is explored in the next few chapters. For now, a brief overview of possible avenues will help round out the introduction to the philosophical basis of JWT.

The first option is simply to say that the ethical restraints imposed by *jus in bello* criteria are merely so much eyewash. This realist position, which is sometimes called "moral nihilism with respect to war,"[30] rejects *jus in bello* criteria as simply inapplicable. On this view, speaking of ethics in war is like speaking of ethics between animals in the wild. There may be good reasons for restraint coming from the fear of retaliation or perhaps concern for international disapproval or historical legacy, but there is no such thing as sensible ethical language in war. This position, which is voiced frequently by beginners in military ethics, is vulnerable to an array of criticisms that are explored later. For now, suffice it to say that it resolves the tension by eliminating one of its poles.

The second option is to adhere to *jus in bello* criteria even at the expense of losing the war. This position, which we might call "absolutist," has numerous thoughtful proponents, mostly arguing from a rights perspective. Some are understandably skeptical of its practicality, but it may be helpful to point out that at least some battles in modern wars have respected both discrimination and proportionality. Historically, much naval warfare has taken place between military vessels staffed exclusively by military members, thus respecting the *jus in bello* criterion of discrimination by its very nature. Air-to-air combat, although increasingly rare, likewise adheres to the discrimination criterion, as does much land warfare that takes place in remote areas.

A third option is to regard the *jus in bello* criteria as defeasible. That is, if winning is impossible without overriding *jus in bello,* but the importance of winning (usually found in the "just cause" criterion) outweighs the rules, the rules nevertheless apply, in contrast to the nihilist position. There are several varieties of this position, including Walzer's famous argument from supreme emergency, but they all grant that the *jus in bello* obligations remain in effect. They are overridden, however, by more important moral criteria. For example, someone taking this position might admit that firebombing during the Second World War violated both proportionality and discrimination, but that these violations were compelled by the importance of winning. Naturally, the stronger the nation is with respect to its adversary, the less tenable such a position becomes. On the other hand, the more that is at stake for the outcome of the war, the more the pressure mounts to override the *jus in bello* criteria.

The tensions between the divisions of JWT are only hinted at in this brief introduction, and many more nuanced positions are emerging, but this overview should help illuminate the branches of the tradition itself. These are treated in the next two chapters.

Notes

1. Sir John Winthrop Hackett, "Today and Tomorrow," in *War, Morality, and the Military Profession,* ed. Malham Wakin (Boulder, CO: Westview Publishing, 1986), 99.

2. Risks like these are not exclusive to military members and their families; they are borne by ordinary citizens who might suffer, say, from bad medical decisions or automobile accidents. I am grateful to Cynthia Wright for bringing this to my attention.

3. Gwyne Dyer, *War* (New York: Crown Publishers, 1985), 101.

4. Plato, *Republic,* trans. G.M.A. Grube Rev. C.D.C. Reeve (Indianapolis: Hackett, 1992): 375a2–376c4; 440d2-d6; 441a3–441b1.

5. It is logically possible that both sides could be equally just, although, as an historical matter, such cases are hard to find. The criterion of just cause, as well as the concept of comparative justice, is treated in chapter 4.

6. F. A. Lord, cited in Lt Col Dave Grosman, *On Killing: The Psychological Cost of Learning to Kill in War and Society* (New York: Little, Brown, 1996), 21–22.

7. S.L.A. Marshall, *Men Against Fire: The Problem of Battle Command in Future War* (New York: William Morrow, 1947), 50–56.

8. Peter Kilner, "Military Leaders' Obligation to Justify Killing in War," *Military Review,* Mar-April, 2002, 25. Kilner attributes this to Roger Spiller.

9. Dave Grossman, *On Killing: The Psychological Cost of Learning to Kill in War and Society,* 6–10.

10. Ibid., 153–154.

11. Ibid., 107–108.

12. David G. Myers, *Psychology: Eighth Edition in Modules* (New York: Worth Publishers, 2007), 737–739.

13. *The Landmark Thucydides: A Comprehensive Guide to the Peloponnesian War,* 5.89–5.90, trans. Richard Crawley, ed. Robert B. Strassler, (New York: The Free Press, 1996), 352. The Melians chose to resist and were ultimately crushed.

14. Ibid., 5.105–5.111, 354–355.

15. Thomas Hobbes, *Leviathan: Parts I and II* (Indianapolis: Bobbs-Merrill, 1958), 106–108.

16. Douglas Lackey, *The Ethics of War and Peace* (Englewood Cliffs, NJ: Prentice Hall, 1989), 2.

17. Carl von Clausewitz, *On War,* trans., J. J. Graham, ed. Anatol Rapoport (New York: Penguin Books, 1968), 101. Italics are in the original.

18. Gene Sharp, *The Politics of Nonviolent Action, Part One: Power and Struggle* (Boston, MA: Porter Sargent, 1973), 67.

19. Heinz Ullstein's memoirs "Spielplatz meines Lebens" (Munich: Kindler Verlag, 1961), 338–340, in Gene Sharp, Ibid., 90. Sharp cites this translation as by Hilda Morris, reprinted in Theodor Ebert, "Effects of Repression by the Invader," *Peace News,* March, 19, 1965.

20. For a provocative critique of the supposed independence of *jus in bello* from *jus ad bellum* considerations, see Jeff McMahan, "Innocence, Self-Defense and Killing in War," *Ethics* 114 (July, 2004): 693–733.

21. John Keegan, *The First World War* (New York: Alfred A. Knopf, 1999), 423.

22. Richard Norman, *Ethics Killing and War* (New York: Cambridge University Press, 1995), 156.

23. Matt 5: 38–46, *New English Bible: New Testament* (Cambridge: Cambridge University Press, 1972), 7–8.

24. Stanley Hauerwas, "Pacifism: Some Philosophical Considerations," in *War, Morality, and the Military Profession,* ed. Malham M. Wakin (Boulder, CO: Westview Press, 1986) 283.

25. Ibid., 279.

26. Elizabeth Anscombe, "War and Murder" in *The Morality of War: Classical and Contemporary Readings*, eds. Larry May, Eric Rovie, and Steve Viner (Upper Saddle, NJ: Pearson Education), 203.

27. Jan Narveson, "Pacifism: A Philosophical Analysis" in *The Morality of War,* eds. Larry May, Eric Rovie, and Steve Viner, 141–147.

28. Jeff McMahan, "The Ethics of Killing in War," *Ethics* 114 (2004): 693–733.

29. To list just a few, Fort Benning, GA, Fort Hood, TX, and Fort Lee, VA all share names of Confederate generals.

30. Richard Wasserstrom has offered an extensive analysis of this position. See his "On the Morality of War: A Preliminary Inquiry," in *War, Morality, and the Military Profession,* ed. Malham M. Wakin (Boulder, CO: Westview Press, 1986), 317–340.

CHAPTER 4

Jus ad Bellum Today

Choosing to resort to war makes ethical as well as political history. No set of criteria could adequately comprehend the intricacies of such weighty matters. Accordingly, the *jus ad bellum* criteria are best used to help frame the issue of whether to resort to war, highlighting considerations of conscience while acknowledging the realities of international life. Properly used, the criteria stimulate hard thinking and provide an ethical context for making decisions.

It is important to bear in mind that thinkers in the tradition have differed a bit among themselves. All agree, for example, that a just war demands a weighty *casus belli*, but not everyone would recognize all of the eight criteria discussed here. Some would add more criteria and others would use fewer or different criteria. Differences notwithstanding, the criteria here are representative of the "state of the art" of *jus ad bellum* thinking at the dawn of the 21st century.

The *jus ad bellum* criteria can be thought of as idealized standards or benchmarks against which the morality of decisions may be objectively considered. Each of the criteria points out a moral obligation, and a perfectly just war would fully meet all of the criteria. Of course, in the real world perfect justice is rare, and coming to accurate judgments about justice and injustice is difficult. Ambiguity plagues practical statecraft. The life of a statesman contemplating war is filled with uncertainty and pressure, and lives are literally at stake. It is well to bear these constraints in mind when considering the criteria. Wisdom and good will are essential under these conditions; indeed, they are likely more imperative in political and military matters of state than in any other field of endeavor.

Modern political leaders usually seek to cast their decisions in the most favorable public light. This descriptive fact points to an important normative one. Being perceived as having justice on one's side is important to leaders. Some may privately deny the relevance of ethical considerations to statecraft, but public pronouncements typically acknowledge and even exploit the ethical aspects of a given decision or policy choice. This suggests that ordinary persons appreciate the point of *jus ad bellum* even if they are unaware of its existence as a moral guide. War is widely understood to be intrinsically evil. Choosing to enter into war therefore requires moral justification for reasons of public relations even if those putting forth the justification do so only hypo-critically.

Some realists suggest that public talk of moral considerations about war amounts to nothing more than power play in politics using the weapon of public opinion. Moral language and concepts are not used to guide political decisions, but instead to provide a cover or excuse for realist political strategy. As a descrip-tive matter, this assertion is often accurate. Indeed, the use of moral language to mask more cynical or egoistic strategies is common in many walks of life. Any set of concepts for making moral judgments can be abused by persons of ill will. That people misuse guidelines, however, does not render the guidelines themselves suspect. The abuse or distortion of ethical principles to fit other agendas says more about the people doing the abusing than it does about the principles, as indeed they are often judged according to ethical principles themselves. Applied ethical thinking in any field is useless in the absence of good will on the part of practitioners. *Jus ad bellum* is no exception. Sympathy toward the idea of limiting war's frequency and destructiveness is necessary if the *jus ad bellum* criteria are to be used appropriately.

Even well-intentioned people make mistakes. Accordingly, it may be helpful to approach some of the *jus ad bellum* criteria as having two aspects. Objectively speaking, there will be a truth of the matter regarding, say, the justice of one na-tion's cause for warring against another. And, objectively speaking, only one nation actually can have just cause for war.[1] Subjectively speaking, however, citizens and soldiers of both nations may *believe* that their side is just. Similarly, history may judge a war to have been heavily disproportionate to the evils it was meant to counter, but the leaders who made the decision to wage war likely did so with-out the leisure and perspective that historians enjoy Thus judgments about the justice of a war need not be consistent with judgments about the moral praise-worthiness or blameworthiness of statesmen. One can make honest mistakes and remain a good person. This is one reason that ordinary soldiers, let alone ordinary citizens, who might be expected to believe their country's cause is just, are not generally held accountable for the *jus ad bellum* criteria. History, after all, provides many examples of seemingly wonderful people fighting in the service of morally dubious causes. It also suggests, however, that statesmen are mor-ally obligated to be competent. Morality demands of statesmen that they make every effort to see the truth of matters and to act honestly. It is uncontroversial that incompetence is unethical in a military member. The moral obligation to be competent binds even more stringently on statesmen.

In liberal democracies, the citizenry share in this obligation. Statesmen act in the name of the citizenry, quite literally representing them. This suggests that the citizens of representative governments are morally obligated to elect only competent leaders. A voting population, although generally justified in trusting its government, does well to make itself as informed and wise as it possibly can.[2]

Just Cause

Just cause is the most important of the *jus ad bellum* criteria. In the absence of a just cause, the other criteria become meaningless or, at best, unimportant, for there would be no moral motive for contemplating the resort to war in the first place.

Historically, three general sorts of causes were said to justify violence: defense, restoring something wrongfully taken, and punishment. Today, defense against aggression is widely considered to be the only uncontroversial just cause. This is especially so since the 1928 Kellog-Briand pact that renounced aggressive war as a policy choice. Other candidates are in play, however, that offer a more liberal interpretation of the criterion, particularly in cases of human rights violations and potential terrorist strikes.

Bearing in mind that the just war tradition presupposes the obligation of states to protect their members, just cause typically consists in some variant of a threat to those very members. The comparison to individual self-defense is helpful here. Although a private individual has the right to fight in defense of his own life, he is free not to exercise that right. States, however, have the *obligation* to keep their members safe from harm. Consequently, a bona fide threat to the lives of its citizens obligates a government to take action to defend those citizens. Indeed, in the case of many nations, the military forces operate under the political umbrella of a "defense" branch of their government.

Michael Walzer has refined this line of thinking into a well-known set of concepts he calls "the legalist paradigm." The legalist paradigm might be thought of as an account of ordinary intuitions about how states ought to behave respecting defense. For Walzer and many other modern just war thinkers, this paradigm serves as baseline set of concepts for both understanding and advancing the understanding of justified war and for coming to a theoretical appreciation of aggression.

The paradigm treats states as analogous to individuals living in a community. Just as individuals have the fundamental rights of life and freedom, states have rights to their territory and to determine their internal governmental arrangements. Indeed, as discussed in the historical overview, this analogy is at the core of Grotius's approach to international relations and the applicability of natural laws to them. The domestic analogy, as Walzer has labeled it, draws parallels between living within a community of individual households and a community of nations. For example, in both cases individuals may negotiate among one another peacefully, enjoy friendships and alliances, and live cooperatively. But in other aspects the analogy does not parallel domestic life. Life within most communities can withstand disputes without existential threat to its members or to the community itself. In the international community, however, disputes can grow out of hand, threatening the future of some of its members or, in extreme cases, the entire community. This disanalogy is due to the lack of any forceful authority transcending international relations that would correspond to a state's government establishing and enforcing domestic law. In domestic situations, disputes are ordinarily handled by a formal judicial apparatus. Even violent disputes are easily quelled by the state's police and security forces, and are both adjudicated and punished by systematic means intended to deter future violent crime and to protect the peaceable public's well-being. Internationally, however, the introduction of violence may lead to a self-reinforcing and potentially unbounded increase. Especially in an era of weapons of mass destruction (WMD), violent acts can have profound and grave consequences that reach far beyond the controversies that gave them birth.

The legalist paradigm captures the idea of one state's physically threatening another's sovereignty or territorial integrity as "aggression."[3] Indeed, Walzer refers to the "crime of war" in just these terms. Aggression in this sense requires its victims to defend their rights or expect to lose them. Both options involve some peril; there is no safe way out of the problem.

The idea of consent can help clarify the idea. Aggression involves people in a situation to which they would not consent. The fundamental right involved is freedom, or, more precisely, the right to be free from uninvited interference. One is free to consent to limits on one's activities (as almost everyone does in any civil society), but in the absence of consent, one should be able to expect to be left alone.

The legalist paradigm evolved to embody these ethical principles in the context of international relations. It provides the underpinnings for a theory of aggression that Walzer has distilled into six propositions. The first two note that there is an international community of independent states, each of which has rights both to territorial integrity and political sovereignty. The right to territorial integrity is analogous to the right to the quiet enjoyment of one's home. Others should never enter one's home without being invited. Should someone violate this right, a crime is committed and policemen ought to take action. The right to political sovereignty is analogous to one's being in charge of the activities in her home without unwelcome interference from outsiders. One is free to decide to eat chicken for dinner, and even though the neighboring vegetarians might find the practice appalling, they are not thereby justified in breaking into the home to change the homeowner's diet. Likewise, a state has the right to govern what goes on inside its borders. Although others in the international community might attempt persuasion or diplomacy to alter the practices within a given state, the right to political sovereignty imposes a duty on them to respect the decisions of that state.

Against this backdrop, Walzer proposes that criminal aggression is "*[a]ny use of force or imminent threat of force by one state against the political sovereignty or territorial integrity of another*."[4] Such aggression warrants war on the grounds of self-defense for the affected state, and it also warrants the use of force by other states on the grounds of maintaining international order.[5] Other propositions restrict just cause to eliminate all reasons other than a response to aggression and note that an aggressor state may be punished after it has been defended against successfully.[6] Aggression, for Walzer, is the only crime that states may commit against one another, and, accordingly, the only just cause for war. Moreover, aggression harms more than the state it victimizes; it constitutes an offense against the peaceable order of the international community. This is one reason that third-party states might be justified in warring against it.

The widely known legalist paradigm sets a convenient starting-point for contemporary work in *jus ad bellum*. One of its strengths lies in its simplicity and intuitive appeal. War being as serious a matter as it is, and noninterference being as cherished as it is, the only clear cause for war is the clear act of aggression. Defense is justified only if the aggression defended against is serious, intentional, and obvious. Going to war over a minor offense or an inadvertent penetration of sovereign territory is not justified. Likewise, the physical aggression that is said to justify resort to war must be genuine and unprovoked. Justifying war on pretenses is unethical on its face.

Not every offense justifies resorting to violence. By way of illustrative contrast, imagine a nation taking an adversarial position in a dispute over trade or fishing–rights; these would hardly seem to be just causes for war. A key element in this use of defense-against aggression as a just cause is that the offense must be tangible, violent harm. A sneak attack against shipping, a missile launch against cities, or a land invasion all represent such a threat; a competitor's seeking economic advantage, even through devious means, does not.[7]

The Japanese attack on Pearl Harbor that precipitated the United States's entry into the Second World War is illustrative of just the sort of aggression that the legalist paradigm condemns.

History is filled with dates and places that stand at the threshold of major events, and the outright violence that characterizes war began, for the United States and Japan, on December 7, 1941. It is important, however, not to mistake discrete events for the continuum of military and political events that actually occur and to which just war thinking (JWT) applies. For purposes of ethical analysis, it is worthwhile to keep in mind the background conditions that play into a decision to wage war.

The neutrality acts, passed in 1935 and 1936, were designed to keep America isolated from the troubles overseas. President Roosevelt asked Congress for revisions to the acts in 1939 to allow the United States to supply arms to Britain and France.[8] Twenty-eight U.S. citizens had been killed when a German submarine sank a British passenger liner just days after the invasion of Poland in September 1939.[9] Aggressive Japanese expansion had been evident to the world for years, perhaps most grimly instantiated in the occupation of China. A sustained U.S. military buildup began in 1940. The United States had placed trade restrictions on Japan in 1940 and 1941.[10]

The attack on Pearl Harbor, especially in the context of ongoing Japanese-American diplomacy to address tensions between the states, is widely acknowledged as constituting a clearly just cause for war. The attack itself was plainly a surprise to those who suffered it and the losses heavily one-sided.

From all appearances, the U.S. entry into the conflict accorded with the just cause criterion.

Just cause for war, however, is not limited to defending one's own state. As in domestic settings, aggression against one justifies a response from anyone in the defense of the victim. That is, should Aggressor A violate the political sovereignty or territorial integrity of Victim V, Victim V can justifiably respond in self-defense. A's offense also justifies third-party intervention on V's behalf. A just cause permits, and arguably obligates, intervention on behalf of V, particularly in cases where V is relatively defenseless against A.

The Second World War became as widespread as it did in part as a result of this principle. Germany's invasion of Poland on September 1, 1939 stimulated defensive reactions by other nations. Both the British and French declared war against Germany two days after the attack. Likewise, just cause or not, Germany declared war against the United States within days of the U.S. declaration of war against Japan.

Comparative Justice

Thus far, just cause has been discussed as though it were part of a binary set, as though a cause is either just or unjust. In the applied realm of political and military realities, however, binary options often fail to capture the facts of the matter. Vitoria's old notion of one side's justice compared to another's may be helpful to considerations of just cause in the modern world. The United States National Conference of Catholic Bishops pastoral letter in 1983 restated the old concept in the context of modern war's destructive potential:

> In a world of sovereign states recognizing neither a common moral authority nor a central political authority, comparative justice stresses that no state should act on the basis that it has "absolute justice" on its side. Every party to a conflict should acknowledge the limits of its "just cause" and the consequent requirement to use only limited means in pursuit of its objectives. Far from legitimizing a crusade mentality, comparative justice is designed to relativize absolute claims and to restrain the use of force even in a "justified" conflict.[11]

The value of comparative justice as a part of *jus ad bellum* considerations may be criticized on various grounds. First, the centrality of aggression as legitimizing cause for war lends itself to a binary view of the matter rather than a comparative approach. The aggressor is the unjust party; defense against the aggressor supplies the justice of the defender's cause. Second, if one is concerned with limiting the destructiveness of war, the *jus in bello* criteria should already supply the morally salient restrictions.

Moreover, as Brian Orend notes, it is difficult to find comparative justice in the claims of Nazi Germany. Orend ultimately discards the notion as helpful to understanding just cause, preferring instead to interpret its spirit as requiring a thoroughgoing examination of any purported just cause claims by any warring party.

To defend the utility of comparative justice, one might first note that it does not preclude making some judgments to the effect that one side is frankly unjust. Nothing in the concept of comparison precludes one side's cause being judged as much worse than another's. There are many cases in which a fair-minded observer might be torn and find the idea of comparative justice helpful. One could point to the U.S. contention in 2003 that Iraq possessed WMD or the 1989 "Operation Just Cause" and suggest that the most helpful way to understand those conflicts is in terms of one side's cause being less just than the other's without having to name one side as unjust. The idea of comparative justice in JWT, sympathetically approached, seems to reiterate the wisdom of renaissance thinking about just wars.

Just Cause and the Idea of a State

It is worth noting here that the legalist paradigm depends on the war's being conducted by states with recognizable geographic and political borders. The legalist paradigm is a starting point for understanding just war between states in the modern era. It should be mentioned, however, that it is inadequate to some present-day challenges, notably problems of preemptive war, terrorism, and humanitarian intervention. This inadequacy is due to the legalist paradigm's reliance on a certain way of understanding what constitutes a recognized member of the international community.

The idea of a state, as it is known today, can be traced to the 1648 Peace of Westphalia. This treaty, which marked the end of the Thirty Years War, did so in part by declaring that states' borders constitute barriers to religious hegemony.

The Thirty Years War was in large part a religious conflict. In this regard, the opponents identified themselves less with their political associations and more with their religious ones. But the war devastated Europe while failing to settle the question of religion. The framers of the Peace of Westphalia hit upon a solution that would contain religious disagreement by establishing political sovereignty as a theoretically impermeable barrier. What went on within states became, so to speak, the business of those states and no one else's. The idea of a state as an international citizen, free to determine its own direction without interference, was embodied by the Peace of Westphalia. Sovereign states were required to respect the sovereignty of other states, leaving them to manage their own internal affairs. No one state need fear the interference of another across recognized political borders.

In light of this notion of political sovereignty, it becomes clearer why the *jus ad bellum* in its present form considers unprovoked aggression to be the only obviously just cause for war. It is also clear how legitimate authority is linked tightly to public declarations by a state's representatives. Furthermore, against this background of sovereign nations coexisting in a global community, it is easy to see why militaries are bound to serve their states instead of individual rulers or political parties within states. The division of moral responsibility between political powers guided by *jus ad bellum* considerations and military members bound by the limitations of *jus in bello* is equally logical under the Westphalian model.

As will become clear later, however, not all conflicts are the products of interstate conflicts. Nonstate-actors are increasingly involving themselves in violent acts in the modern world. Defense is required against all sorts of harm, not just the harm posed by recognized states. The notion of political sovereignty is challenged by violations of human rights within states. Modern just war thinkers are increasingly considering the ethics of humanitarian intervention, even when such intervention is considered unwelcome by the government in the state where humanitarian crises are taking place.

The legalist paradigm's clear simplicity is adequate to capture much thinking about just cause, but there are more complex and difficult issues in play to challenge modern statesmen and militaries. *Jus ad bellum* is evolving.

Modifications to the Baseline Case for Just Cause

Response to unprovoked deliberate physical aggression is widely accepted as a just cause, but other candidates for just cause require more nuanced treatment as competing values can come into play. Clear cases, such as Poland's right to defend itself against the German invasion, are relatively easy to address both in terms of ordinary moral intuitions and the legalist paradigm. But less obvious cases, particularly in defense against threats that originate outside of recognizable states, require more thought. Grotius's sensitive and insightful treatment of how difficult determining what constitutes a just cause can be is worth bearing in mind. Today, many military ethicists are challenged by the issues of anticipatory strikes, aid to third parties including political communities that do not enjoy status as full-blown states, and terrorism.

War in Anticipation of Harm

One state might detect a deliberate building of armed capability on the part of a potential adversary, along with a tense or hostile political environment, and reasonably conclude that a war is forthcoming. If responding to aggression after it occurs is justified under the traditional interpretations of *jus ad bellum,* would not launching a defensive war in anticipation of aggression be likewise justified? After all, the very notion of defense itself suggests deflecting an oncoming attack before suffering its effects.

As aggression can often be seen coming well before violent damage is suffered, anticipatory defense against it makes both practical and moral sense. To help clarify the issue, Brian Orend suggests using a distinction between descriptive defense and normative defense. The first requires that the defender must actually suffer a violent assault before responding. The second might morally permit a first strike if it is defensive in the sense of warding off an imminent attack. "A just war is one that is normatively defensive—it defends people from aggression and seeks, in response, to resist and repel it—whereas the tactics which may be employed, within the context of such a just war, may be either empirically defensive or offensive."[12]

Although the justice of normatively defensive preemption is widely accepted, its nature is delicate. The real-world situation is often not at all as clear as one might at first suppose. Whether a preemptive war is genuinely normatively defensive depends in large part on what is taken to be indicative of a potential attack. On the one hand, if defense is justified, preventing aggression would seem doubly so, as the victims of an aggressor's first strike have just as much right to their lives and happiness as anyone else. This would suggest that early warning signs of a planned strike would constitute just cause for an anticipatory attack. On the other hand, lowering the evidentiary threshold from the clarity of having suffered a blow to having "sufficient evidence" that an aggressive war is forthcoming courts both strategic disaster and moral peril.

One concern is that this sort of logic can justify far too much. It might be used to mask aggression under the camouflage of perceived threats. This cynical use of preemption would obviously conflict with the spirit of *jus ad bellum,* but violence could result from even innocent uses. Normatively defensive preemption might be used to justify an honestly defensive anticipatory attack when in fact no threat was intended by the supposed aggressor. As with a child swatting at unoffending but nearby bees, it would be the very fear of harm that leads to harm when otherwise none would have occurred. Perhaps worse, the claim that anticipatory attacks are justified can cut both ways. Country A may justify aggression against country B by claiming that, say, the massive military exercises B is conducting just over A's borders are in reality preparations for an imminent war against A. A accordingly mobilizes its forces to strike B before suffering an invasion. But if A does so, notice that country B would be, all things being equal, justified in preempting country A's preemption. Such logic can spiral, with each nation's fear of the other intensifying in a mutually reinforcing suspicious apprehension. This spiral can substantially lower the threshold of going to war, with each side arguing, perhaps justifiably, that it had to strike first in self-defense. The case is especially serious if the forces involved are, or could escalate to, the use of nuclear missiles and other fast-moving, highly destructive and irrevocable weapons. What begins as suspicion can end in warfare that no one intended. This hardly meets the *jus ad bellum* purpose of making war less frequent—indeed, it does precisely the opposite.

To a large extent, the complexities plaguing the justification of preemption lie in questions about the degree of certainty regarding the threat. In the paradigmatic case of having received a physical blow, there is no doubt that one has suffered aggression. Even in this traditional case, however, there could be doubts over who struck the blow and even over whether the strike was deliberate or the result of a human mistake or technical glitch. Things become murkier when attempting to predict physical aggression that has not yet been made manifest by tangible violence. Justifiably striking in advance necessarily presupposes that one *knows* an attack is coming. Prudence, however, may urge that to wait until one is certain is to be reckless with the lives of one's citizens. Conclusions about the future are always subject to correction, and the further into the future one looks the less clear things may be. This is especially so given the duplicity that often accompanies hostility even though no violence has yet occurred. Still, there are cases where the signs of an oncoming attack are unmistakable, even if its magnitude may be uncertain. Much of moral consequence hinges on how soon an attack will come.

JWT addresses the problem by specifying a distinction between two sorts of anticipatory attack. Preemptive war is widely viewed as ethically permissible under certain conditions. Preventive war, however, is generally judged as impermissible.

Preemption. Michael Walzer offers an analysis of justified preemption composed of three elements that together constitute "the point of sufficient threat." These are "a manifest intent to injure, a degree of active preparation that makes that intent a positive danger, and a general situation in which waiting, or doing anything other than fighting, greatly magnifies the risk."[13] Using Israel's preemptive strike in the Six-Day War as an example, Walzer concludes that preemption is warranted when waiting for the opponent to strike first would put the state at grave risk.[14] Brian Orend prefers the label of "anticipatory attack" for first-strikes justified under this set of circumstances, but he agrees in principle with Walzer's analysis. Notice that in cases of justified preemption, the notion of imminent threat carries much of the moral load. As in the case of individual self-defense against an assailant, waiting for a blow to fall can be a fatal error. The practical problem, however, of understanding just what constitutes sufficient evidence that "the point of sufficient threat" has been reached remains. Determining what signals a "serious risk" is a serious practical problem.

The issue of preemption's moral justification is particularly relevant as more and more threats are presented by rogue states and indeed by political actors, such as Al Qaeda, that act on the authority of no state. Threats from these sources certainly justify defense, but most work in the past century or so has focused on the behavior of Westphalian-style states. Chapter 6 addresses these emerging issues.

Preventive War. Historically, arguments that seek to justify preventive war do not appeal directly to self-defense but rather to a defense of the "balance of power" in a world in which future conflicts are inevitable. That is, the war is waged to prevent any one state's becoming so powerful in relation to other states that it could act without fear of adverse future consequences. In the absence of countervailing powers, such a state might be likely to initiate wars in the future; therefore, waging war against that state today would prevent harm in the future. A preventive war is said to be justified on behalf of a community of states, all of which benefit from no one state being able to overwhelm others. Unlike preemptive war, which defends against an imminent and actual threat, preventive war attempts to deal with potential threats.

As with preemptive war, the issues surrounding what constitutes sufficient evidence of a forthcoming war are crucial to establishing the just cause for *jus ad bellum*. But if preemptive war faces problems of evidence, preventive war faces exponentially increased problems of evidence. A moment's reflection reveals that justifying preventive war requires almost impossibly close calculation of what constitutes a trend toward an irreversible imbalance of power. The issue is complicated by considerations of how seriously imbalanced power must become to justify preventive war. Accurate forecasting is required to establish when the purported threat to peace will exist. Worse, "spin" may be applied quite easily in the face of ambiguities that characterize predicting a political future.

These worries call the defensive nature of preventive war into serious doubt. Indeed, it is hard to see how a preventive war could ever satisfactorily be considered normatively defensive because of the very nature of defense. To defend implies that there is an attack already in evidence against which to defend. Defense, in other words, *presupposes* that there is an attack of some nature. But in the case of preventive war, the attack is exactly what is purportedly being prevented from ever coming into being.[15]

In the face of these difficulties, most just war thinkers regard preventive war as morally dubious, as it is much like, or even indistinguishable from, aggression. If one remembers that JWT seeks to limit both the frequency and destructiveness of war, one can easily see that permitting war today to prevent war in the future is self-frustrating. It involves trading, in Jeffrie Murphy's phrase, "a certain evil for a possible good."[16]

Aid to Other States and Enforcing International Law

A state that enjoys rights may not possess the military power to defend those rights. As noted earlier, the powerful often dominate the weak, regardless of philosophical discoveries or the imperatives of ethics. Relatively weak states may be especially at risk of aggression if respecting their sovereignty is perceived to be inconsistent with the interests of stronger states. To address this asymmetry, modern JWT recognizes that one (usually relatively powerful) state may justifiably respond to aggression on behalf of another political community or that a coalition of communities may justifiably act on behalf of a weak one. In the present era, a UN resolution may specify the just cause and serve to legitimize the violence.

Self-determination is one value at stake here, as is respect for international law and order. As Brian Orend has pointed out, war is always about how a particular community will be governed.[17] Violent aggression against a state impedes or destroys its capacity to determine its form of government for itself. Should a rescuer state respond, the response must be in the service of the members of the victimized community. Doing so as a pretext for a war that is otherwise motivated is not justified.

Similarly, enforcing international law can constitute a just cause for war in the defense of others. Here, the aggressor state is punished both to deter further aggression and to maintain international law while the rights of the victimized state are defended. Some see this punishment as a form of collective self-defense, akin to the deterrent effect that punishing criminals is said to have in domestic life.[18]

The "Second Gulf War" of 1990–1991[19] provides one of the best examples of international action in accordance with these ethical principles.

Iraq invaded Kuwait on August 2, 1990. The United Nations Security Council issued Resolution 660 the same day, demanding that the Iraqi forces return to their preinvasion positions. The Arab League condemned the invasion as well. Iraq continued to occupy Kuwait throughout the fall of 1990, in spite of numerous UN resolutions condemning the invasion and occupation. Various other means short of war, including trade and economic sanctions, proved ineffective in pressuring Iraq to withdraw. On November 29, the Security Council adopted Resolution 678, authorizing "States co-operating with the Government of Kuwait . . . to use all necessary means to uphold and implement resolution 660" unless Iraq complied with it by January 15, 1991. As is well known, Iraq did not comply, and, accordingly, the coalition forces took violent action. The coalition itself was composed of more than 30 nations, including Egypt, Saudi Arabia, Syria, Senegal, Bangladesh, Pakistan, Oman, the United Arab Emirates, Qatar, and Bahrain. Monetary aid for the war was provided by both Japan and Germany.

The Second Gulf War was both one-sided and short. The coalition air strikes began on January 17, 1991, with the land attacks into Iraq beginning on February 24 and ending after 100 hours of fighting with a cease fire. Kuwait was liberated and the resolution enforced. UN Resolution 686, dated March 2, 1991, embodied the willingness of Iraq to comply with all of the relevant resolutions.

The war illustrates the difference between defeating an adversary and defending a third party. The war did not aim to destroy Iraq or establish new rule over it. Rather, the objective was to defeat the aggression that Kuwait had suffered.

Civil Wars and Wars of Liberation

History is replete with cases in which a political community considers itself to be inadequately represented by the governing powers of its own sovereign state. The United States provides examples both of a revolution against its own government in the1770s, as well as a civil war in the 1860s. In both of these cases, commissioned officers led armies against the governments that had commissioned them. And, in both cases, foreign powers involved or nearly involved themselves on the side of these armies.

Understanding just cause in cases like these requires understanding the relationship between a political community and the state. Volumes have been written about this relationship; a general sketch of the issues will have to suffice here.

In the idealized case, a political community is identical with its state. That is, the political identity of the community is perfectly represented by its ruling authorities. In such cases, there is no question of a government's legitimacy. Its power to rule derives from the free consent of the governed and, to the extent that states have rights, they flow from the rights of their citizens. Although criticisms have been leveled at this model,[20] it remains in wide use.

In some cases, however, a given political community may be only poorly represented by its state. This is often the case with colonialism, for example. It may also result from ethnic or religious clashes. In many parts of the world, the political boundaries were drawn during times of colonial governments that have since ended, leaving lines on maps that correspond poorly or not at all to the various political identities in the same geographic region. Much of the Middle East, for example, is plagued with a poor correspondence between states boundaries and political communities. Kurdish, Shiite, and Sunni political communities are all found within the legal boundaries of Iraq.

In such cases, the legitimacy of a government may come into question. Should the government and the political communities be unable to resolve the problem, the political community may resort to violence, as indeed happened in some of the North American British colonies during the 18th century.

The question of just cause for a third-party's involvement can be complex. On the one hand, the right to political sovereignty enjoyed by the government of the affected state would seem to prohibit armed intervention on behalf of the revolutionaries. On the other hand, the revolutionaries may be able to make a good case that their government should not enjoy political sovereignty just because it is not legitimate. Chapter 6 examines in depth tensions such as these.

Legitimate Authority

In the historical overview it was noted that much of JWT was intended to advise rulers regarding when and why to wage war. The underlying premise was that rulers have the authority to make such decisions as an ordinary and necessary aspect of being rulers. Citizens, accordingly, no matter how wealthy or influential, do not enjoy this authority. At least at first blush, the criterion therefore prohibits armed civil unrest. Sovereigns may raise armies and wage wars, but insurrection and civil war are illegitimate avenues to achieve political goals. The domestic order provided by a state is defended by the criterion of legitimate (sometimes called "competent") authority.

In modern liberal democracies, governmental authority rests on the consent of the governed. The government explicitly acts in the name of the people. For modern JWT, then, at least in liberal democracies, the only legitimate moral authority for a state's waging war lies with its citizens, even as the legal authority lies with their representatives. Violence is done on behalf of the state's members by agents of the state, who are formally identified as such by credentials and, in many cases, uniforms. Wars waged in accordance with this criterion are "popular" and enjoy wide support among the population. For the United States, the Second World War exemplifies the popular support that the criterion requires. The declaration of war that followed the Japanese assault on Pearl Harbor was passed quickly, with virtually no debate. The legal requirements for legitimate authority were satisfied. Perhaps of more significance, volunteers flooded military recruitment offices soon after Pearl Harbor, the civilian population accepted rationing and other wartime deprivations willingly overall, and there was almost no political opposition to waging the war. Indeed, even the results of subsequent presidential elections seem to reflect popular approval of senior leadership in the Second World War. Harry Truman, who, as a result of the death in office of Franklin Roosevelt, served as president for the last days of the Second World War, was elected to the office in 1948. His successor, Dwight Eisenhower, who had served as Supreme Allied Commander, served two terms as president.

The U.S. involvement in Vietnam provides an interesting contrasting example. Resistance to the draft, civil unrest, and domestic political events reflected substantial disagreement regarding the war. Like Truman, Lyndon Johnson came to be president as a result of the death of his predecessor. In contrast to Truman however, Johnson announced that he would not seek reelection in March of 1968, soon after the North Vietnamese Tet offensive. As the Second World War and Vietnam illustrate, popular support for a war, or its lack, may be reflected in both the political rhetoric and the results of democratic elections.

The question of conscription offers additional perspective on the matter of legitimate authority. A draft may offer a mechanism to hold a democratic state to the legitimate authority criterion, as it engages a representative cross section of a state's citizens in the consequences of war. Put another way, one can test whether a state has legitimate authority for waging war if one spreads the risks of that war equitably across the citizenry. If the burden of military service, including the possibility of death or maiming, is shared across all socioeconomic levels, then one will have a gauge for the popularity of a war. Everyone, so to speak, will have a stake in the fight. On the other hand, an all-volunteer military may be composed disproportionately of the socioeconomically disadvantaged. In this case, the risks are borne unequally across the society and the matter of legitimate authority may be less clear.

Declaration of Cause

Sunshine makes unethical behavior less likely; the *jus ad bellum* requirement for a public declaration of cause exploits this fact. It is true that states place value on popular opinion about their decisions. History judges the actions of states and their statesmen, at least in part, through the lens of morality. For example, the use of Nazi Germany to represent an aggressive evil regime is commonplace. Britain's aerial self-defense in the Second World War, on the other hand, is widely regarded as her "finest hour."

States do generally explain their violent actions publicly. The explanations may not be truthful, but even in their attempts at deception, the ethical imperative to justify violence is acknowledged.

Declaring one's cause truthfully and publicly serves a practical and important purpose: it announces to the world what conditions the adversary must meet to end the war and return to peaceable international relations. Assuming that Clausewitz is correct that war is politics "by other means,"[21] declaring the cause makes the political goal of the war public knowledge and accordingly makes the continuation of violence after the political goals are met subject to harsh global judgment. Perhaps more important, subjecting the political goal to the international public eye helps ensure that seeking that goal is justifiable in the first place. Few would judge repelling an aggressor's unprovoked invasion as unjustified; all would want to reserve the right to defend against aggression for their own use. On the other hand, most would judge overt hegemony as unjustified, and even in those cases where a "cover story" was in place, many would suspect it.

The Second Gulf War exemplifies the appropriate use of this criterion on the part of the coalition forces. Iraq's aggressive acts against Kuwait were widely condemned and the injustice of its occupation publicly declared as the *casus belli*. Although Iraq's military was soundly defeated, coalition forces ceased violent operations after the stated goal, embodied in United Nations Resolutions, of restoring Kuwait's territorial integrity and sovereignty had been accomplished.[22]

The Second World War provides some intriguing instances of declarations. The formal declaration of war against Japan appealed explicitly to self-defense, but also to bad faith on the part of the Japanese government. Vengeance seems to have constituted at least a part of the public sentiment when the war was entered, and that sense is conveyed by Franklin Roosevelt's address seeking a declaration of war, which reads, in part:

> Always will we remember the character of the onslaught against us.
>
> No matter how long it may take us to overcome this premeditated invasion, the American people, in their righteous might, will win through to absolute victory.
>
> I believe I interpret the will of the Congress and of the people when I assert that we will not only defend ourselves to the uttermost but will make very certain that this form of treachery shall never endanger us again.[23]

Terms such as *absolute victory* in the second paragraph, and the third paragraph in its entirety read today as testimony to justified outrage. In a similar vein, the Allied Powers' Casablanca Conference of January 1943 resulted in a declaration by Franklin Roosevelt that the Allies would end hostilities only on the unconditional surrender of the Axis powers. Demands for unconditional surrender are criticized by some military ethicists and strategists, as they tend to foster increased resistance on the part of a weakened adversary, thereby prolonging the suffering that war entails.[24] Indeed, as late as early August, 1945, U.S. Secretary of the

Navy Forrestal suggested that "the Japanese cabinet seemed to have decided 'that the war must be fought with all the vigour and bitterness of which the nation is capable, so long as the only alternative is unconditional surrender.'"[25] The fire-bombings and nuclear strikes against Japan in 1945, when the severely weakened nation plainly presented no aggressive threat, have made their mark on history as extremely controversial. Some argue that these bombings were required in order to cause the Japanese to capitulate. But, as Michael Walzer and others have noted, this assertion in turn raises the issue of whether demands for unconditional surrender can be morally justified. The demand for unconditional surrender gives the outcome of the war extremely high stakes.

Right Intention

The criterion of right intention was meant historically to rule out hatred for one's adversaries as a motive for war. Notice that the object of the criterion is a state of mind. The criterion captures an important distinction between the justice of the war itself and the attitude with which war is decided upon. One may decide to resort to a war, which would otherwise be just, on motives that fail the criterion of right intention. For example, if one were to wage an otherwise justified defensive war against a theocratic adversary, but wage it out of hatred for the theology the adversary practices, one would fail to have right intention.

The Christian thinking that influenced JWT's development is in play here; there is a requirement to love one's enemies even as one wages war against them. Indeed, it may not be too much of a stretch to suggest that modern Christian pacifism derives much of its philosophical potency from the insights of right intention to "hate the sin but love the sinner." That is, under right intention, the target of justifiable violence is not people, but rather ideologies or policies. Right intention requires that war be waged with the intention of attacking and defeating moral evil only. This criterion therefore rules out waging war for nationalistic, racial, religious, or tribal motives. Wars of genocide or "ethnic cleansing" have people as their targets, not ideas, and accordingly fail to meet the criterion. Likewise, hatred of the adversary or the enjoyment of violence is prohibited, as they are inconsistent with the more properly regretful or mournful attitude toward even a just war.

Most modern secular thinkers view the criterion as an important way to limit both the frequency and destructiveness of war, exploiting the important distinction between persons and politics. For example, the motives of defending rights and the international peaceful order would meet the criterion, whereas other motives, obtaining resources for example, do not.

It is interesting to consider war propaganda in the light of this criterion. One can find propaganda that is consistent with right intention as well as propaganda, which evidently seeks to inspire or reinforce attitudes that would run counter to it. For example, some of the propaganda in the United States during the Second World War appealed to racist attitudes regarding the Japanese adversary—a clear violation of right intention. But other appeals, for example Norman Rockwell's "Freedom" paintings, reflect a motive to restore the sorts of human rights that the Axis powers offended. Both, evidently, were intended to motivate viewers to the war effort, but only one harmonized with JWT.

Victor David Hanson, a classicist and military historian, has argued that armies that fight with explicitly moral goals in mind have often performed far better than might otherwise have been expected. In *The Soul of Battle,* Hanson illustrates his contention by studying three armies: Thebans under Epaminondas, in 370–369 BC, federal troops under General Sherman in 1864–1865, and American soldiers under General Patton in 1944–1945. In all three cases, these armies performed feats astonishing to both their adversaries and comrades, changing history for the better. The Thebans ended Spartan slavery, the federals did the same for the American South, and Patton ended the Nazi occupation of Western Europe. In each of these cases, the soldiers were primarily nonprofessionals, mobilized for the war and then rapidly disbanded after the cause had been won.[26]

Hanson's claims about the multiplying effect of having a moral cause present to mind are echoed by nonviolence theorists. Gandhi's *satyagraha,* or "truth-struggle," required practitioners to suffer to achieve a political goal that was of sufficient moral import to justify the suffering. The object of *satyagraha* is to convert the will of the opponent. It rules out any personal animosity toward the adversary, instead focusing on changing the opponent's mind.[27]

Proportionality

Jus ad bellum proportionality considerations reflect consequentialist lines of moral evaluation. That is, the proportionality criterion focuses on the cost-benefit ratio of predicted outcomes, seeking to minimize the harm suffered by all who are affected by a given decision.

The criterion is both backward- and forward-looking. The forward-looking aspect can be quite difficult to apply, as it requires predicting the future. The backward-looking aspect is less difficult, as it requires a measured response to an evil act.

Looking forward, the proportionality criterion requires forecasting the disvalue of the evil the war will create and comparing it to the good that the war is likely to achieve. That this is difficult may help temper subsequent historical judgments about the individuals involved, but it does nothing to diminish the obligation to forecast accurately. A just war ought to prevent substantially more evil than it causes. This criterion acknowledges that war, like surgery, always causes harm, but the evil prevented can be of such magnitude as to justify doing some harm of lesser magnitude in order to prevent it.

Thinking back to December 1941, the forward-looking question of proportionality undoubtedly appears differently from today's perspective than it did then. The Japanese attacks that day were not limited to Pearl Harbor. Wake, Guam, Hong Kong, the Philippines, and Midway were all attacked within a day of the strike against Pearl Harbor. The precise extent of losses suffered by U.S. forces was almost certainly unknown to statesmen in Washington, although it seems clear that they knew the losses were severe. Still, the United States, with its mighty industrial and manpower capacities, most likely seemed adequate to the task. The Japanese treatment of China, which it had invaded in 1937, could be used as a yardstick for the harm that Japanese victory would entail. The aggression and brutal occupation there that followed provided substantial evidence that Japanese rule would be harsh.[28] Although today it is impossible to say with accuracy how the situation would have appeared on December 7, it is clear that the U.S. government judged that it would be in for a fight, but that winning the fight would be worth its cost.

Considerations of proportionality should continue through wartime. Wars have a way of expanding in both scale and viciousness. A war that begins in proportion to the good sought may become disproportionately harmful to it as the conflict continues. Failure to meet the criterion over time can constitute a good moral reason to seek an end to the violence. The First World War is a good example. Few today can describe what evil that war was supposed to prevent, but there is no doubt that the war itself killed and maimed millions. More is at stake today. The possibility of a modern conflict leading to a widespread nuclear exchange is real, and obviously any such exchange would do far more harm than it could prevent.

Looking backward, applying the criterion in response to aggression should not be disproportionate to the aggression itself. Offensive acts that morally invite retaliation vary in the harm they do, and accordingly the response ought to vary as well. By way of illustration, the Soviet invasion of Afghanistan in 1979 would not justify nuclear retaliation, but the Nazi depredations in Europe did justify massive defensive response.

The backward-looking aspect may also apply to punishment. States engage in unjust acts and punishment is warranted. But, as in domestic law, the punishment should be crafted in relation to the offense. Again, the question of the United States waging war against the Axis in the Second World War seems settled. The question, however, of waging a war for unconditional surrender, with its attendant increase in the resistance offered, is not. It may be suggested that the demand for unconditional surrender was justified as a punishment because of the extremely brutal policies by at least some of the Axis nations.

Some modern pacifists suggest that the proportionality criterion can never be met. Modern war, they argue, with its unimaginably destructive potential, is always disproportionate, and therefore nonviolent methods offer the only possibility of a proportionate defense against evil. Richard Norman has rightly noted that such a position must always be open to revision as new facts emerge. One might have held a pacifist position after the First World War, plausibly believing that that war was vastly disproportionate. But then the Nazis appeared, and they represented such a magnitude of evil that an even more destructive Second World War was indeed justified.[29] One might revise one's position again in light of massively destructive weapons, only to modify it again if such weapons might be successfully neutralized.

Reasonable Hope of Success

The requirement for a reasonable hope of success is meant to preclude futile struggle. The idea is that if the outcome of an armed conflict is foreseeable in advance of entering the conflict, little purpose is served by fighting, but the harm suffered by all would increase. If defeat is inevitable, why suffer the evil of war?

The inevitability of defeat is not always clear in advance. As with other forward-looking criteria, deciding just what constitutes a "reasonable hope" is rarely straightforward. In the summer and fall of 1940, the British resisted the Nazis successfully during the Battle of Britain, although the German Army had occupied almost all of Europe during its Blitzkrieg and forced the British to evacuate their military forces at Dunkirk.

Despite uncertainties regarding the future, some propose that the very act of resistance serves a moral purpose even if it fails. To make peace with oppression, even when defeat is inevitable, raises moral issues involving the relative moral attractiveness of peace and justice. If injustice is to be endured regardless of resistance, one might be tempted to say that suffering injustice would be preferable to suffering both injustice and the evils of war; but ordinary intuitions offer countervailing considerations. One such consideration has to do with deterring aggression. If aggression is said to be a criminal act in the international community, a failure to engage against it may suggest that it is condoned. Arguably, there is great moral value in registering a courageous objection to injustice even though suffering it remains inevitable.

Appeasement is controversial for this reason among others. As with Thucydides's account of the Athenian's confrontation with the Melians, resisting injustice may rightfully be seen as futile but nonetheless morally compelling. To submit to force against the imperatives of morality seems inevitably to invite controversy. Submission in the face of oppression rubs against the grain of ordinary moral intuition. Put more starkly, one might suggest that obligations to justice trump obligations to survive.

The obligation to one's citizens counts as well. Their lives are the proper object of a state's protection, and no morally decent government could properly put those lives at risk unless there was some hope that the risk would be worthwhile. In cases where the protection of lives might require the sacrifice of justice, it is not hard to see why the citizens themselves might argue in favor of the criterion's utility.

Reasonable hope of success must be on the minds of those contemplating surrender. Defeat and suicide are both unwelcome, but the former is less final than the latter. When defeat is inevitable, it seems clear that further resistance as an alternative to surrender places both lives and justice in peril. Surrender, however unpalatable, generally does preserve life.

Czechoslovakia's acquiescence to Nazi aggression in 1938–1939 provides a good historical example of this reasoning. Hitler, having brought Austria into his control in March 1938, believed that he was in a position to annex the Sudetenland, the western part of Czechoslovakia, which was populated largely by people of German descent. It was also where many Czech military defenses were located. Hitler denounced the treatment of German-speaking Czechs in the Sudetenland and called for its secession from Czechoslovakia. Violence seemed imminent, especially as tensions over the same region in the spring had seemed to threaten the outbreak of a war involving France and Britain. In an attempt to avoid going to war, representatives of Britain and France met with Hitler and Mussolini. Britain and France had no intention of going to war over the issue of the Sudetenland. There was no Czech representation at the meeting. The Munich Agreement, signed on September 30, 1938, was the result. This agreement permitted the Germans to occupy parts of the Sudetenland but required it to respect the integrity of the rest of Czechoslovakia. The Czechs suffered a fait accompli in the Sudetenland. Perhaps worse, Czechoslovakia was left alone to face German threats to the rest of its territory. When the German military moved to occupy remaining areas of Czechoslovakia in March 1939, it seemed clear that no allied help would be offered and that any resistance would fail.[30] Consequently, the Czech government capitulated, avoiding a war that would be almost certain to end in defeat.

Many seem to find the Czech decision in this case to be a reasonable one, but they judge the behavior of France and Britain more harshly.[31] This is likely due to underlying presuppositions about the nature of freedom and necessity. Alone against Hitler's looming military, a Czech decision to fight may well have been unreasonable. They found themselves in a position analogous to a defenseless citizen threatened with the option of "your money or your life." In one case, the citizen loses his money and his life. In the other, he loses his money but remains alive. Cutting losses is the best choice. The Czechs acted under compulsion that they could do nothing to avoid and so are generally regarded sympathetically. France and Britain, on the other hand, did have the option to go to war over Czechoslovakia, but chose not to exercise that option, preferring instead a policy of appeasement.

Last Resort

War's intrinsically destructive nature demands that it be the option of last resort. Particularly if one understands Clausewitz's conception of warfare as "a mere continuation of policy by other means,"[32] this criterion helps one to seek to do politics by political means instead of violent ones.

The existing international community offers many routes to resolving disputes. All of the practical routes offered by the community ought to be attempted in good faith before engaging in warfare.

Like many of the other criteria, it can be difficult to understand with precision. Just what does a *last* resort amount to? It seems clear, however, that the criterion is to be understood as requiring those who would adopt violent means to view war as the least attractive means to their ends. That is, the concept of "last" is to be understood as "least preferred"—that other means should be considered preferable to going to war. The analogy to medicine is helpful here. Although surgery may be an effective way to fight a patient's affliction, it is ethically inappropriate if other, less drastic treatments are available. If a physician can effect a cure through a change of diet, prescribing medication, or performing surgery, all things being equal, she ought to begin treatment with the least costly and least harmful option available. Should the change of diet prove ineffective, then she might choose to try the use of drugs. Only after that method fails should she resort to surgery.

On the other hand, the criterion does not require "last" to be understood in temporal terms. A first-strike is consistent with the criterion if such a strike is the only option left open after other means have been honestly and thoroughly explored. It may help to think of an unhappy marriage. If both parties genuinely desire to keep the marriage intact and, consistent with this, make good faith efforts toward that end, only to find that their efforts fail, then divorce might be considered as a last resort. It is sincerely unwanted, but there is no better choice given the circumstances.

In the case of a surprise, the matter is more straightforward. If one is physically assaulted while walking down a remote street at night, physical self-defense is justified. Similarly, if a nation suffers deliberate and overt physical aggression, the last resort criterion is met. For example, America's formal entry into the Second World War, although widely anticipated, was precipitated by a surprise attack at Pearl Harbor and the German declaration of war against the United States. Indeed, Japanese and American leaders were engaged in diplomatic negotiations to reduce the tensions in Indochina when the talks were ended by the Japanese attack.

End of Peace

Remembering that JWT aims to limit the harm that nations and individuals willfully do to one another, it only makes sense to wage war with the goal of peace in mind. It is easy to appreciate this if one thinks about the resolution of disputes within a modern liberal democracy. If negotiation between the parties does not solve the matter, appeal is often made to the judicial system. The legal battle may be a fierce one, but all parties enter it with the end of peace as an assumption. It is reasonable to believe that one may lose a lawsuit, but it is unreasonable to believe that peace will be seriously disrupted. Living well is possible even after an adverse outcome if one may live in peace.

Peace within the global community facilitates the well-being of all, whereas conflict puts all potentially at risk. Thoughtful statesmen are particularly sensitive to the threat of instability, given its tendency to generate long-lasting animosities even after active hostilities have ceased. The political wounds of war can take generations to heal. Wars can lead to more wars, defeating their own point.

Waging war only with the goal of peace in mind means that the adversaries can have a better chance of negotiating an end to the war in good faith regardless of who prevails. The appropriate aspiration is for a future of peaceful coexistence. A good understanding of this on the part of the warring parties may temper damning rhetoric about one's adversary, facilitating a peaceful outcome.

Some are quite skeptical about this criterion. The doubt results from two related issues. First, it requires adversaries to peer into the future and envision a just peace. Given the chaotic evolution of wars, it can be difficult to anticipate events. Alliances form and dissolve, third parties enter the fray, astonishing military reverses occur. But even if one could predict the future of a war with reasonable accuracy, different parties likely have different ideas about what would constitute a just peace. Indeed, this difference of opinion lies at the root of many wars. Everyone wants peace in the long run—it is the terms of that peace that complicate matters.

The Second Gulf War on the coalition's side seems to have satisfied this criterion. The multiple UN resolutions that condemned the Iraqi aggression and that ultimately authorized the use of forceful means reflect a sensitivity to the spirit of the criterion. Resolution 678, dated November 29, 1990, authorized "all necessary means," but only to implement the previous resolutions regarding the Iraq-Kuwait conflict. Although these resolutions required, among other things, that Iraq withdraw from Kuwait (Resolution 660) and suffer economic sanctions, they did not, for example, require regime change or the occupation of Iraq. The Security Council Resolutions coincident with the cease fire required that Iraq "accept in principle its liability for any loss, damage, or injury arising in regard to Kuwait and third states" but did not require that the Iraqis suffer the loss of territory. In short, the resolutions authorizing the war, as well as the quick conclusion to hostilities, seem consistent with the idea of restoring peace and maintaining it into the future.

Applying the *Jus ad Bellum* Criteria

There is an unfortunate tendency among some to approach the *jus ad bellum* criteria as though they constituted a list of discrete items to be checked off like a shopping list. This tendency can result from an innocently immature understanding of JWT's purposes and insights, but it can also be the result of a more sinister mindset. Some wishing to justify a war simply go through the criteria one by one concocting more-or-less plausible-sounding reasons to explain why a given decision to wage war meets all of the criteria. This shallow approach can be used to "justify" just about anything, as even a cursory overview of any century's wars will reveal. Examples of such a cynical use of the criteria abound. The Nazi invasion of Poland in 1939 was "justified" by Polish "provocations" including, among other pretexts, an orchestrated attack on a German radio station at Gleiwitz near the Polish border.[33]

Historical events such as the Glewitz incident highlight an interesting feature of international relations and ethical judgment. Regardless of how jaded a view a state's leaders may take about military ethics, *appearing* ethical matters to them. Hypocrisy, as de La Rochefoucauld noted, is indeed the "homage that vice pays to virtue." Putting a morally upright face on a decision to do violence seems important even to those who more privately may discount morality's applicability to international relations.[34]

Less cynically, Immanuel Kant suggested that "the homage which each state pays (at least in words) to the concept of law proves that there is slumbering in man an even greater moral disposition to become master of the evil principle in himself (which he cannot disclaim) and to hope for the same for others. Otherwise the word 'law' would never be pronounced by states which wish to war upon one another."[35]

Serious students of JWT appreciate that the *jus ad bellum* criteria are morally worthless if they are not used in good faith. Using the criteria appropriately requires a commitment to seeking the ethical heart of the matter, regardless of whatever political rhetoric might be uttered. As with other sorts of ethical judgments, it may be necessary to sort through self-serving discourse and misleading representations of fact. Part of being serious about the criteria is admitting that they can be hard to apply with exactitude. The criteria are guides to making good judgments; they are not substitutes for it. The criteria help highlight many appropriate considerations, but they are neither perfect nor set in stone. Like much of applied ethics, JWT is a work in progress.

Instead of using the *jus ad bellum* criteria mechanically, it may be helpful to think of them as ways of framing the various morally laden aspects of the decision whether to wage war. The criteria can be usefully thought of as a constellation of considerations that reason and experience have handed down to modern statesmen and citizens. Each consideration likely has multiple dimensions, and the criteria interweave in ways peculiar to each case. This means that proficiency in making good ethical judgments regarding war requires a certain amount of education and experience.

The same is true for many other sorts of judgments about war. Students of military history will recognize that military strategy and tactics do not reduce to a checklist composed of the principles of war or a field-manual's guidance. Nor by any means does leadership. Political and military wisdom require study and experience. The same is true for ethical judgment.

Notes

1. Many suggest that this bipolarity is too stark to capture many real-world cases. The notion of comparative justice is discussed later.

2. I am indebted to Dr. Dan Zupan for this point. Walzer makes a similar point by noting that in a perfect democracy, every citizen "can rightly be called to account" for state policies. Michael Walzer, *Just and Unjust Wars* (New York: Basic Books, 1977), 299–300.

3. This term is also prevalent in the language of international law.

4. Walzer, *Just and Unjust Wars*, 62.

5. Ibid.

6. Ibid., 61–62.

7. Brian Orend illustrates the point this way: "We do not think getting fired is a sufficient reason to retaliate with violence even if the firing sharply harms our interests." Brian Orend, *The Morality of War* (Peterborough, Ontario: Broadview Press, 2006), 32.

8. C. L. Sulzberger and the Editors of American Heritage, *The American Heritage Picture History of World War II,* David G. McCullough, editor in charge (n.p. American Heritage Publishing Company, 1966), 129.

9. Martin Gilbert, *The Second World War: A Complete History,* rev. ed. (New York: Henry Holt, 1989), 4.

10. C. L. Sulzberger and the Editors of American Heritage, *The American Heritage Picture History of World War II,* 131.

11. National Conference of Catholic Bishops, *The Challenge of Peace: God's Promise and Our Response* (Washington, DC: United States Catholic Conference, 1983), 29.

12. Brian Orend, *The Morality of War,* 76.

13. Michael Walzer, *Just and Unjust Wars,* 81.

14. Ibid., 85.

15. This is not to suggest that preventive *force* might not be used justly, as in the case of inspection teams or peacekeeping operations. For more insight into the issues of anticipatory attack, see papers on the topic from the Joint Services Conference on Professional Ethics, 2005, at http://www.usafa.edu/isme/JSCOPE05/jscope05.html.

16. Jeffrie Murphy, "The Killing of the Innocent," in *War, Morality, and the Military Profession,* ed. Malham M. Wakin (Boulder, CO: Westview Press, 1986), 341–364.

17. Orend, *The Morality of War,* 3.

18. I am indebted to Dr. Carl Ficarrotta for this point.

19. This war is now sometimes referred to as the Second Gulf War, with the Iran-Iraq conflict of the 1980s known as the first Gulf War and the 2003 invasion of Iraq constituting the third.

20. See, for example, David Rodin, "War and Self-Defense," in *The Morality of War,* eds. Larry May, Eric Rovie, and Steve Viner (Upper Saddle River, NJ: Pearson Education, 2006), 261–271.

21. Carl von Clausewitz, *On War,* ed. Anatol Rapoport, trans. J. J. Graham (New York: Penguin Books, 1982), 119.

22. See United Nations Resolution 660–662; 664–667 and 678 (August-November, 1990).

23. "Declarations of a State of War with Japan, Germany, and Italy," 77th Congress 1st Session, President Roosevelt's address to joint session, December 8, 1941 (Washington, DC: U.S. Government Printing Office).

24. Elizabeth Anscombe is representative. See Elizabeth Anscombie, "War and Murder," in *The Morality of War,* eds. Larry May, Eric Rovie, and Steve Viner, 209.

25. Martin Gilbert, *The Second World War: A Complete History,* rev. ed. (New York: Henry Holt, 1989), 710.

26. Victor David Hanson, *The Soul of Battle* (New York: The Free Press, 1999).

27. Gene Sharp, *The Politics of Nonviolent Action, Part Three: The Dynamics of Nonviolent Action* (Boston: Porter Sargent Publishers, 1973), 707–708.

28. Some historians have estimated that there were 200,000 Chinese deaths in Nanking alone. David M. Kennedy, *Freedom from Fear: The American People in Depression and War, 1929–1945* (New York: Oxford University Press, 1999), 401.

29. Richard Norman, *Ethics, Killing and War* (Cambridge: Cambridge University Press, 1995).

30. John Keegan, *The Second World War* (New York: Penguin Books USA, 1989), 39–41.

31. See, for example, Orend, *The Morality of War,* 45–46, and Walzer, *Just and Unjust Wars,* 67–72.

32. Clausewitz, *On War,* 119.

33. William Shirer, *The Rise and Fall of the Third Reich* (New York: Simon and Shuster, 1959), 518–519.

34. Others have made note of this phenomenon. See, for example, Martin L. Cook, *The Moral Warrior: Ethics and Service in the U.S. Military* (Albany: The State University Press of New York, 2004), 40, and Michael Walzer, *Just and Unjust Wars,* 12.

35. Immanuel Kant "Perpetual Peace" trans. Lewis White Beck in *Kant on History* ed. Lewis White (Indianapolis: Bobbs Merrill, 1963), 99.

CHAPTER 5

Jus in Bello Today

It is not hard to understand that *jus ad bellum* serves the interests of the international community over time. When properly applied. it will reduce the frequency of war.

On the occasions that statesmen satisfy themselves that a war is appropriate, they call on military forces to wage it. At first blush, it would seem that if a war is just, it would be proper to do what it takes to win it. Making sense of limits on the conduct of war therefore seems challenging. Moreover, war by its very nature appears to be immune to ethical limits.

Nevertheless, militaries usually do follow rules of war, in part, because of the political ends that motivate war—not every *casus belli* is worth wholesale destruction. Although the record is by no means perfect, military forces historically have refrained from acts that would constitute murder or disproportionate destruction. Indeed, military actions that do not respect these limits are notorious.

In April 1942, the Japanese took about 76,000 prisoners on the Philippine peninsula of Baatan. About 64,000 of the captives were Filipino, with the remaining 12,000 being Americans.[1] During the subsequent infamous "Bataan Death March," these prisoners were force-marched about 65 miles to a prison camp. Although some prisoners were treated humanely, many were not. Denied food, water, and rest, many of the captives fell from exhaustion and were killed by their guards. At least 600 Americans and 5,000 Filipinos died on the march.[2] Once they arrived at their prison camp, disease and continued maltreatment felled another 40 percent within six months.[3]

Atrocities have been committed by the militaries serving liberal democratic states as well. On March 16, 1968, during the Vietnam conflict, the U.S. Army's Lt. Calley led his platoon in murdering about 500 unresisting Vietnamese civilians. Many victims of what has become known as the My Lai massacre were women and children, including babies. Some were raped before being murdered. The soldiers also mutilated some of the corpses.[4]

Such acts are morally offensive on their face, and so they draw attention to themselves and their perpetrators on the grounds of moral intuition alone. But massacres and war atrocities are also notable just because they are unusual given the vast number of military operations that have taken place and continue to take place.

The fact that ordinary responsible people are morally outraged by such acts testifies to the relevance of ethics in conducting warfare. No one is outraged when a natural disaster kills or wounds thousands of people. In those cases, the ordinary reaction is generally sadness and a sense of compassion for the victims. But when militaries bring about the same sorts of effects, most react with indignation because intuitions suggest that the harm occurred as a result of humans making decisions. Gratuitous violence on the part of military members offends and embarrasses professional military members as it disgusts the thoughtful layperson. This fact relies on a foregoing assumption that the soldier is accountable for his actions in a way that weather patterns or earthquakes are not.

Most militaries accept surrender, for example, sparing the lives of the defeated. Prisoners are taken and cared for humanely in at least most instances and are generally repatriated. Moreover, most armies respect the rights of noncombatants to remain unmolested by the bad fortunes of war, and they do what they can to assist them. They also limit the sorts of weaponry used. Nuclear, biological, and chemical weapons may be stockpiled, but they are rarely actually used.

Jus in bello, or justice in war, frames major moral considerations on the conduct of war, providing guidance for military operations. It is not concerned with whether any given war itself is just, but rather with fighting justly. Before examining *jus in bello,* however, the practical concepts underlying the principles are worth considering.

The Idea of Rules of War

Although it may seem counterintuitive at first, the rules of war are in place to benefit both military members seeking to win a war and the ordinary citizens affected by the fighting. Some who think about war focus on the drive to victory and so see the idea of restricting violence as running counter to the goals for which the war is fought. There is much to this contention, as will become more obvious soon. For now, however, note that wars always involve inflicting harm, and, accordingly, somebody suffers that harm.

Jus in bello restricts inflicting harm to legitimate military targets, thereby sparing civilians from deliberate attack. It also restricts the amount of harm to which military personnel and other legitimate targets may be subjected. Accordingly, *jus in bello* grants that combatants may be killed, but that does not mean that they can be treated wantonly. For example, it affords protection to unresisting wounded soldiers, so that they might outlive the war.

To help ground understanding of why rules of war make good sense, it is helpful to refer to a well-known modern approach deployed by Richard Brandt.[5]

Brandt has applied some concepts to warfare that were first published by John Rawls in the 1970s. Rawls famously argued for a brand of social contract that would produce just policies that any rational, self-interested person would find acceptable.[6] The following thought experiment is illustrative.

First, make the assumption that one's own state will be involved in violent conflict in the future. The exact nature and timing are unknown, but sooner or later combat will take place. Given this assumption, one is behind a veil of ignorance[7] regarding two matters of vital import: the military power of one's own state relative to the other warring state(s) and the role one will personally play in the conflict. One may find that her state is unable to defend against a new secret weapon that an adversary has produced, or one may possess such a weapon while others do not. At the individual level, one may find oneself a non-combatant or a combatant; a private or a general; wounded, a prisoner, a refugee, or something else. Involvement is certain, but the specifics are unknown. The fortunes of war being what they are, experienced military members will admit that the veil of ignorance is more than a mere mental exercise.

Others who will be involved are also behind this veil. Citizens and soldiers of other states know that they will be involved in conflict, but they are unaware of their specific future role as well.

All of these rational and self-interested participants are then asked what rules, if any, they would propose for conducting future conflict. The idea is that the group would agree on rules that would maximize utility to one's own state and that would still be acceptable to the least-advantaged person in the future conflict. Such rules, for example, may permit killing only certain classes of people and prohibit maltreatment of those who are wounded or captured. If one faces the prospect of being disadvantaged in the future, the rational choice is to create rules that even the disadvantaged can accept. One would not, however, be likely to accept rules that would seriously impede the chance of victory because wars are indeed waged to be won, and no state would be likely to accept a rule that prevented its deploying all power possible to overcome the adversary. The result, Brandt suggests, would be similar to the current state of *jus in bello*.[8]

Under *jus in bello*, just war thinking (JWT) offers guidance to the military practitioner that may at first seem much less complex than the *jus ad bellum* criteria. There are only two main criteria for *jus in bello*: discrimination and proportionality, although military necessity is sometimes included. Applying these criteria, however, is not always straightforward. Satisfying one criterion may court violating another in at least some tough cases.

Military Necessity, Discrimination, and Proportionality

Military Necessity

It is important to understand that any harm deliberately inflicted in warfare must meet a condition of military necessity. This notion is frequently misunderstood.

Military necessity does *not* justify any and all acts that commanders or soldiers deem necessary to achieve an objective. Rather, it requires that all harm inflicted must be the result of legitimate military requirements; doing harm capriciously or wantonly violates military necessity. Military necessity is to be understood as necessity *within* the constraints supplied by *jus in bello*. *Jus in bello* offers criteria regarding what may be harmed and how badly it may be harmed. It does not permit violations of the criteria in order to achieve a military end. Put differently, there must be a military reason to justify inflicting harm, but that harm must still meet the *jus in bello* criteria.

Discrimination

People sometimes think of discrimination as a bad thing because the word has come to be associated with unfair treatment of a class of persons, but not all discrimination is unfair. Under *jus in bello,* discrimination is required for solid ethical reasons.

It is unfair to deny a job to an otherwise qualified individual on the basis of ethnicity or gender because neither ethnicity nor gender has anything to do with whether an individual is capable of being proficient at a given job. Being male or female, for example, bears no relationship to whether one can meet check ride standards as an airline pilot.

It is not unfair, however, to require reasonably good eyesight for airline pilots. Pilots have to be able to see well enough to fly safely. The requirement for a certain standard of visual acuity is in the functional role of airline pilot itself. In other words, the discrimination is not arbitrary, but rather required by the function of flying airplanes. It is relevant to the job at hand, and discriminating in that regard seems reasonable to at least most of those affected by the discrimination. It is in this positive and helpful sense that the *jus in bello* principle of discrimination is meant to be understood.

Killing and Murder. Far from being unfair, discrimination in *jus in bello* is intended to *preclude* the unfair treatment of individuals. Its point is to foster treating people as they ought to be treated, even during a war. In a nutshell, those doing violence are required by the principle to discriminate between legitimate and nonlegitimate targets. This criterion is intended to spare noncombatants from the harms that warfare entails.

A six-month-old baby is not a legitimate military target, regardless of geographic position. Despite the risks to which she may be exposed, there is nothing about being a baby in a war zone that makes her *deserve* to be harmed. An armed soldier, by contrast, is a legitimate target and may ethically be targeted. Ordinary intuitions reflect this sort of discrimination, especially when viewed in light of self-defense. The baby offers no threat to anyone. If she is deliberately killed, ordinary people, let alone military ethicists, would think of it as murder.

The soldier, on the other hand, does appear to offer a palpable threat of violence. This is true even if he is secretly a pacifist and has no intention of ever firing his weapon, for there is no way an adversary can be expected to know that. Hence, although people might think of the soldier's being deliberately killed as a sad or tragic event, they do not think of it as unjustified killing. In the cases of the baby and of the soldier, a human being is deliberately killed, but in only one of the cases is the killing murder. One way of thinking about the principle of discrimination, then, is as allowing killing in war while ruling-out murder.

The principle of discrimination refers to *deliberate* harm to noncombatants. In cases where the baby is harmed, but the harm is contrary to the sincerely held desires of those doing the harm, the principle of discrimination is not violated. In this case, the harm to the noncombatant is analogous to the harm suffered in a traffic accident. No ordinary driver intends to harm anyone; the intention is rather to get to the destination safely. Should a child suddenly dart out into the car's path and be struck and injured despite the driver's efforts to avoid him, however, ordinary moral intuitions hold that the harm was accidental. The driver is unlucky, but not guilty of intending any harm. This unintended harm is sometimes referred to as "collateral damage." That is, given the limitations of weaponry's precision and the fortunes of war, unintended harm can occur. This distinction between intended and unintended harm is open to abuse, and ethicists have developed methods to avoid it. Some of these are described later in the modern version of double effect.

The principle of discrimination is often discussed in terms of rights theory. Rights theorists take the right to be free from unwanted interference as fundamental. Indeed, it is that very freedom that often justifies violent defense. The baby does not have any interest in war, but—Trotsky's insight from chapter 1 comes to mind—war may be interested in her. She is too feeble to defend her rights to life and liberty, but she has them nonetheless, and they impose duties on everyone, including combatants. Whether one has rights has nothing to do with where one happens to be located. The infant has a right to be left unmolested, even in a combat zone.

By contrast, her father the soldier—call him Dan—is in the business of interfering with others. He has given up his right to noninterference by his very presence as a soldier in combat. He may wish he were elsewhere, and he may even have been drafted, but his adversary has no way of discerning that and Dan knows it. The arms he is carrying and the uniform he is wearing would seem good evidence to anyone that he is ready for and plans to do violence. These facts signify his giving up his right not to be targeted. Put differently, a soldier in the opposing military would have excellent reasons to believe that Dan intended to do him harm. To exaggerate the point, there is a sense in which Dan *consents* to being a target. He has given up his claim on others not to kill him. He should not be surprised that others view him as a threat and may well seek to harm him.

With the distinction between Dan and his daughter in place, it may be proper to clarify terminology that military ethicists have evolved to capture the difference in practical terms. Dan is a combatant and therefore a legitimate target. His baby is a noncombatant and therefore not a legitimate target. The distinction between legitimate and nonlegitimate targets does not turn on whether someone is a morally good person. Rather, as a practical matter, it turns on whether it is reasonable to believe that a palpable threat is presented that would justify violent self-defense. Dan may be an extraordinarily good man, filled with sorrow over the war and desiring to harm no one, and his grandmother may be filled with racist hatred toward her country's adversary. In practical terms of selecting targets, this distinction makes no difference, because the combatant doing the targeting must discriminate on the available evidence.[9]

Limiting Harm to Soldiers. From an ethical point of view, Dan is not vulnerable to any and all harm. It may not violate the principle of discrimination to target him, but moral limits remain. He retains some rights even in war because he is a human being even as he is a soldier. As a human being, Dan would present no threat to the adversary. The act of going into battle to do harm is done on behalf of the state that armed Dan in the first place and trained him to fight. It is in this role, and only because of this role, that Dan is in combat.

JWT captures this concept by considering Dan as having two aspects—as a human being and as a state-actor. Dan has the human aspect just by virtue of being, but he acquires the combatant aspect at the behest of his state. Although the combatant aspect is temporary, the human one is not. When Dan becomes a combatant, he acquires certain special sorts of freedom such as the freedom to kill other humans under tightly controlled circumstances. He also loses certain protections, such as the right not to be targeted. But these special conditions do not undo his humanity. He remains human regardless of what roles he acquires.

Suppose that Dan receives a disabling wound while engaged in combat. This causes him to lose his combatant aspect. He no longer presents a threat to the enemy and as such is to be regarded primarily in his human aspect. The enemy ought to treat Dan's wound and care for him as a human being in their custody. Likewise, Dan ought not to try to harm his previous enemy; he has lost his status as combatant.

Bearing these two aspects in mind while considering applied military ethics helps illuminate many commonly accepted practices. Taken broadly, the principle of discrimination distinguishes Dan's combatant aspect from his human aspect across multiple dimensions. Understanding that war takes place between political entities and not between people in themselves makes it possible to attempt to harm the political entity while regretting the death or disfigurement of the soldier. The enmity is not personal between the opposing soldiers. Reconciliation, even future alliance, is facilitated, as is the humane treatment of prisoners, the wounded, and shipwrecked.

Legitimate Targets. To wage a modern war requires effective contributions from lots of people, many of whom are not in the military. A modern combatant like Dan depends on the efforts of thousands to supply him.

The principle of discrimination is said to justify the adversary's deliberate killing of Dan. Because he is a combatant, killing Dan is not murder. But if Dan is a good soldier and, especially if he is equipped with armor, he may be extraordinarily hard to wound or kill. He can be counted on to use every tool at his disposal to keep himself and his comrades alive. Dan is a "hard" target, but the factory that manufactures parts for his vehicle or the ammunition for his weapon may be considerably more vulnerable. It would make sense to consider targeting these relatively soft parts of the supply chain. Perhaps Dan's grandmother is taking care of his children in a major population center and so is equally or more vulnerable than the factory. Killing them might demoralize Dan enough to render him unwilling to continue fighting. It is not surprising, then, that attacks on a nation's manufacturing base, and even the civilian populace, have appealed to military strategists.

At first blush, such attacks would appear to violate the principle of discrimination, as the targets are not, strictly speaking, military personnel or military bases. Without the arms industry, however, Dan would not be able to inflict as much harm as he can if he has sophisticated equipment designed for the purpose.

Military ethicists have wrestled with this problem and offered some helpful distinctions to handle it. Jeffrie Murphy has suggested thinking of two avenues that support combatants with equipment, food, and other needs.

The first means of support he labels "causal." Those in the causal chain supply the combatant with what he needs to live, as well as what he needs to fight. Those building his armored vehicle are included, as are the farmers who grow the food that the combatants eat. His grandmother and children may be included as well, as they supply motivation and psychological support to his war-fighting. In the modern era, the causal chain involves lots of people, including, arguably, every taxpayer. Harming or eliminating links in this chain would weaken the combatant's lethality. Dan may be weakened as much by, say, extreme hunger, as he would be by being wounded.

The second means of support Murphy labels a "chain of agency." This chain is much smaller and is included in the causal chain. The links in this chain support Dan's destructive efforts, but not others. Put another way, the chain of agency supplies Dan as a combatant; the causal chain supplies him as a person. The causal chain would be required to support Dan outside of his violent role. Whether or not Dan is in a military role, he still needs to eat, and so farmers will grow food for him to eat in both peace and war. This suggests that the farmer, although causally required for Dan's activities, is nonetheless not a legitimate target. But at least certain links in the chain of agency are legitimate targets because those links make no sense outside of an intention to inflict harm.[10]

By way of example, Dan is supported by both grenades and applesauce; however, children eat applesauce, too. Manufacturing applesauce makes sense outside of an attempt to harm others. Grenades, however, have no purpose outside of destructive ones. Consequently, the grenade factory can be considered as a legitimate target, as can the people laboring in it. But to target the applesauce factory would be to violate the principle as Murphy interprets it, as manufacturing apple-sauce makes sense outside of an attempt to wage war.

For Murphy, then, a combatant is someone whose activities make no sense outside of an attempt to harm, and noncombatants are everyone else.[11] His analysis illuminates the principle of discrimination without restricting targeting solely to military persons.

One can think, then, of the principle of discrimination as offering protection of the rights of noncombatants at the peril of the combatants. Those who choose not to take on that role remain safe, at least in theory, because someone else has taken on the role. If there is anything noble about being a combatant, surely part of that nobility is found in this concept.

Adhering to the principle may seem to make winning a war more difficult, and that is probably sometimes the case. But to violate it is to violate human rights. It is to commit murder. The deliberate killing of the innocent is murder, regardless of the motives behind it. Murdering a witness may make a criminal's life easier because, if she gets away with it, she may escape being convicted for another crime, but ordinary moral intuitions prohibit that attempt at "justification." The same intuitions suggest that crimes such as murder are not rendered justifiable because they serve a state's interests.

Some military ethicists have proposed another view of the matter. Instead of viewing the principle in absolute terms, they propose that if the stakes are high enough, the principle of discrimination might be overridden. Before moving to that contention, however, it is important to appreciate the principle of proportionality as it applies to *jus in bello*.

Proportionality

The principle of proportionality in *jus in bello* is similar to that in *jus ad bellum*. Indeed, this dual use of the criterion introduces complexities between the two arenas. Considered in the context of *jus in bello* only, proportionality requires the harm caused by a military activity to be offset by a greater good. An aerial attack that killed 200 combatants yet relieved a besieged city of millions would likely meet the criterion. For a negative example, soldiers ought not to destroy an entire city in order to disable one antiaircraft battery. And at this level, following the proportionality criterion makes good military sense. Achieving one's objective efficiently is as laudable in military operations as in any other endeavor. Thus, and in accordance with the notion of military necessity, if there is a way to achieve quick victory with relatively little suffering overall, soldiers ought to prefer that path to others.

Like all forward-looking ethical principles, the *jus in bello* criterion of proportionality is often inexact in application. It requires combatants to make estimates of harm done and harm prevented. Inexactness, however, does not render the principle useless. The spirit of proportionality makes good common sense and is applied in many aspects of professional ethics. Doing more harm than good is never desirable.

Proportionality and Weaponry. Considerations of proportionality may be applied at the level of weapons. If one thinks in terms of defending oneself against an armed and determined adversary, say a sniper, the clear goal is to eliminate whatever threat that adversary presents. This is the "evil prevented." Many means may be used to accomplish that goal, and plainly some of those would more closely respect the principle of proportionality than would others. Viewed as a continuum, with end-points exaggerated to make the point, one could imagine destroying the sniper via a massive artillery bombardment or via a stealthy, temporarily disabling blow. The bombardment, covering acres of ground, would be so intense that, even if he tried to flee, he would still most likely be killed. Such bombardment would almost assuredly remove the threat, but it would do disproportionate additional damage. On the other end of the spectrum, one could imagine creeping up on the sniper and giving him a quick blow to render him temporarily unconscious and then capturing him while he is unable to resist. The latter method is preferable to the former, as it accomplishes the same objective with substantially less harm. Although the extremes of the spectrum are perhaps so extreme as to be unrealistic, more moderate intermediate positions are not.

A disabling wound renders an adversary unthreatening just as effectively as killing him does. And, to make the point more finely, not all disabling wounds are equally harmful to the victim. Being disabled by a concussion from which one may recover in time is far less debilitating than suffering the loss of both legs. Hence, most militaries foreswear the use of exploding bullets or glass-filled projectiles. Weapons such as these would do more harm than the good (disabling an opponent) they are expected to achieve. A bullet wound alone is generally sufficient to stop an adversary; to have it explode within his body would do more harm but no additional good. Similarly, metal shrapnel can be seen on an x-ray film, making the treatment of a wounded soldier easier to accomplish, but other substances are much tougher for medical personnel to detect. Indeed, weapons such as these have been prohibited by international law. Exploding bullets were specifically forbidden by the 1868 St. Petersburg Declaration.[12] Weapons "calculated to cause unnecessary suffering" were ruled out by the Hague Convention of 1907.[13] Note, however, that some weapons that would be disproportionate when used against a person would not be so when used against a machine of war. An exploding bullet used against an enemy aircraft would likely not be disproportionate.

History offers numerous instances of controversy over the permissibility of weapons. The neutron bomb was designed to harm persons, but spare buildings and other property. Its radioactivity was enhanced while its explosive power was relatively low. Today, land mines are under scrutiny, in part because they render the areas where they were planted dangerous for years, thus violating proportionality and likely discrimination as well.

The principle of proportionality has driven technology. Weapons have grown more precise, as has the capacity to accurately fix targets. This is particularly true of aerial bombardment. Whereas the accuracy of bombing in the Second World War was sufficiently poor to require masses of airplanes to reduce a single target,

today, using more recent technology, one aircraft or cruise missile is often sufficient. The increasing availability and popularity of precision weapons, coupled
with the principle of proportionality, have interesting implications. As the harm
required to achieve a particular objective diminishes, the set of objectives that
might offset the lessened degree of harm grows. In a preceding example, it was
noted that it would be disproportionate to destroy a city in order to disable one
antiaircraft battery. But with the increasing availability of very precise weaponry, it
may be possible to target the battery without harming the city. Thus the set of targets that meets the principle of proportionality has a tendency to grow. The barrier that was once constituted by unacceptable levels of collateral damage drops
as weaponry's precision increases.

This phenomenon may also be seen in the use of nonlethal weapons (NLW).
These weapons provide commanders with a range of options to clear an area or
disable an opponent without having to inflict death. The caltrop, a small set of
spikes that may be scattered in mass before an advancing adversary, is an ancient
device that is still effective today, especially against vehicles with pneumatic tires.
More innovative weapons include a very slippery antitraction material that can
be sprayed over an area to make it unusable by vehicles and hard for people to
negotiate. Large but nonlethal flash-bangs can be use to disorient an adversary
or incapacitate temporarily. In 1995, the United States Marines evacuated 2,500
UN peacekeepers from Somalia using NLW, including caltrops and sticky foam.[14]
There were no fatalities among the Marines, the peacekeepers, or the Somalis.[15]

Proportionality's Dual Nature. Proportionality's range of application is wide
insofar as it regards one enemy soldier. Many avenues are available to harm one
individual, and they are not all equally respectful of proportionality. Plainly, the
complexity of finding proportionate means increases exponentially when applying the principle on a larger scale. This is particularly true of nuclear weapons
and other weapons of mass destruction. It is perhaps most weighty, as Grotius
warned, at the level of war itself.

The *jus in bello* criterion of proportionality should not be understood in isolation from the companion criterion in *jus ad bellum*, which holds that war itself
must be proportional to the good it is to achieve. What may be seemingly disproportionate to a commander at the level of *jus in bello* may be proportionate
at the level of *jus ad bellum* and vice-versa. Consider, for example, a case of an
extraordinarily costly operation that a commander views as clearly disproportionate to the military objective achieved. At the level of *jus in bello,* the decision
to conduct the operation fails proportionality, but the same operation may serve
as the decisive event in winning the war itself. If that is the case, the operation
may be critical to meeting the *jus ad bellum* criterion. On the other hand, waging
war in strict accordance with proportionality at the level of *jus in bello* may pro-
long the war to the degree that it fails the *jus ad bellum* proportionality criterion.
Perhaps most intriguingly, as it becomes technically feasible to destroy targets
with precision, or render troops ineffective with nonlethal methods, the harm

that a war is expected to inflict decreases. This suggests, then, that the *jus ad bellum* criterion of proportionality becomes easier to satisfy, raising the morally weighty implication that war could become more frequent as the threshold of proportionality decreases.

Some just war thinkers contend that, in at least some cases, *jus ad bellum* considerations outweigh *jus in bello,* but others resist this claim. They often do so on the grounds that, if *jus in bello* criteria cannot be met, avoiding war in the first place is the best option.

Tensions between Discrimination and Proportionality

Cases can arise where respecting one of the *jus in bello* principles can interfere with adhering to the other. This is especially frequent in the event that adherence to discrimination results in greater overall harm than would violating it. A number of factors account for this. The first is that combatants are frequently hardened targets. That is, they are more difficult to harm than noncombatants. They are anticipating attempts to harm them and take extensive security measures, in many cases occupying fortifications or camouflaging themselves. Noncombatants on the same side may be mostly undefended and concentrated in cities. For example, if destroying a few of these relatively soft cities would compel the adversary's capitulation relatively quickly and would therefore involve fewer wounded and killed overall than would fighting a long and hard battle against combatants, it would seem proportional to destroy the cities and end the war. Indeed, such a justification has been put forth, controversially, to justify the use of atomic bombs against Japanese cities in the Second World War. The argument compared two strategies for compelling Japan's unconditional surrender. The first option, an invasion of the islands of Japan, was said to entail a toll of at least a half-million military casualties. The second, using nuclear weapons against cities to compel capitulation, would cost far fewer lives, but most of the lives lost would be noncombatants. On this account, proportionality is best served by violating discrimination.

The same logic comes into play regarding strategies of nuclear deterrence. Put starkly, one can attempt to deter a nuclear war by one of two means. First, consider a counter-value approach. A counter-value strategy deters war by preselecting targets of very high value to the adversary. The civilian population is such a target, and with nuclear weapons it is possible to threaten millions of people. Further, the delivery system for the weapons need not be all that precise. Nuclear weapons destroy large geographic areas and foul even larger areas with radioactive fallout. Thus, using a counter-value approach, it may be necessary to have on hand only 100 or so missiles, each loaded with warheads designed to destroy cities. If such missiles are housed securely, say, aboard stealthy submarines, most or all would be able to survive a first strike. This would preclude the need to build a large arsenal that would cause the evil of proliferation. For such a strategy to work, however, the intent to murder must be credibly held.

Counter-force strategy targets only combatants and their equipment. That is, a counter-force approach respects discrimination by targeting only enemy military *forces*. More, a counter-force strategy can respect proportionality as smaller warheads, delivered with precision, are sufficient to destroy military bases, enemy missile sites, and other legitimate targets. A counter-force strategy, however, requires a large arsenal to prevent a conflict from escalating unnecessarily. One would want to be able to assemble a proportionate response to any threat or strike. This implies that one would need an array of nuclear weapons and delivery methodologies, thereby contributing to the potential for an arms race. A further worry looms. If one were to contemplate fighting a nuclear war against enemy forces only, one would naturally expect to have some of one's own forces targeted and lost. This requires having an even larger supply of nuclear weapons at the ready so as to be able to afford losing a portion of one's forces without thereby having to lose the war. This further contributes to proliferation, but the alternative is to be forced into a "use or lose" posture. That is, one would be compelled to launch one's own weapons as soon as credible information is received that one's forces were under attack, as failure to do so would mean that one one's own arsenal might be destroyed without ever being used. Thus counter-force advocates usually recommend policies that lead to the existence of greater and greater numbers of weapons. This not only costs lots of money and effort, but puts the world at greater risk of the weapons being lost, stolen, or inadvertently detonated. Perhaps even more worrisome, a counter-force approach might suggest that the *jus ad bellum* criterion of proportionality could be met along with the *jus in bello* approach. This lowers the threshold of nuclear war, thereby defeating the purpose of deterrence in the first place. In sum, it looks as though the policy that comes closest to meeting the *jus in bello* proportionality criterion is arguably even more morally dubious than the policy that requires an intention to murder. This was indeed the conclusion reached by the U.S. Catholic Bishops in their pastoral letter of 1983.[16]

The problem is that murder remains murder. An active intention to do murder under certain conditions is, to say the least, morally unsettling. In the case of Hiroshima and Nagasaki, the intention was carried out, and even if the decision did save lives, it remains controversial for that reason.

Interpretations of the Principle of Discrimination

Military ethicists have wrestled extensively with the tension between discrimination and proportionality, and two general responses have evolved. The first, which might be called the "absolutist" position, holds that the principle of discrimination must always be respected. The second position holds that the principle may be overridden by other weighty moral values.

Absolutist Interpretation of Discrimination. The absolutist allows no exceptions to discrimination. If that means that more death and destruction occurs than would have been otherwise, the absolutist might reply that this is an appeal to an *outcome* and therefore irrelevant to the morality of a given *act*. Moreover, it is just when people have a strong temptation to violate a principle that adherence to principle itself is most morally praiseworthy. A moral prohibition against murder is needed most when the temptation to murder is the strongest. This is in the very nature of moral commitment itself. Absolutists often turn to the do/allow distinction as well, noting that the prohibition against murder is a prohibition against a particular way of *acting*. Absolutist interpretations of discrimination do not require one to *prevent* murder. Virtually everyone fails that standard. But the requirement not to murder is both morally binding and achievable as a practical matter. The fact that respecting human rights might end up allowing lots of harm is tragic, but it would be immoral to violate rights to prevent the harm. In cases like the use of nuclear weapons against Japan, the absolutist might grant that combatants would have suffered more harm than they did had the bombs not been used; but the combatants accepted a chance of being harmed by the very act of becoming combatants, whereas the children of Hiroshima and Nagasaki did not. Although the harm to combatants may cause suffering, it does not violate their rights.

To illustrate this concept, consider an economic analogy. With wealth, more is better. But money is not the only value in play—rights matter, too. No morally acceptable economic scheme builds wealth through the deliberate violation of human rights. To violate human rights in pursuit of wealth is to commit a crime. For example, regardless of how much money it might generate, human trafficking violates human rights. And, should the criminal suggest that he would never commit a crime for only a small amount of money, but in his case there are very large sums at stake, and so an exception ought to be made, he would be regarded as morally ignorant at best and monstrous at worst. Rights put a set of side constraints on the pursuit of wealth. More wealth is better, but not every avenue to wealth is permissible.

The absolutist holds this perspective regarding proportionality's relationship to discrimination. Less destruction is always better, but not every method that would reduce suffering is morally permissible. The principle of discrimination binds *absolutely*—no amount of reduced suffering can justify violating it.

Nonabsolutist Interpretations of Discrimination. A second approach to discrimination regards it as binding only prima facie, or on first appearance. In other words, it always binds, but it does not bind absolutely. There may be cases in which the principle of discrimination may be justifiably overridden.

This approach grants that violating discrimination is always evil, but that other values can nonetheless render the violation the best choice. To give an extreme example to make the point, consider a hypothetical case where the deliberate killing of one innocent would save the lives of 10,000 combatants and that these options were the only two available. Those holding an absolutist position would refuse to murder, thereby condemning the 10,000, but most would likely find the decision tough to make. This difficulty highlights the strength of the second approach that holds the principle of discrimination to be binding, but not to the exclusion of other values. Although the deliberate killing is wrong, the choice is still the best possible choice under these constraints.

Those who hold the principle of discrimination to be binding only prima facie sometimes justify their position by appealing to utilitarian considerations of proportionality. There are at least two general lines of argument. The first holds that any act that shortens a war significantly must be considered in light of both proportionality and discrimination. The deliberate destruction of a few of the adversary's population centers, it might be argued, would substantially shorten a war that is costing, say, an average of 1,000 lives daily. The lives that are saved would far outnumber those killed in the cities, so from the point of view of consequences, the optimal decision is to bomb the cities. Many of the lives saved would be those of combatants, but many noncombatant lives would be saved as well. In arguments of this sort, the combatant-noncombatant distinction is sometimes deployed to the disadvantage of the noncombatant, as in the case of counter-population bombing in the Second World War. Governments expect their soldiers to die, but when they cannot defend their civilians from violent attack, the argument goes, the civilian population would pressure its government to sue for peace.

The second line of argument follows the same logic but is more straightforward. Here the claim is that adhering absolutely to the principle of discrimination costs lives in the short term, as well as the long term. Taking the time and effort required to avoid population centers or innocent bystanders adds greatly to the combatant's burden. This is especially true in urban environments in which the combatant and noncombatant may be quite close together. Suppose, for example, that a small city is known to house multiple small munitions manufactories, as well as active combatant adversaries working in them. The munitions are in daily use against friendly forces. The friendly forces do not know which buildings house the small factories and the combatants, and even if they did, they are likely moving around as a security measure. The friendly commander is faced with a problem. If he sends small units to secure the city building by building, he will be more able to discriminate between active combatants and their noncombatant families. Moreover, he will be able to remove the manufacturing equipment, stored munitions, and raw materials, as well as stand a good chance of capturing a prisoner. But to enter each building individually is both time consuming and dangerous. Doing so requires facing the strong possibility that there will be armed adversaries waiting inside ready to pounce the moment the door is opened. This is to court risks to one's own combatants that could be avoided if, say, the building were simply set afire or blown up. Adopting this latter tactic for each building may clear a city relatively quickly. Doing so may well cost the lives of the building's inhabitants, but at least some of them are combatants. The munitions will be destroyed quickly and the friendly troops become available for another task.

Both of these approaches override the discrimination criterion in the name of reducing overall suffering. Naturally, they both run into objections that rights are meaningless if there is some price that is worth an innocent life. The absolutist might suggest that destroying the cities or the buildings treats the noncombatants in them merely as objects or tools in ways to which they would not consent. Relying on the do/allow distinction, the absolutist would likely grant that the alternative methods of fighting, which respect discrimination fully, may result in ugly consequences of a longer war or more combatant casualties, but these are not the *doings* of the friendly forces. There are many causal factors to account for the suffering the war entails, but the deliberate murder of the noncombatants is a *doing* of evil.

Murder in the Case of "Supreme Emergency". It is also possible to approach the issue of discrimination's absolutism from the point of view of fundamental rights and necessity. Michael Walzer's argument from "supreme emergency," although by no means universally accepted, is a substantial contribution to the literature on the topic.[17]

For Walzer, a genuine supreme emergency is present only rarely. It is composed of two essential elements. First, the threat must be morally extraordinary; that is, the threat to moral values must be unusually high. Second, the threat must be imminent. Both of these elements are required. A grave threat to rights that is foreseen but not immediate is not enough to constitute a supreme emergency. An immediate threat that is not gravely serious is insufficient as well, but an imminent, grave threat that morally demands defense is sufficient. If a nation faces such a threat, and it is possible to defeat the threat short of violating *jus in bello* limits, then the nation is required to fight according to *jus in bello*. In a case where such a threat can be defeated only by violating the rules, however, violating the rules is the only possible choice. In other words, breaking the rules must be necessary to meet the emergency.

Walzer is clear that a genuine supreme emergency is an extraordinary event— extraordinary, but not unknown. Emergencies occur with some frequency in war, but few rise to the level he has in mind. One might propose that losing a war would be sufficient to constitute a supreme emergency, but this would suggest that any nation facing imminent defeat would face a supreme emergency, and Walzer does not permit that. In the case of a supreme emergency, moral gravity is required as well as imminence. Most often, being defeated does not mean being eliminated. Nor do most adversaries threaten to dominate much or all of the world. But in the rare circumstance where the foe is so powerful, so evil, so determined, and so close as to constitute a supreme emergency, committing the evil of murder may be the only avenue of escape from even greater evil.

Walzer cites a potential Nazi victory over Britain in 1940 as an historical example of a real-world supreme emergency. He suggests that the British counter-population bombing of Germany may have been permissible because the only possible way for the British to strike offensively was through the use of their bombers, which lacked precision-targeting capability. They could find a city, but targeting specific buildings such as factories was unrealistic. Putting together the nature of the threat with the fact that the only means of fighting was too inaccurate to respect the principle of discrimination, the violation of discrimination was necessary.[18]

Whether Britain could have survived without conducting counter-population air raids is, of course, an unsettled question. From an ethical point of view, however, the important point is Walzer's exploration of the idea that, in some cases, the moral obligation to defend human rights may override discrimination, itself a principle that relies on rights. In this case, rights are violated deliberately, although regretfully, with the defense of rights as the primary goal.

Double Effect

A single act may have more than one effect. Ethicists sometimes frame this fact through updated versions of St. Thomas Aquinas's insights that were mentioned in chapter 2.

There are various formulations of the modern principle of double effect (PDE), but only one representative description is provided here.

The PDE grants that evil may result from intentional acts, but the acts may nonetheless be justifiable. This can be so if four conditions are met:

> The act itself must be morally permissible.
>
> The good effect must be proportional to the evil effect.
>
> The evil effect must not be the means to the good effect.
>
> The morally good effect must have been what was sincerely intended. The evil effect may be foreseen, but it must not be intended or desired.

Note that the PDE features aspects of both deontological and utilitarian thought. Both aspects, however, must be met in full. In other words, all four of the conditions must be met for the act in question to be morally permissible. Failing to meet any one of the conditions means that the act is not permitted.

The notion of collateral damage is illuminated by the PDE. Consider a case in which an adversary locates artillery pieces in close proximity to a population center. The enemy is using the artillery to strike at one's own forces as they advance toward a legitimate military objective. The commander of the friendly forces, intending to reduce the threat to his own troops by destroying the enemy's weapon, uses artillery to strike back at the enemy's weaponry. The artillery is destroyed, but, at the same time, civilians near the artillery piece are wounded.

In this case, the artillery strike is morally permissible, as its target was legitimate. The destruction of the enemy's weapon is the good effect, and the harming of the civilians, although regrettable, is proportional to the friendly lives saved. The good and bad effects occurred simultaneously, and one was not the means to the other. In this case, although some evil is suffered, the PDE's conditions are met.

Now alter the case a bit. Suppose the commander tortured the civilians to discover the location of the artillery piece and then used the information to target and destroy it. In this case the PDE would not have been satisfied. Torture is evil in itself, so the case fails the first condition. The case fails on the third condition as well, as the torture was the means to the good effect, but it treated the civilians as mere tools to the commander's goal. It may be true that the evil suffered by the civilians is less than the evil prevented by the destruction of the weapon, but that is not a relevant consideration, as the act itself was impermissible.

Notes

1. Gilbert, *The Second World War: A Complete History* (New York: Henry Holt, 1989), 316.

2. Ibid.

3. C. L. Sulzberger and the Editors of American Heritage, *The American Heritage Picture History of World War II* (n.p.: American Heritage Publishing, 1966), 169.

4. Joanna Bourke, *An Intimate History of Killing: Face-to-Face Killing in Twentieth-Century Warfare* (n.p.: Basic Books, 1999), 160.

5. Richard Brandt, "Utilitarianism and the Rules of War," in *The Morality of War,* eds. Larry May, Eric Rovie, and Steve Viner (Upper Saddle, NJ: Pearson Education, 2006), 236–245.

6. John Rawls, *A Theory of Justice* (Cambridge, MA: The Belknap Press of Harvard University Press, 1971), 11–22.

7. Ibid., 136–142.

8. Richard Brandt, "Utilitarianism and the Rules of War," in *The Morality of War,* eds. May, Rovie and Viner, 238–244.

9. Jeffrie G. Murphy, "The Killing of the Innocent," in *War, Morality, and the Military Profession,* ed. Malham M. Wakin (Boulder: CO: Westview Press, 1986), 343–345.

10. Ibid., 346–347.

11. Ibid., 346–348.

12. Michael Ignatieff, *The Warrior's Honor: Ethnic War and the Modern Conscience* (New York: Henry Holt, 1997), 115.

13. Hague Convention No. IV, Respecting the laws and Customs of War on Land, October 18, 1907. art 23, e. in *Treaties Governing Land Warfare* (n.p.: Department of the Army Pamphlet 27–1, December, 1956), 12.

14. F. M. Lorenz, "Non-Lethal Force: The Slippery Slope to War?" *Parameters* 26 no. 3 (1996): 56.

15. Graham T. Allison and Paul X. Kelley, "Nonlethal Weapons and Capabilities," *Report of an Independent Task Force sponsored by the Council on Foreign Relations.* (New York: Council on Foreign Relations Press, 2004), 10.

16. National Conference of Catholic Bishops, *The Challenge of Peace: God's Promise and Our Response* (Washington, DC: United States Catholic Conference, 1983), 58–60.

17. Michael Walzer, *Just and Unjust Wars* (New York: Basic Books, 1977), 251–268.

18. Ibid., 255–261.

CHAPTER 6

Adapting to Contemporary Challenges

Just war thinking (JWT) has evolved as a result of multiple historical influences, as well as related political and philosophical developments. It continues to evolve today as challenges emerge and as the study of ethics advances. The challenges and influences are many, but only three major areas are treated here: growing problems presented by international crime and terrorism, humanitarian intervention, and the influences of nonstate actors such as the media. Each of these comes into tension with the Westphalian model of state sovereignty.

Westphalia and the Modern State

The *jus ad bellum* described in chapter 4 relies on certain preconditions, some of which are no longer to be taken for granted, thereby sparking controversy over *jus ad bellum's* relevance to emerging threats to peace. Common to some of these controversies is the apparent JWT assumption that it typically states that exercise violence in the service of political ends. Increasingly, the problems facing both statesmen and soldiers have to do with violence perpetrated by nonstate actors. Some military ethicists working today believe that the Westphalian underpinnings of JWT apply to relatively fewer cases than they did, say, 100 years ago, and so JWT must evolve to address those issues that do not fit comfortably under the Westphalian model for at least three reasons, which in some cases become interrelated.

First, the Westphalian model no longer accurately describes the sorts of violent threats that militaries are expected to handle. The emergence of violent actors engaged in criminal activities or acting in the name of their political or religious identities instead of a state presents challenges to the present model and demands that military ethicists respond. Second, states themselves may commit acts under the guise of sovereignty that are morally intolerable. Human rights abuses remain human rights abuses whether they are committed under a state's authority and within its borders or not. Third, terrorists may seek shelter within a state that cannot control what goes on within its borders, or that does not fully will to control nonstate-actors in its territory. Those nonstate-actors, however, may prepare a violent act against a victim under the cover of the sovereignty of their host nation. Together, these three challenges motivate reconsideration of the legalist paradigm that holds the only clear just cause for war to be aggression.

International Crime and Terrorism

Although some nonstate-actors foster respect for ethical concerns, others operate in blatant disregard of moral decency. Two of these, organized criminal bodies and terrorist organizations, offer obvious threats both to law-abiding citizens and their states.

Organized Criminal Bodies

International crime is not new, but its importance to military ethicists has increased greatly in the latter half of the 20th century. The cold war that polarized much of the globe served to inhibit commerce, legal or illegal, across many borders. Since the early 1990s, however, it has become both easier and more attractive for many nations to participate in the economic benefits of global trade. The resulting softening of trade restrictions and travel limitations has permitted illegal trafficking, especially in arms and drugs, to blossom. The same, however, cannot be said for state-sanctioned security organizations. These are limited by the Westphalian notions of sovereignty. This asymmetry between law-abiding security forces and law-breaking criminal organizations obviously puts the security forces at a disadvantage. Although the asymmetry is addressed in part by increased international cooperation in law enforcement, the problem of international crime continues to pose challenges. Some suggest that *jus ad bellum* criteria, particularly the requirement for a just cause, ought to be revisited in light of the threats to stability and well-being that international criminal organizations present. In the case of illegal arms trafficking, including, potentially, weapons of mass destruction (WMD), it may be argued that intercepting weapons trading constitutes a just cause for a violation of sovereignty, especially in those cases where the criminal activity cannot be stopped domestically because of a relatively weak law-enforcement capacity.

Common sense might suggest that cooperation is the obvious solution to challenges such as these. In the ideal case, the weak law-enforcement capacity of a state might be supplemented by assistance from more capable states, especially those whose interests are affected by the crime. In other words, territory might be invaded with the permission, or even the gratitude, of a relatively weak state. This approach respects both sovereignty and the need for international defense against criminal activity.

Still, one must be prepared for the case in which common sense does not prevail. Should a weak state grant that crime ought to be suppressed but nonetheless deny permission to other states to enter its territory for the purpose of law enforce-ment, respect for territorial integrity under the Westphalian model would suggest that the criminal activity must be allowed to persist. But allowing that activity permits threats to other states, as well as threats to human rights to proliferate, and so there seem to be good reasons to violate sovereignty in the name of de-fense. At least one entailment of this argument makes for apprehension having to do with justifying the violation of sovereignty (aggression) through appeal to law enforcement. Should state D be the favored locale for criminal activity that poses a threat to state A, state A may claim a just cause for invading state D. The inva-sion, however, although affecting the rights and interests of state D, is not said to be justified on the grounds of state D's actions. Instead, it is said to be justified by what amounts to a geographical accident. This claim, not surprisingly, gener-ates worries that the idea of sovereignty itself could lose primacy in international relations.

Terrorist Organizations

Criminal organizations are frequently involved with terrorist organizations. The crime provides financial support and other advantages. But it is terrorism itself that is most prominently in the public eye since the al-Qaeda attacks on New York and Washington on September 11, 2001. These attacks have inspired substantial, and controversial, reinterpretation of *jus ad bellum*.

Plainly, the terrorist attacks of 9/11 constituted a wrong received and justified an armed response, but the common presupposition of state involvement in ag-gression proves problematic in framing that response. Had a traditional state's military attacked the twin towers and the Pentagon with missiles or bombs, the target for a response would be easily identified and a declaration of cause straight-forward. But al-Qaeda plotted and executed the attacks, and al-Qaeda is not a state. The nexus of the challenge has to do with both terrorism's methodology and the threshold of a just cause. In particular, terrorist acts are designed to strike without specific warning to their targets and more or less randomly against non-combatants. This also means that terrorism relies on murder as a tactic, a clear violation of *jus in bello*.

States and nonstate-actors alike have engaged in terrorism. Terrorism is a method to achieve political ends. Like war, it is designed to compel an adver-sary to do what one wills. An inherent part of terrorism's method, however, is the deliberate violation of discrimination. The terror bombings of the Second World War were designed to drive a wedge between the population of a state and its government. If that wedge were driven effectively, the population would no longer consent to supporting the war, and the adversary would soon capitu-late. The al-Qaeda likewise seeks to drive a wedge between populations and their governments with the goal of changing the behavior of states. In particular, the al-Qaeda seeks to compel the withdrawal of foreign non-Islamic presence from Islamic soil.

Al-Qaeda's methods of striking illegitimate targets and relying on surprise make open warfare against the terrorist organization difficult, as pitched battles, for which a Westphalian-oriented state's militaries are likely best prepared, are unlikely. This drives an interest in reconsidering the just cause criterion toward a more liberal approach to preemption or even preventive strikes.

JWT can be adapted successfully to the challenges posed by nonstate-actors within the tradition. This suggestion is especially plausible if one thinks back to the JWT before the Westphalian Peace. Augustine's Rome, for example, was faced with threats that in some ways are much like those posed by terrorist organizations today. It is the assertion within the legalist paradigm that aggression must be suffered before defending against it that needs to be modified, and that modification can take place comfortably within the just-war framework to address both threats from states and from nonstate-actors. Indeed, as Brian Orend has pointed out, neither just war thinking nor international law claims that aggression must be committed by a state.[1] The aggression is undeniable, and so a response is justified.

Preemptive and Preventive War against Terrorism

Responding to terrorist organizations where the aggression has already occurred and the perpetrators solidly identified is one thing. Eliminating terrorist threats is another, and it is here that the ethical issues most clearly require further scrutiny.

In the absence of a clear and practical standard, the likelihood that justified preemption will be abused rises. Almost anything could be said to constitute a threat, or indeed, *feeling* threatened might be said to be sufficient. This is especially true if the threat presented involves WMD, as the consequences of waiting to receive the attack could be horrific. If waiting to receive the first blow would prove too costly, what threshold *would* constitute sufficient moral cause for violent anticipatory action?

This question has received much attention since the terror attacks against the United States in 2001. The *National Security Strategy* of 2002, as well as that of 2006, explicitly reserves the right of preemptive strikes as a part of U.S. strategy, noting that the attendant risks to not striking preemptively increase with the potential effects of WMD in the hands of terrorist adversaries. Hence, according to the *National Security Strategy*, the United States will strike preemptively "when necessary."

Martin Cook has insightfully suggested one practical approach to help determine whether a certain perceived threat actually rises to a level that could justify preemption. He proposes that, at a minimum, one ought to be able to convince friendly states that such a cause exists. Suppose that nation D believes it has just cause war for going to war preemptively against nation A. If the belief is justified, nation D ought to be able to elicit a like judgment from its allies, if not from the international community as a whole. In the absence of agreement from even one's allies or friends, just cause is likely absent as well.[2] Naturally, one would need to be cautious before giving too much credence to the stated views of other nations. It is always possible that one's allies might have realist motives for supporting a contemplated military action.

Cook's suggestion does not clarify what would justify preemption but rather serves as a check to ensure that one does not engage in unjustified preemption. Put differently, using Cook's idea, one might consider the agreement of friendly states that preemption might be warranted as a necessary but still insufficient condition for justifying an anticipatory attack.

Anticipatory strikes against states, such as the Six Days' War of 1967, have been considered previously. In the case of an anticipatory strike against a state, JWT grants that there may be cases where a state has just cause to strike preemptively before suffering bona fide imminent aggression. But strikes against nonstate-actors are more problematic, because the strike may require violating the sovereignty of a state that bears no malice toward the state that the terrorists are planning to attack.

In cases where the state willingly hosts the terrorists, the traditional notions of just cause are operative. This is the case of the Taliban government's sponsorship of the al-Qaeda. The U.S. strikes against the Taliban and the al-Qaeda fit the traditional account of just cause. But in cases where the terrorists take harbor without their host's knowledge (as indeed, the 9/11 hijackers did in the United States), or where the state is incapable of enforcing its own laws, the matter becomes more ambiguous.

As with the problem of international crime, in these sorts of cases the values of sovereignty and security seem to work against one another. To respect the sovereignty of a weak state that is home to terrorist preparations is to allow the risk to the target state to grow. In the ideal case, of course, such issues would be handled by mutual agreement between the state that claims to be defending itself and the state in which the terrorists hide. In this way, the two states cooperate in what amounts to an exercise in law enforcement. But should the host state consider intervention within its own borders to be unwelcome, the legalist paradigm would seem to tie the hands of the target state. It is in this context that many feel divergent moral tugs. On the one hand, states have the right to defend themselves against terrorism. This right derives easily from the rights of noncombatants to be free from murder. Citizens properly require that their states defend their human rights against terrorism. On the other hand, the Westphalian system, which usually serves to help secure the rights of citizens, seems to require that outsiders respect the sovereignty of every state unless the state itself has provoked military response. A state infested with organizations that act without its consent, but that is aware of that infestation and is taking action, however embryonic, to address the problem might properly appeal to the Westphalian notion of sovereignty to require that other states keep their forces to themselves.

The controversial Bush doctrine, formalized in the *National Security Strategy* of 2002, is in part a result of this problem. In essence, the Bush doctrine holds that anticipatory strikes against terrorists are not prevented by considerations of sovereignty. It bases this assertion on the right of self-defense:

> Given the goals of rogue states and terrorists, the United States can no longer solely rely on a reactive posture as we have in the past. The inability to deter a potential attacker, the immediacy of today's threats, and the magnitude of potential harm that could be caused by our adversaries' choice of weapons, do not permit that option. We cannot let our enemies strike first
>
> The greater the threat, the greater is the risk of inaction—and the more compelling the case for taking anticipatory action to defend ourselves, even if uncertainty remains as to the time and place of the enemy's attack. To forestall or prevent such hostile acts by our adversaries, the United States will, if necessary, act preemptively.[3]

The National Security Strategy was updated in 2006, but the argument favoring preemption is essentially unchanged:

> If necessary, however, under long-standing principles of self defense, we do not rule out the use of force before attacks occur, even if uncertainty remains as to the time and place of the enemy's attack. When the consequences of an attack with WMD are potentially so devastating, we cannot afford to stand idly by as grave dangers materialize.[4]

Although no threshold for what constitutes a just cause for preemption is specified, the Bush doctrine does stimulate reflection regarding the applicability of the Westphalian model to the present day.

Humanitarian Intervention

There is a growing acceptance for waging war on humanitarian grounds. The ethical tugs for intervention have become especially vivid since the advent of widespread media coverage of humanitarian crises. It is also likely that the widespread evils of 20th-century political history stimulated thinking about the evil that states can do to those under their dominion. Although many feel the obligation to help those in other states, however, this imperative presents challenges to the Westphalian assumptions that underlie much of recent JWT.

Human rights are universal; ethically speaking, one has these rights regardless of political circumstances. The practical question is whether those rights are respected by others. When rights are violated, especially when the violations are systemic and egregious, a just cause for outside intervention may come into being. This idea is not new. Grotius noted that "the will to govern and the will to destroy cannot exist together, and so a king who declares himself the enemy of all his people by that act renounces his very kingdom."[5]

Ethically speaking, one human's rights obligate everyone to respect them. Human rights do not depend on national borders or accidents of geography and neither does the duty to respect them. The same logic is in place with regard to the defense of rights. It follows then that it is not only self-defense that can justify violent action—defense of the rights of other communities may do so as well, even in those cases where it is the local government that is violating their rights. Ordinary moral intuitions suggest that there is an obligation to help victims of oppression. Pol Pot's genocide in Cambodia in the 1970s and the mass killing of close to 1 million Tutsis in Rwanda in the mid-1990s brought the obligation vividly to the public mind. It is probably fair to suggest that many in the developed world now regret the failure to take military action to stop the killing in these cases. There is substantial controversy, however, over just how stringently states are bound to intervene when the rights of members of other states are violated.

Some ethicists, like David Luban, argue that intervention to defend against human rights violations is morally obligatory. Others, like Walzer in his *Just and Unjust Wars,* suggest that although there are cases in which humanitarian intervention is appropriate to free an oppressed community, the real burden lies on the oppressed to liberate themselves.

There are other values at stake, however. An armed intervention on humanitarian grounds will almost certainly violate the territory of another state, as well as undermining the authority of its government. This violation of a state's sovereignty may itself be viewed as a case of aggression against that state. The line between humanitarian intervention and engaging in, or appearing to engage in, imperialism can be a thin one. It is one thing to intervene on behalf of the oppressed and then withdraw after their safety is established. It is quite another to use their oppression as a pretext for narrowly self-interested motives to mask a goal of occupation or acquiring territory.

Perhaps more profoundly, justifying war on humanitarian grounds calls into question fundamental assumptions about the nearly absolute value of state sovereignty in the international arena.

Walzer's 1977 analysis relies in part on the precedent work of John S. Mill. Mill argues that the very nature of self-determination requires that its genesis occur within the community that has been denied it. Others cannot impose freedom; by its very nature it must find its wellspring within the community that desires it. This requires that those whose rights are being violated take matters into their own hands; however, in some cases, this is simply impossible. Even while acknowledging the persuasiveness of Mill's position, Walzer suggests that third parties are obligated to intervene in cases of massacre.[6]

Walzer's more recent position has softened a bit. Although he maintains the overall position that states should enjoy their sovereignty unmolested by others, there are cases in which intervention is justified on humanitarian grounds.[7] Of importance, however, he notes that those who would intervene must concern themselves with an "exit strategy."[8] After all, if the intervening nation does not exit, the intervention may become something more like an occupation. Two factors make this especially complex. First, it is often difficult to know just how things will proceed in advance. It may be the case that the intervention simply works to remove an oppressor and then the oppressed are capable of organizing themselves into some governmental form that respects human rights and is capable of defending them. That scenario may not play out, however, and the intervening power may become drawn ever more deeply into a succession of seemingly unending tasks of nation-building. Second, any declaration of an exit strategy will become public knowledge. This may encourage the oppressive powers simply to wait out the intervention, reemerging once the forces have withdrawn in the knowledge that the domestic politics of the intervening nation may well make reengagement unlikely.

The question of casualty aversion arises as well. Casualties are commonly accepted, even if they are regretted, in a war of self-defense. But when violence is suffered in the course of defending others, soldiers and citizens may begin to wonder whether the costs are justified. Even if just cause is satisfied, the authority for military interventions, which lies with the will of the citizens of a state, may be lacking.

Some of David Luban's most intriguing insights involve the inconsistency between the reality of humanitarian crises and the Westphalian model of the state that underlies modern notions of just cause. He notes that in many cases of widespread rights violations, legitimate governments are absent. Accordingly, the legalist paradigm is difficult or impossible to apply, and if that is the case, the notion of just cause being restricted to a state's defense against aggression is unhelpful at best. For Luban, the morally salient considerations have to do with the violations of basic human rights instead of states rights.

Luban relies on earlier work by Henry Shue[9] who defended a concept of "socially basic" rights as those that are necessary if any other rights are to be enjoyed.[10] Rights of this nature include rights to security, subsistence, and the basic necessities for healthy living such as clean water and shelter.[11] Hence, Luban proposes reorienting the idea of justified defense from the defense of *states* rights to the defense of *human* rights. Naturally, epistemic problems remain even if this shift in the moral center of gravity were to be made. The problem of what constitutes a sufficiently grave offense against human rights is troublesome, but it seems clear that cases such as Rwanda in the 1990s or Cambodia in the 1970s would be sufficient.

The moral quality of humanitarian intervention as a just cause is plainly unsettled. The tension between states rights and human rights that is at the ethical core of the problem challenges the Westphalian model, and it is important to distinguish between babies and bathwater.

Brian Orend has put forth a suggestion to relieve the tension. Reminiscent, perhaps, of Grotius, he proposes that in the case of widespread state-sponsored rights violations, the state loses its rights as a state.[12] In such cases, any moral obligation to respect state sovereignty is overridden by the failure of a given state to perform its duties as a state. Because the purported state's ethical orientation or governmental competence fails to rise to the assumptions underlying the Westphalian model, the tension is reduced.

The relative simplicity of the legalist paradigm, with its binary account of aggression as evil and defense against aggression as just, is easy to understand. Its clarity, however, comes at a cost; following it unmindfully can endanger human rights. Indeed, almost any such binary model is bound to prove far too blunt an instrument when applied to cases in the real world. This does not suggest that the Westphalian model should be discarded, but rather that it is incomplete. Good will and good judgment are necessary supplements to any model, whether it be political or ethical.

The Influence of Other Nonstate-Actors

Present-day international relations reflect the activities of more than states and other political communities. Much influential power is wielded by nongovernmental agencies such as the International Committee of the Red Cross (ICRC) or Amnesty International. Moreover, the globalization of economic relations and advances in news gathering and dissemination have changed the international landscape in ways relevant to military ethics.

Aid Agencies

Most humanitarian organizations promote activities that are generally consistent with JWT. The ICRC in particular has worked for more than a century to alleviate the suffering caused by war. Indeed, 175 years ago, it was not uncommon for wounded soldiers to receive little assistance from their own governments.[13] The ICRC, which has its roots in Geneva, Switzerland, was formed to enable medical organizations to care for the wounded, regardless of which state they had served. The first Geneva Convention, in 1864, was a result. This convention formalized the practical ethical observation that ambulances, hospitals, medial practitioners, and the like should be immune from deliberate attack.[14]

Under international law, the ICRC enjoys rare power to perform humanitarian acts.[15] It observes strict neutrality regarding whom it aids. This is a logical extension of the just-war distinction between a human being and a combatant representing a state. The ICRC's policy regarding neutrality seems to embody the fact that, although soldiers fight on behalf of others, their suffering is their own. Political values, however just or unjust, are both morally and logically distinct from the obligation to alleviate suffering in the wounded.

Media

The global media presence increasingly influences thinking about and judging the moral aspects of war. Arguably, in some cases the media's influence has spurred ethical improvements in the conduct of warfare and the treatment of the suffering. In others, the media has exerted the opposite effect by portraying people or events dishonestly.

Although written descriptions of the evils of war have a long history, war reporting literally became much more graphic after advances in photography made the effects of a battle visible to everyone. The devastation and suffering caused by the American Civil War were revealed with unprecedented realism. Photographs of bloated casualties still on the battlefield, hospitals, and burial brought the human cost of war close. It may not be mere coincidence that drafting and adoption of the first Geneva Convention took place in 1864. At around the same time, the telegraph made reporting much more timely. Civilians' distance from the battlefield and from the morally problematic dimensions of war began to diminish.

Technical advances over the past 150 years or so have diminished that distance even more. Inventions such as movie cameras and, of late, the Internet and digital photography have made fast and graphic reporting the norm for professional news reporters. At the same time, cameras and video recorders have become smaller, and their use by ordinary people, including soldiers, has become commonplace. In the present day, it is possible for participants to record their own battles using a cell-phone camera and to post the resulting images on the Web.

All of these advances combine to increase the probability that soldiers' activities will become widely known, especially in controversial or spectacular cases. The prison scandal at Abu-Grahib and the mutilation of American contractors in Fallujah, both of which were revealed in 2004, are both well known and widely condemned. Their long-range strategic impact remains to be assessed fully, but it seems a safe bet that history will judge both as having damaged the causes of their perpetrators.

Notes

1. Brian Orend, *The Morality of War* (Petersborough, Ontario: Broadview Press, 2006), 71.

2. Dr. Martin L. Cook, personal communication, July 2008.

3. National Security Strategy of the United States of America, (Washington, DC: The White House, 2002) 19.

4. The National Security Strategy of the United States of America, March 2006, http://74.125.47.132/search?q=cache:VATwAg3qM-MJ:www.marforres.usmc.mil/docs/nss2006.pdf+national+security+strategy+united+states&cd=3&h (page 28).

5. Hugo Grotius, *The Law of War and Peace,* trans. Louise R. Loomis (Roslyn, NY: Walter J. Black, 1949), 65 .

6. Michael Walzer, *Just and Unjust Wars* (New York: Basic Books, 1977), 106.

7. Michael Walzer, "The Politics of Rescue," in *Arguing about War* (New Haven: Yale University Press, 2004), 67–81.

8. Ibid., 72.

9. See Henry Shue, *Basic Rights: Subsistence, Affluence, and U.S. Foreign Policy,* 2nd ed. (Princeton: Princeton University Press, 1996).

10. David Luban, "Just War and Human Rights" in *The Morality of War*, eds. Larry May, Eric Rovie, and Steve Viner (Upper Saddle, NJ: Pearson Education, 2006), 276.

11. Ibid.

12. Brian Orend, *The Morality of War,* 35–36.

13. Michael Ignatieff, *The Warrior's Honor: Ethnic War and the Modern Conscience* (New York: Henry Holt, 1997), 113.

14. Ibid., 111–112.

15. Ibid., 124.

CHAPTER 7

Cultural Ethical Issues

Matters involving the application of force have occupied most of the literature in military ethics. Although questions of killing and dying seem to be at the forefront in popular conceptions of the field, however, it is safe to say that the most common morally laden concerns facing military members have little or nothing to do with violence. Talk of and preparation for violent conflict are widespread in the modern military, but actual combat engagements are statistically relatively rare.

As with any large organization, militaries must deal with emergent ethical challenges as a product of societal evolution and advances in the study of ethics. The issues are many, but only three are considered here: the integration of women, military policies regarding homosexuality, and the role of religion in the military.

It is important to bear in mind a central problem while discussing each of these issues. Those who view the military sympathetically will understand that, ideals of integrity notwithstanding, not every conscientious military member agrees with public policy. Indeed, the disharmony between the duties of public office and the dictates of private conscience is a substantial element of military ethics, although little has been written about it.

Women in the Armed Forces

With a few exceptions across history, the military has been an almost exclusively male enterprise. And even when women did fulfill military roles, they were typically classified into "auxiliary" components of the military. Historically and culturally speaking, military women were a rarity.

In the middle of the 20th century, things began to change. In part this was driven by the severe need for military recruits incident to the Second World War. The historical dictates of necessity, however, have since been replaced by moral controversy as the societal issues of women's rights and gender equity have evolved. At issue is the question whether discriminating between males and females in a military context is ethically justified. Put differently, there is controversy over whether the practice of restricting military service, or certain forms of service, to males discriminates unfairly against women.

Many military specialties are open to women, but those involving direct combat remain closed. This policy is sometimes referred to as the "combat exclusion." This is not to say that women are not harmed in modern military operations, however. Between 2003 and July 2009, 111 female U.S. service members died in Iraq, about 2.5 percent of the total fatalities for that period.[1]

It is important to note that combat experience, or at least operational assignments, tends to foster military members' career prospects. Excluding women from some of the operational fields, such as infantry, therefore tends to put women at some disadvantage for career advancement.

Concerns about Women in the Military

The case for gender segregation in the military is multifaceted, appealing to assertions about function, cohesion, psychology, and biology. The matter is accordingly complex and requires nuanced consideration.

As noted previously, discrimination in and of itself is not necessarily immoral. The moral quality of discrimination pivots on the reasons that are said to support the discrimination. Under *jus in bello*, it is a moral requirement to discriminate between combatants and noncombatants because each class is deserving of different treatment. On the other hand, just war thinking (JWT) prohibits discriminating on the basis of ethnic identity, because, all things being equal, ethnicity has nothing to do with whether a person is a legitimate military target.

Discrimination is unethical only if it is unfair. For example, it would be unethical to refuse military opportunities to someone who has red hair simply on the grounds that red hair is relatively uncommon. On the other hand, denying military opportunities to those unable to read is permissible because the discrimination is relevant to the role of military member. Literacy is required on the grounds of function. Put differently, a person who is unable to read cannot perform well in a modern military, and so precluding military opportunity to the illiterate is not unfair.

Consent provides a good indication of whether any given discrimination policy is morally justified. When the individuals who are most adversely affected by a given policy can appreciate why that policy is in place, there are good reasons to believe that the policy is a fair one. Notice that one may dislike a policy but still appreciate why it is in place. Combatants accept that they are legitimate targets, and the illiterate can understand that they may harm others as well as themselves were they to try to operate complex military hardware without being able to read the manual or warning placards.

With these examples in place, it is easy to see that discrimination's *justification* is the central issue in denying a person a given role in a community. Should the role be denied unfairly, then the discrimination is morally objectionable, and the ethical community is obligated to modify its policy. Should the discrimination be justifiable in terms of functional requirements attached to a given role, then the discrimination is not unethical, even though some may dislike it. Accordingly, one can understand the controversy over full integration in the military as a disagreement over whether there is anything about women as a class that renders discrimination between men and women in the military as fair.

A comparison to racial discrimination may be helpful. Racial integration of the military is uncontroversial today, although segregation was practiced, at least in the United States, within living memory. Racial integration has succeeded overall in large measure because race has nothing to do with being able to function effectively as a military member. But gender integration is a tougher issue. With the possible exception of certain genetic dispositions for disease, there are no important biological differences among races, but it is indisputable that there are important differences between men and women. Indeed, the defining differences among various races would seem to have nothing to do with any one person's capacity to perform military functions. There is nothing about being white or African American that would have any obvious effect on fitness to serve. But the same is not true for gender differences. There, the defining qualities arguably may affect a person's capacity to perform military functions to the point of justifying discrimination.

Pregnancy. For many who oppose the integration of women into the military, the most salient difference between men and women is that women may become pregnant. Pregnancy is incompatible with many military functions that may involve extended deployments at some distance from hospitals or duties that require exposure to hazardous conditions, including combat. Of course, men may succumb to illness or injuries that would render them unsuitable for certain forms of duty as well, but the limitations that pregnancy impose are exclusive to women. Furthermore, to the extent that a fetus bears rights, a woman combatant who suffers death or debilitation by combat has put the child she is carrying at an unjustifiable hazard. Even if she is willing to bear the burdens of combat, it is not at all clear that she can morally expose an obviously innocent unborn child to those burdens.

The argument against having women in the military, let alone combat, may also find support in certain conceptions of teleology. The argument hinges on the claim that women, as women, are outfitted for the reproductive and child-rearing role by virtue of natural biology. Motherhood, inescapably a feminine role, occupies a substantial span of a mother's life. And the mother's well-being is critical to the well-being of the child. Hence, any policy that exposes females to the risks inherent in combat also exposes the innocent child. It might be noted from the perspective of rights theory, that the son or daughter has an interest in the mother's well-being but is not offered an opportunity to defend that interest. Men, by contrast, require little time to fulfill their reproductive function. Whereas the child certainly has an interest in his father's nurture, that interest can be met by other men in a way that the child's interest in the mother cannot.

Physical Strength. The differences are not only limited to reproductive functions but also have to do with upper-body strength, average height, and stamina. Together, these raise concerns that women will require assistance in performing some tasks, inhibiting the unit's effectiveness and cohesion because some members will be unable to "pull their own weight." The concern is especially acute in combat settings, where, for example, a soldier might be required to carry a wounded comrade to safety or haul heavy equipment over substantial distances. But the worry exists in other settings as well. Much military equipment weighs a great deal, and in a heavily mechanized modern military, maintaining it requires strength. The same is true for the routine shipment of consumables. In both direct combat operations and those that support combat, the ability to carry and maintain heavy things at a rapid pace for sustained periods of time is critical.

Favoritism and Cohesion. There are distinct differences in the sorts of relationships men and women enjoy. This is said to inhibit or complicate the sorts of cohesive bonds that military virtue requires. Men—particularly young men—bond with one another freely and rapidly under almost any conditions. The introduction of women into a group of men complicates this bonding, as sexual and romantic interests may ensue. As romance by its very nature involves favoring one individual over others, group cohesion is said to be adversely affected. Whether or not such favoritism would result in increased risks for other members of a unit when under fire, the perception that favoritism was a possibility would likely complicate the trust that an all-male unit would enjoy.

Socialization and Cultural Roles. The military function involves deliberately deploying violent means against fellow humans. Although most men become accustomed to violence through their socialization, women are typically viewed as alien from it. Men are viewed as naturally comfortable with the use of force; women are more typically viewed as naturally nurturing. This perception in turn suggests that females may be less likely to behave with appropriate aggression in combat.

Integrating women into the United States service academies in the 1970s was controversial for just this reason. Although the policy is now a settled matter of law, for some, the ethical considerations opposing that law remain.

Military academies, at least until women were admitted to them in 1976, were bastions of masculinity. The opposition to integration, articulated in a 1979 *Washingtonian* article by Naval Academy graduate James Webb, centers around the disharmony between the military lifestyle and feminine identity.

The military is said to require leaders who have been through an extraordinarily stressful experience, which the all-male academies provided. The academic education that cadets and midshipmen receive is secondary to the military education, which is what is essential to successful leadership in combat. Once women were admitted to the academies, those institutions lost their capability to provide the requisite stresses, because women could not meet their demands successfully.

Therefore the military would be impeded in its preparation of leaders for the inevitable stresses of future battles. Part of that masculine identity is the capacity to endure privation, harassment, and stress that are said to be essential to prepare combat leaders.[2]

Advocating Full Integration

Many advocates of integration grant that the concerns about fully incorporating women into the military have merit, but argue that these concerns can be addressed satisfactorily without discriminating against women. In general, their approach to the problem involves distinguishing between qualities essential to women or men as such and the qualities essential to military functions. The advocates of full integration challenge discrimination on the basis of gender alone, but are comfortable with fair discrimination based on functional imperatives. The question is not whether to consent to certain discriminatory policies or practices, but rather what justifications are offered to support them.

Pregnancy. There is little controversy over whether pregnant women should be in combat; like other physically strenuous and mentally stressful activities, combat is inconsistent with a healthy pregnancy. Moreover, on the assumption that an unborn child bears rights, the principle of discrimination obligates the pregnant combatant to keep her fetus out of harm's way. In accordance with these considerations, governmental policy dictates that materials and working environments that may jeopardize a healthy pregnancy be reduced to the practical minimum. If it is impossible to eliminate health hazards, policy restricts female military members from duties that may interfere with a successful pregnancy, including combat duties, and to avoid risky deployments.[3]

These considerations preclude only *pregnant* women from combat and other hazards. They do not provide grounds for saying that women should not be in combat, let alone in the military, just by virtue of their sex. The fact that a person is capable of becoming pregnant does not imply that the person actually is pregnant any more than the fact that a person can become ill implies that a person actually is ill at any given time. Furthermore, the ready availability of birth control, not to mention the option to abstain from sexual activity, gives female soldiers control over the likelihood of pregnancy. A woman whose unit is depending on her to deploy with them is therefore arguably obligated to avoid pregnancies that would interfere with her doing her part for the unit.[4]

Based on the preceding argument, concerns about pregnancy do not justify prohibiting women from combat assignments. Instead, there is an ethical obligation to ensure that one does not become pregnant when there is a risk of becoming involved in combat. Although male military members cannot become pregnant, they are similarly obligated to avoid conditions that may affect their combat readiness. A male who breaks his leg playing football or riding a motorcycle places a burden on other members to close the gap that his injuries cause.

Concerns about pregnancy, even where combat is not foreseen, can be addressed in the same way that other impediments to military functioning are handled. There is no question that a pregnant soldier must limit certain sorts of activities for the good of the fetus and her own health, but the same is true for many other medical conditions that afflict both men and women. The soldier with the broken leg, or even severe sunburn for that matter, cannot function as effectively as a healthy one.

This common-sense approach to balancing the imperatives of family life with those of military life grants that pregnancy is incompatible with certain endeavors, and resolves the apparent tension between the two by yielding to both but at different times. This approach is already embodied in some military policy. The U.S. Navy advocates family planning practices that would voluntarily limit pregnancy to times when the female member is on a shore assignment.[5]

Similarly, it is granted that a child has an interest in growing up in a secure and loving home, but this does not require that women be excluded from hazardous military duties because the child's interest can be met without the presence of either biological parent. Fathers are killed or maimed as a result of their military activities, and, although tragic, it does not morally preclude fathers from combat. Other men can fulfill the father's role. The same is true for mothers.

Physical Strength. Those who suspect that female military members lack sufficient strength to perform military tasks overlook several facts. First, although it is true that women as a group have less upper body strength than do men as a class, there are large variations in upper body strength among members of each group. Put differently, some men are weaker than some women. If this is the case, and there is a clear functional requirement for a certain amount of strength, then the appropriate discriminator is not gender, but rather an individual service member's strength. Assignments to particular specialties and tasks ought to be based on what the position actually demands. The capacity to accomplish given tasks is the important criterion, and it is the one that other members ultimately depend on. By way of example, one retired female military pilot mentioned to me that her sense of smell helped her detect and diagnose malfunctions in her airplane (e.g., leaking hydraulic fluid) more quickly than her male crewmembers.[6]

If the same functional approach is applied more broadly, it becomes evident that certain physical characteristics that tend to be associated with females may well have greater functionality for some tasks than those associated with men. One example might be the functional requirements for avionics maintenance in military aircraft. Here, the openings behind panels and within access covers are often very small and cramped; this presents more impediment to those with large hands, however strong, than it does to the typically smaller-handed female. The same is true for many sorts of maintenance involving sophisticated equipment and tight spaces. Where male technicians may need to perform a disassembly to access the malfunctioning component, the female's smaller physique may allow her to access it without having to tear down as much equipment. In cases like this, the addition of a female may increase a unit's effectiveness by permitting more specialization within a team.[7]

Favoritism and Cohesion. The tendency of men and women to pair off and form relationships is also susceptible to a common-sense solution that will preserve unit effectiveness. A commitment to the military virtues will preclude favoring any one person, regardless of gender, over any other in the military workplace.

Militaries already prohibit favoritism because of its ill effects. The threat to good order and discipline that favoritism can present is not limited to romantically involved couples at all. Men form unique friendships within any group, but the military functions adequately despite this fact. Not all dispositions to like, or to dislike, another member of one's unit pose a threat to effectiveness because one can have a disposition and yet refrain from acting on it. The rank hierarchy itself is in place in part to ensure that members of a given stratum are treated equitably. For a male officer to befriend an enlisted man and show favoritism on that account would be to violate professional ethical obligations as well as regulations. The same structure should preclude favoritism between men and women. Indeed, a practical appreciation of military ethics would regulate romantic relationships in the same way that it would all other relationships. The issue is best understood as tied to a policy regarding professionalism rather than integration.

Avoiding favoritism, however, may not be sufficient to preserve the cohesion that is critical to military effectiveness. Introducing women into previously all-male groups is said to inhibit the ability of the group to cohere.

Proponents of full integration argue that, although the willing subordination of the self to the good of the unit is undoubtedly a military virtue, there is no clear relationship between single-sex groups and greater cohesion. Few with experience in the modern business world would deny that men and women can gain one another's trust in the same way that single-sex groups gain it—through competence, communication, and good moral character. These are the individual qualities that lead to unit cohesion, and there is no monopoly on any of them by either sex. The relevant determinant is not gender, but a shared commitment to effective, high-quality work, and good leadership. No organization that wishes to compete seriously in business should limit its pool of potential talent to only half of the population. Indeed, it ought to put forth substantial effort to recruit and retain the most effective, trustworthy, and competent people for every position and ensure that they were well led. The same should be true for military units.

Still, it might be pointed out, the demands of competition in a free market are of a different kind than those faced by military units. The stakes in business life do not approach those of military life. Hence, an acceptable level of cohesion among men and women in the business environment fails to show that women would not disrupt unit cohesion in the military.

Before proceeding, it is important to avoid confusion between social cohesion and task cohesion. Social cohesion might be likened to friendship, a good thing to be sure, but of dubious relationship to unit effectiveness. Task cohesion has to do with a shared devotion to achieving a result. Task cohesion has a demonstrable correlation to performance. Social cohesion does not and may, in some cases, actually work against effectiveness.[8] Accordingly, it is task cohesion that is essential to military effectiveness.

A 1997 RAND study examined the effect of gender integration on task cohesion and found that gender, considered in isolation, "did not appear to erode cohesion."[9] As might be expected, the study found that unit cohesion was influenced much more strongly by command climate, mutual respect, and shared hardship than by gender.[10]

Socialization and Cultural Roles. Women's integration into all military units may increase unit effectiveness by expanding the options available to commanders because, depending on local cultural mores, women may be able to accomplish what men would find difficult. The nurturing image commonly associated with women can be a distinctive advantage when interacting with women and children in a foreign nation, especially if their associated culture views women as less threatening than men. The reaction of a suspicious villager to a male infantryman seeking information may well inhibit gathering helpful intelligence, but the mere fact of being a woman may project a less threatening air. On the other hand, the very presence of a woman in uniform may be considered an insult. As with other leadership responsibilities, assigning the appropriate tasks to each unit member is imperative.

The same sort of approach might be taken toward psychological suitability for violence. Advocates of full integration grant that socialization for violence is more widespread among men than it is among women, but it does not follow that no women are psychologically prepared to suffer and deliver violence. To the contrary, an effective military develops methods to prepare its troops for violence as a part of the training process for combat. Many men serving in the military are poorly socialized for violence in the absence of deliberate training to that end, as the empirical data reviewed in chapter 3 suggest. Gender is not the determinant of psychological suitability; socialization is. And if there is one capacity the modern military has mastered, it is the capacity to socialize people.

Inequity, Informal Associations, and the Role of Ethics. In interviews with numerous female veterans and active duty military members, two themes have emerged when the topics of ethics and gender integration come under discussion. First, many women discover that there exists an "old-boy's club" in the military. The ethical dimensions of this club's existence may be easily overlooked by many male military members. In the same way a fish is said not to notice that it is surrounded by water, military men may be unaware that their majority status is ethically laden with implications of unfair discrimination against women. Second, women's minority status in the military gives them vivid insight into the functional nature of military ethics. There are at least two discernible dimensions to this vivid appreciation. First, the woman is aware that judgments about her will reflect on fellow females. Second, judgments about her will sometimes be made against a presupposition that women are unsuitable for military service. Where a man may be able to rely on his military brethren to "carry" him through a failure, a woman will likely find no such informal support network. Hence, the woman military member is under scrutiny for her actions in ways that men are not, and this seems to improve focus on the functional nature of ethics.

To illustrate these factors, consider the case of a new second lieutenant (the entry-level position of the commissioned officer ranks) in 1972, assigned as the squadron section commander of an otherwise all-male Air Force squadron in the northern tier of the United States. Squadron section commanders are responsible for the administrative oversight of a squadron, including disciplinary matters. This officer, who recently retired as a major general in the Air Force Reserves, was among the first females to occupy such a position.

Soon after her arrival, she performed an inspection of the enlisted dormitories as part of her official function. She was accompanied by the first sergeant, the enlisted man responsible for morale and discipline in the squadron. The dormitory walls had been specially prepared for her arrival with centerfolds from adult magazines.

Many male military officers never face leadership challenges of this nature, possibly to their developmental detriment. This sort of real-world challenge to authority is not covered by typical officer-training curricula. Significantly, in this case, the lieutenant realized that the only way to meet the challenge long term was to earn the respect of the squadron's men. Instead of relying on the formal authority her rank granted her, she resolved to perform so well and to become so valued by her subordinates that they would remove the centerfolds themselves. This took several months, but the strategy worked. Perhaps more significantly, this officer learned about the functional effectiveness of earning respect as opposed to demanding it—a lesson she took with her through her obviously successful career. To advocates of full integration, this is just the sort of evidence that shows women belong in all facets of military service. Troops recognize that leadership is what matters, not gender, and perform accordingly. Women who succeed in the way this lieutenant did have to be good leaders; otherwise they would be unable to overcome the additional obstacles that sexism places before them.

The issue of women's integration would not be an issue if it were settled, although it appears clear that women are already in combat *de facto,* and their formal full integration is likely only a matter of time. Passionate and good-hearted people continue to debate the issue, and the empirical data available, although growing, remain limited. Still, two aspects of the issue seem to be uncontroversial.

First, regardless of how the future evolves, the present proportion of women in the military fails to provide them with a "critical mass." This entails that, justified or not, the feminine voice is often drowned out. The "old boys' club" is as obvious to military women as it is invisible to most of its members. Many women seem to feel powerless in its face, as the military is still about 85 percent male. The informal relationships among the men may have a deleterious effect on meritorious women's accessing formal power or retaining it. To some women, it seems clear that to be accepted by the dominant male culture is to be "safe"—that is, properly in one's place as a female military member. In essence, this means being a female whose behavior accords with the standards informally set by the club.

Second, women are at risk regardless of policy. In spite of whatever rights they may bear as noncombatants, women, children, and the unborn have suffered mightily in war. The attacks of 9/11 did not exclude women, pregnant women, or children. This leads some of those advocating full integration to point out that the issue might best be framed in terms less emphatic of protecting women from harm and more insistent on granting them the right to fight. Women have suffered violence regardless of policies; policies that preclude their taking up arms cannot therefore be based on appeals to women as a special class immune to violence.

Gays and Lesbians in the Armed Forces

For most of the 20th century, the United States Armed Forces permitted only heterosexuals in its ranks. Since 1993, the policy has been to permit service for gays and lesbians, but to preclude "open" homosexuality through a "don't ask, don't tell, don't pursue" (DADT) rule.

As in the case of females in the military, the most relevant applied ethical issue has to do with the justification of discrimination. There is no restriction on heterosexuals serving "openly" in the military, and any policy that would discriminate against gays and lesbians requires justification on grounds relevant to sexual orientation's effect on military functionality.

It is worth noting that, as an empirical matter, militaries have likely been composed in part by gays and lesbians regardless of publicly stated policies. This point has been made repeatedly in recent years by those advocating a change in policy.[11] That fact, however, does nothing to settle the question of whether they *ought* to be permitted to serve in the military.

Concerns about Homosexuality in the Military

Some who oppose allowing gay men and lesbians to serve openly in the military today do so because they hold that homosexuality itself is immoral. Often this claim is based on religious convictions that are beyond the jurisdiction of applied military ethics, and so those objections to homosexuality in general are not considered here. Instead, the discussion assumes the existence of considerable social disapproval of homosexuality, regardless of that disapproval's moral justification. The role of religion within the military is discussed in the next section.

Most who oppose permitting openly gay men or lesbians to serve describe their opposition in functional terms. They contend that the integration of openly gay people in the military might be corrosive to good order and discipline and unit cohesion. Given societal attitudes against homosexuality, worries arise over whether the presence of openly gay men and lesbians would inhibit or even preclude cohesiveness. As unit cohesiveness is vital to military effectiveness and, in some cases, survival, allowing unrestricted service threatens both mission accomplishment and individual safety. Accordingly, policies that preclude openly gay men or lesbians to serve are morally justified, as they foster cohesiveness and effectiveness.

The animosity heterosexuals are said to harbor regarding gays and lesbians might introduce a schism in a unit that would render it less effective and therefore potentially threaten lives. Although this societal attitude does not prohibit openly gay people's working in more ordinary occupations, the military member's lifestyle is no ordinary occupation. Living under conditions that might be called "forced intimacy" severely interferes with the privacy members of most other occupations take for granted. Military members sometimes live in cramped quarters, especially in training environments and during deployments. These conditions are said to exacerbate the risk that an openly gay orientation poses to unit cohesion.

A related concern is the discomfort some heterosexuals may feel when sharing living arrangements with gay people. Opponents of openly gay service often make note of the necessity for communal showers as a way of illustrating this concern.[12]

The military recognizes the imperatives of modesty and does its best to respect them. When women were integrated into military units, the services provided separate sleeping quarters, bathrooms, and shower facilities. One can imagine the objections that would have been voiced had this accommodation been denied. But whereas men and women are distinguished by obvious physical signs that are nearly impossible to disguise, a sexual preference may be hidden successfully for an entire lifetime. Hence, if one is sharing such facilities with gays or lesbians, one may be subject to embarrassment. This discomfort has consequences that adversely impact unit cohesion. Worse, given the diminishing but still palpable societal prejudice against homosexuality, mere suspicions regarding a unit member's sexual orientation may be disruptive. A detriment to cohesion in itself, this disruption may further result in overt hostility directed at some unit members given the backdrop of disapproving societal attitudes. Then, as with other sorts of disputes within a unit, the schism may spread to the point of threatening effectiveness.

Advocating Unrestricted Service

Any policy that excludes a group of people from military service is clearly treating people unequally. Just as in the case of denying certain military roles to women, the fundamental issue has to do with the justification for the unequal treatment; many think that the justifications offered here are insufficient to support discrimination.

Those who advocate allowing gay men and lesbians to serve openly point to the fact that they are already in the military and have been throughout history. A 2004 study found that there are an estimated 36,000 gay men and lesbians on active duty in the United States military.[13] The same study found that there were nearly 1 million gay and lesbian veterans.[14] This fact suggests to many that regardless of policy, gay men and lesbians have served and continue to serve with no significant adverse effect. Put differently, the presence of gay men and women in the military evidently has no discernible impact on military effectiveness. This suggests that the social antipathy cited here is overstated.[15] Even if the military were to discard DADT, gay men and lesbians would likely continue to exercise discretion about revealing their orientation, especially if they were to sense hostility in their immediate environment.[16] Gay men and lesbians are aware of the antipathy that some feel against them and so will remain discreet if revealing their orientation were likely to cause disruption. Consequently, concerns that doing away with restrictions regarding homosexuality would inhibit unit cohesion or good order and discipline are largely unfounded. Evidence from military services in Australia, Great Britain, Israel, and Canada supports this point. In all of these militaries, restrictions on gay men and lesbians have been lifted, and there has been virtually no impact on military effectiveness.[17]

More important, from an ethical point of view, the fact that some members of one class of people feels antipathy for another is a morally dubious reason to discriminate against a class of people. Gay men and lesbians have rights regardless of whether others feel antipathy for them as a class. That societal antipathy exists does not make it morally justifiable. If one were to accept the existence of social antipathy as a driver of policy, one would add a second moral wrong to the first. Indeed, the moral obligation to respect and defend rights becomes especially vivid in the face of social antipathy.

Racism was widespread in the United States, and the military integrated nonetheless. It is widely accepted that the military has been in the vanguard of the ethically laudable movement to eliminate discrimination based on race, but it is in the rear guard regarding discrimination based on sexual orientation. This is especially ethically troublesome because the military, perhaps uniquely among large organizations, can exert control over discriminatory behavior within its ranks. Advocates accordingly might suggest that the most praiseworthy policy choice would be to do away with overt policies of discrimination against gay people and to establish clear guidelines within the services that discriminatory behavior against homosexuals will not be tolerated.

Moreover, as concerns about cohesion and discipline are ultimately concerns about military effectiveness, the adverse effects of discriminating against gay men and lesbians should be considered. For example, the military's discharge of Arabic language specialists on the grounds of sexual orientation decreases military effectiveness and increases the burden on the remaining specialists.[18] Even if one were to grant that the presence of openly gay men and lesbians in the military might result in a decrease in effectiveness because of cohesion issues, that decrease may be less costly than expelling those who have critically needed skills from the military, especially during times when national security is endangered in a way that those skills directly address.

Religion

Although entry to the military engages individuals in a special role as state-actors, matters of private conscience remain their own. The state may require certain behaviors on the part of its soldiers, and it may try to influence their internal lives. But attitudes, preferences, and spiritual commitments ultimately belong to individuals. The moral equality of soldiers extends to their ability to disagree with the decisions of their governments and to their (almost certainly unique) perspectives on matters of ultimate importance.

This combination of public office and private conscience poses issues for military ethics, both when waging war and during peacetime. For individuals, the questions revolve first around the compatibility of certain sorts of commitments with military service, and second around the unique power relationships that exist in the military. In the first case, religious beliefs may come into varying degrees of harmony or tension with the requirements of military service. In the second, the issues have to do with the authority that military superiors may use to influence the religious beliefs of those junior to them.

A further ethical issue regarding religion and the military emerges at the level of states. Here the international arena's perception that warfare may be religiously motivated can have important strategic influence. There are important differences between a crusade and a just war.

Religious Commitments and Military Service

Opinions vary widely regarding the proper relationship of private religious belief to public military service. Indeed, it is this very issue that provided much of the creative tension behind the development of Western JWT.

At the individual level, a variety of options are available, each of which is supported by intriguing arguments. Some hold that reconciliation between religious commitment and military service is impossible, and if this is the case, the obvious choice is to avoid military service, or at least certain forms of military service, on the grounds of personal religious belief. This is perhaps most vividly represented in the case of Christian pacifism. Here, the Christian is forbidden from doing violence, even on the orders of a state. In the United States, conscientious objector status is available to those who would otherwise be conscripted into military service.

If it is granted that military service and religious commitment are compatible, the question of the proper role of each emerges. Certainly, there is no obvious reason why a person should be compelled to change religious beliefs merely on the grounds of entry into the military insofar as those beliefs are consistent with the functional requirements and legal restrictions that accompany military service. Military life may in fact intensify a person's belief. The old adage that there are no atheists in foxholes points out that military members facing combat must confront the imminent and real possibility of their own death or disfigurement.

Likewise, many former prisoners of war have pointed to their religious beliefs as critical to their enduring captivity and maltreatment. In circumstances such as these, it seems clear that denying religion's importance to the military function contradicts the facts of experience. Accordingly, religious commitment, far from being inconsistent with military life, may, at least for some, be essential to it.

Religion as Beneficial to Military Service. Some military ethicists suggest that effective leadership is difficult, or perhaps impossible, without a meaningful religious commitment on the part of individual leaders. This commitment supplies ethical guidelines as well as motivational force to act in accordance with them. Some may suggest that it is possible to have a spiritual devotion to ideas, such as those embodied in the Constitution, or perhaps to the military itself; but others disagree, insisting that the commitment must be, at base, religious in nature. For example, in a piece on military ethics entitled "A Message to Garcia: Leading Soldiers in Moral Mayhem," James Toner suggests that the U.S. Army values are "meritorious, secular reflections of transcendent sacred virtues."[19] Through multiple references to the Bible, Toner goes on to argue that the "standard of right" comes from "leaders at all levels, insofar as it conforms to the eternal [Christian] standard."[20]

Arguments for a strong and obvious religious presence in military life rely in part on the idea that motivation sufficient for the military function must be simultaneously intangible and profound. This is particularly important in combat, as life itself is at risk, and any merely tangible motivators are accordingly incommensurate.

Religion as an Impediment to Military Effectiveness. Others argue that proper ethical commitments are entirely possible in the absence of religious ones and note that in at least some cases, religion acts counter to the ethical imperatives of military service. Indeed, it was in part the excesses of religiously motivated warfare that preceded the Treaty of Westphalia and that spurred the development of modern, secular JWT. Although it seems certain that many warriors have been motivated by religious commitments, it is equally clear that these sorts of motivations are not always consistent with the core notions of JWT, which emphasize the secular ethical obligation to defend human rights. Religious motivations are in play for many of the West's adversaries, including the al Qaeda. Hence, if one is to argue that religion enhances military effectiveness, one would also have to argue for only certain sorts of religious commitments. This in turn would, at least in the United States, involve serious legal issues with First Amendment rights. For these ethicists, then, religious commitments ought to remain essentially matters of private conscience.

Religious identity may also create problems with cohesion and equal treatment. The worry is that members of a given faith tradition may hold other members of that tradition in higher regard than their peers. This preference may go unnoticed by the person who has it, but it is unlikely to remain unnoticed by members of the same unit who do not share the same religious commitments. This is particularly true for members of minority sects. For example, if 85 percent of one's unit overtly identifies as members of a particular faith tradition, the remaining 15 percent may sense pressure to conform, despite the fact that religious commitments are personal matters. In the case of conformity under this pressure, it is arguable that rights to religious freedom have been infringed; in the case of nonconformity, a schism may emerge within the unit.

Religion, Private Conscience, and Rank

The relationship between military authority and private conscience can be delicate. On the one hand, some faith traditions explicitly require that adherents seek to bring others into the tradition. And even for those traditions that do not, most religious people are religious just because they find something satisfying about it and are accordingly happy to share their faith with others. No one is required to abandon religious commitments simply on account of entering military service. And, for at least some religious traditions, public ritual and discussion of matters of conscience is an inherent part of a faith commitment. Hence, the argument goes, any restriction on that public side of religious life in the military is an unjustifiable barrier to military members' rights to their own faith. Moreover, it hardly seems as though people should lose their right to express religious belief just because they rise in rank. The right to free expression is part of what modern Western militaries defend.

On the other hand, however, things are complicated for the military in a way that they are not for most other institutions. The military structure explicitly requires obedience and subordination, and the detailed rank structure embodies power relationships. Accordingly, certain forms of expression that are permitted to private citizens are restricted by both law and military ethics.

An analogy may be helpful. Certain forms of social interaction, including dating, can raise ethical concerns when the parties are of differing ranks. In the event that a mid-grade officer took a romantic interest in a young, first-term enlistee, the problem of rank asymmetry would be obvious. There is serious doubt over whether a person substantially junior in rank *can* consent freely to a relationship with a superior. For this reason, among others, military ethics warns against romantic relationships where there is a substantial inequality of military rank.

A similar worry is in place regarding religion and rank. Religion is a private matter, but rank is not. Should superior officers make their faith commitments clear public knowledge, those of inferior rank could feel as though their careers would be enhanced by adopting faith commitments similar to those of their superiors. Perhaps worse, the junior members may sense, rightly or wrongly, that their career prospects may be harmed by their privately held religious commitments. If this is the case, then public office begins to influence what ought to remain private matters. The military is obligated to defend the rights of everyone to enjoy free religious conscience. Thus, allowing into the equation the power that rank and position can wield, even unintentionally, is to violate an ethical obligation.

Strategic Implications

This issue has strategic consequences that ought not to be overlooked. As the Western nations find themselves working to resolve conflicts that have religious animosity at their core, the impression they make regarding religious tolerance is of significant import. To the extent that an adversary justifies doing violence in religious terms, the impression that one is threatening a faith can serve to heighten that motivation. The consequences of allowing military operations to be cast by a religiously motivated adversary in terms that can heighten ill feeling are obvious.

Notes

1. iCasualties.org, http://icasualties.org/Iraq/Female.aspx (accessed July 18, 2009).

2. James Webb, "Women Can't Fight," *Washingtonian Magazine,* November, 1979, available at http://www.washingtonian.com/articles/people/2182.html. See also Brian Mitchell, *Weak Link. The Feminization of the American Military* (Washington, DC: Regnery Gateway, 1979), 47–90, and Mitchell, *Women in the Military: Flirting with Disaster* (Washington DC: Regnery Publishing, 1998), 35–76.

3. See, for example, Army Regulation 40–501, *Standards of Medical Fitness*; 7–19 (Washington, DC: Headquarters, Department of the Army, December, 2007, revised 10 September, 2008): 76–77 or OPNAVINST 6000.1c, *Guidelines Concerning Pregnancy and Parenthood* 102–103 (Washington, DC: Department of the Navy, 14 June, 2007): 1–5—1–8.

4. One female field-grade officer of the author's acquaintance has illustrated this point by proposing that female soldiers of childbearing age receive contraceptive implants 10–12 months before any scheduled deployment.

5. According to OPNAVINST 6000.1c, *Guidelines Concerning Pregnancy and Parenthood* "Servicewomen are expected to plan a pregnancy to successfully balance the demands of family responsibilities and military obligations," 101 e (1), 1–3.

6. Lt. Col. Lori Salgado (USAF, retired). Personal communication to the author, n. d.

7. Accounts like this are abundant. See, for example, Lorry M. Fenner and Marie E. deYoung, *Women in Combat: Civic Duty or Military Liability?* (Washington, DC: Georgetown University Press, 2001), 9–10.

8. Robert J. MacCoun, "Sexual Orientation and Military Cohesion: A Critical Review of the Evidence," in *Out in Force: Sexual Orientation and the Military,* eds. Gregory M. Herek, Jared B. Jobe, and Ralph M. Carney (Chicago: University of Chicago Press, 1996), 157–160.

9. Margaret C. Harnell and Laura Miller, *New Opportunities for Military Women: Effects upon Readiness, Cohesion, and Morale* (Santa Monica, CA: RAND Corporation, 1997), 54.

10. Ibid., 54–55. A compendium on Women in Combat from the U.S. Army's War college contains similar observations. One senior leader's narrative, recounting his experiences as a commander in Iraq, notes: "I found essentially no difference in the performance in combat situations between male and female junior officers. I found that male and female soldiers performed essentially the same." Paul L. Grossskruger, "Women Leaders in

Combat: One Commander's Perspective," in Michelle M. Putko and Douglas V. Johnson II, eds, *Women in Combat Compendium* (Carlisle, PA: Strategic Studies Institute, U.S. Army War College, 2008), 49.

11. See, for example, Randy Shilts, *Conduct Unbecoming* (New York: St. Martin's Press, 1993).

12. Communal showers are a rarity in the modern U.S. military, although they are still common in training environments.

13. Gary J Gates, "Gay Men and Lesbians in the U.S. Military: Estimates from Census 2000" (Washington, DC: Urban Institute, 2004), iii.

14. Ibid., iv.

15. There is substantial polling data regarding the social acceptance of homosexuality. See, for example, http://www.washingtonpost.com/wp-dyn/content/story/2008/07/18/ST2008071802580.html.

16. Gregory Herek and Aaron Belkin, "Sexual Orientation and Military Service: Prospects for Organizational and Individual Change in the United States," Prepublication draft to appear in T. W. Britt, A. B. Adler, and C. A. Castro, eds., *Military Life: The Psychology of Serving in Peace and Combat*, Vol. 4: *Military Culture* (Westport, CT: Praeger Security International, 2005), 119–142.

17. Aaron Belkin, "Don't Ask, Don't Tell: Is the Gay Ban Based on Military Necessity?" *Parameters* 33, no. 2 (Summer, 2003), 110–113.

18. As of June 2007, 58 Arab linguists had been dismissed from the military on the grounds of homosexuality since 1993, when DADT became policy. Stephan Benjamin, "Don't Ask, Don't Translate," *New York Times* Op ed, June 8, 2007. Available at http://www.nytimes.com/2007/06/08/opinion/08benjamin.html?_r=1&scp=1&sq=arab%20linguist%20homosexual&st=cse.

19. James H. Toner, "A Message to Garcia: Leading Soldiers in Moral Mayhem," in *The Future of the Army Profession,* ed. Lloyd J. Matthews (Boston: McGraw-Hill Primis Custom Publishing, 2002), 323.

20. Ibid., 334.

CHAPTER 8

Modern Military Identity

Many military members view their uniformed predecessors as a long line of tra-dition and identity. Indeed, some service members report that gaining a specific identity was one of the elements that attracted them to the military in the first place. As noted in chapter 3, there are well-established cultural themes in military life for any initiate to discover and emulate. A large part of military indoctrination is devoted to just such a process, and those who have been through it often do think of it as a meaningful and positive shift in self-concept.[1]

A serious ethical question looms, however, in light of the ever-changing world that modern military members face. Just what sort of identity is appropriate for the military or for individual components of the military? The problem is best approached through an examination of a few dimensions of identity that exhibit tensions. Although it is impossible to provide an in-depth examination of all of these tensions, this chapter surveys a few of the most obvious.

The first tension has to do with the huge role of military tradition as a constitu-ent of identity. Buildings and streets are named for iconic figures, and reverence for tradition is common in most military communities. But not all traditions are equally relevant for the present world.

The second tension has to do with obedience to military hierarchy. Although military effectiveness demands obedience, there are cases in which it is func-tionally inappropriate. This is especially so in cases where a superior may be unaware of crucial facts; in such cases it seems likely that disobedience would be excused. But the issue also crops up where adhering to guidance or orders would be ethically problematic, and doing so would cause people to be harmed or killed unnecessarily.

The third tension is similar, but on a larger scale; it lies in military subordination to civil control. This subordination helps ground a sense of service in the military community and a sense of respect, during at least some historical periods, for the military itself. But does subordination require silent compliance with decisions that rub against firmly held professional military opinion? The relationship between professional dissent and subordination can pose tough ethical issues.

A fourth tension for military identity involves how professionalism is to be understood. Much has been written about the military's identity as a professional identity. This is unsurprising, as many military training environments emphasize "professionalism" and typically convey the message that "being professional" is an ethical obligation. But these terms are used to mean different things in varying military contexts. The question is not whether a military member ought to "be professional," but rather just what professionalism means.

Tradition, Hierarchy, and Innovation

Traditions serve an important and ethically salient sociological purpose; they help to provide a self-concept for the members, both individually and collectively. Military members understand themselves as situated in a particular societal niche, and this in turn helps in framing the ethical dimensions of any given situation. A sense of tradition also aids in the functional imperatives of unit cohesion and devotion to the group. But there is more to tradition's role in the military. It provides a sense of connection to military members who have served in the past, especially to those who suffered greatly or died in the military. Here, a sense of obligation may be engendered that helps members both to understand the nature of the military and to motivate faithful service.

This tradition-minded and obedient self-concept, however, can be a double-edged sword. Times change and successful militaries must adapt to them. A reverence for the past can result in inadequate relevance to the present. The conservative-minded nature of some military practices may impede functionality in a world that does not adhere to tradition, or when an adversary exploits a reverence for military tradition. It is commonplace to hear that a given military is fighting "the last war." Examples abound. The widespread slaughter of the First World War was in large measure due to the advent of the machine gun's effectiveness against the sorts of massed infantry assaults that had characterized earlier wars. The Nazi assault into Poland was mechanized, but some of the defenders were on horseback. It may be impossible to know with certainty just what innovations the future will hold, but an uncritical reliance on "the way we've always done things" obviously courts peril.

Similarly, military identity is connected in strong ways to the notions of obedience and subordination of self. The obligation to obey lawful orders makes sense in a context where accomplishing a task requires the interlocked coordination individual efforts, especially when time is short. In some cases, the very survival of others depends on this obedient coordination. But in other cases, obedience can result in tragedy. The My Lai massacre of 1968 resulted, in part, from following orders that ought not to have been followed. The My Lai atrocity is especially illustrative in that an officer who witnessed part of it from a helicopter took the initiative to save a group of Vietnamese who would likely have been slaughtered in the absence of his actions. Witnessing the event from aloft, Warrant Officer Hugh Thompson landed his helicopter between a group of Vietnamese and the advancing American soldiers. Thompson ordered his gunner to shoot the Americans if they tried to harm the Vietnamese. The helicopter crew rescued one wounded child and flew him to safety. About 30 years later, the army awarded Thompson the Soldier's Medal for his heroism.[2]

None of this is to suggest that tradition and obedience should be jettisoned. It is, however, to suggest that military thinkers do well to consider tradition and obedience in light of the ethical obligation to keep a military as effective against present-day security threats as possible, and to be on the lookout for policies, practices, and mindsets that might impede adaptability or corrode respect for human rights. Whereas obedience is a functional imperative for the military, independence of mind is crucial as well.

Civil-Military Relations

Militaries are subject to civil authority in liberal democracies. This subordination is consistent with just war thinking (JWT) and further is justified on the grounds that the military exists to defend the rights of the citizenry who support them.

Concerns emerge, however, in the practical implementation of this hierarchical relationship. Two are mentioned here. First, there is the question of the military's commonality with and regard for the society it protects. Second is the matter of military subordination in the face of what it considers ill-informed direction.

A "Higher Calling"

Some say that the military is a microcosm of society at large, and this is likely true if universal military conscription is in place. But in an all-volunteer military, the assertion can come into serious doubt. At least in the case of the United States, in some ways the military does not reflect the population it protects. Both demographically and culturally, there is a palpable distance. And far from considering this a problem, as some might in a democracy, many military members seem to exude a sense of moral superiority over the citizenry.[3] This sense of a "higher calling" is palpable in much writing about military ethics. General Sir John Winthrop Hackett famously remarked that "A man can be selfish, cowardly, disloyal, false, fleeting, perjured, and morally corrupt in a wide variety of other ways and still be outstandingly good in pursuits in which other imperatives bear than those upon the fighting man. . . . What the bad man cannot be is a good sailor, or soldier, or airman. Military institutions thus form a repository of moral resource that should always be a source of strength within the state."[4]

This pride in moral character has both healthy and unhealthy consequences. On the one hand, the military virtues discussed in chapter 3 are to be valued whether those who embody them are in military service or not. What is imperative for the military member is a boon to civil living as well. On the other hand, cultivation of these virtues may tend to imbue the military, both individually and collectively, with a self-regarding sense of nobility that may rub against the idea of civil control of the military. Pride in military identity requires balance by an appropriate humility.

Subordination to Civilian Control and Military Hierarchy

Military members are expected to face dangerous situations on behalf of noncombatants. This relationship is well established. Ethical issues arise when military judgments about which dangers to face conflict with those of the civilian leadership.

An analogy may help clarify the matter. Consider an airliner in flight with 8 crewmembers and 80 passengers. The flight crew determines that continuing to the destination courts unjustifiable risk, and accordingly they make a decision to divert the flight to an alternate airport. This decision is based on professional expertise and carried out safely.

The decision may disappoint passengers, but few would consider second-guessing the flight crew's decision. And should someone do so, the final decision remains with the crew. It is worth noting that in an airliner, the client and the professional share the consequences of a decision together.

Move now to think of a physician and a patient. Here, the professional's fate is independent of the client's, but nonetheless a conscientious physician will always give the patient the best possible expert service. If the client ignores the doctor's advice, she may suffer harm, but the physician is likely to be unaffected.

In the case of civilian control over the military, however, the client's decisions are binding. This places special ethical burdens on the military professional, as professional expertise may render a judgment that is at odds with obedience to the client's commands.

The best known case of this sort of conflict culminated in the July 1944 assassination attempt against Adolf Hitler. In that case, a plot was hatched among senior military officers to kill Hitler and take the political reins of Germany before it was destroyed by the encroaching Allied armies. Few crises in military ethics make it to this point, but the tension is nonetheless a relevant one today. In the United States, the phenomenon is most usually made manifest to the civilian populace by retired military officers criticizing civil authority's policies or decisions. But within the military, it is no secret that professional conscience may urge what obedience forbids.

Numerous options emerge in the face of such a tension. One is simply to resign from office, allowing the supposedly misguided policy to remain in effect but not participating in it oneself. This option may offer some sort of relief to conscience, but it is less than ideal for two reasons. First, from an ethical point of view, the sort of person who is bothered enough to contemplate resignation on grounds of professional conscience is probably just the sort of person who should stay in the military. Second, the resignation does nothing to ameliorate the problematic order or policy.

A second option is to allow the ethical obligation of obedience to trump the dictates of professional technical expertise. Often, this may be the best option, as few military members have all of the knowledge that senior civilian leadership has. Moreover, the ethical backdrop to military ethics demands that professional militaries act only on the legitimate authority of the states that support them. Although it is true that authority and wisdom are not always coextensive, the alternative to military subordination may be much more ethically distressing. In other words, it is a virtue to have trust in the system and humility about one's own perspective. Of course, it may remain the case that a given policy or order is ill-conceived.

A third option, which is likely closer to the ideal, is to confront the matter to try to discover how professional expertise might be deployed to address the tension. Under this option, harmony may emerge as the professional concerns inform superiors in a way that might improve their leadership. Ideally, the professional military expertise, including ethical expertise, is sufficiently compelling to persuade one's superiors.

Professional Issues

Career military members often describe themselves as professionals. But what military professionalism amounts to is controversial, as is the question of what constitutes a profession in the first place. As Martin Cook has noted, in the military use, the term *professionalism* can take on many meanings, from denoting good moral character to evaluating how neatly an officer's desk is arranged.[5]

Models of Professionalism

The idea of a profession has stimulated many analyses over the years. Capturing the essence of what constitutes a profession, as opposed to an occupation or job, is surprisingly difficult. From the point of view of professional ethics, two lines of attack seem promising. The first conceives of a profession as defined by the peculiar expertise it exercises. This approach understands a profession as a specialized occupational jurisdiction requiring extensive formal education. Licensing is often in place to recognize the expertise and to preclude laymen from encroaching on the professional domain of practice.

The second approach emphasizes the societal function the profession provides. Here, the profession is characterized by its service to an enduring societal need. On this model, although the techniques may vary over time, and with them the education and expertise required, the function does not.

Jurisdictions. Professional identity may be understood in terms of a delineated jurisdiction in which a specialized expertise is applied.[6] To appreciate this approach, consider how the medical professional practices.

Physicians may be thought of as working in a protected occupational space. For example, they may prescribe drugs for their clients, but lay persons cannot.

To prescribe drugs requires specialized knowledge, acquired by an equally specialized educational regimen. Moreover, access to the jurisdiction is controlled by practicing members. They set the standards of professional conduct required for entry and evaluate success or failure to meet those standards. An individual wishing to become a physician is required to attend medical school and master a particular body of knowledge. To become a licensed physician is to subject one's capabilities to strict scrutiny and to commit to recurrent education as the field advances. Those who fail to meet these standards are not permitted the privileges that those who do enjoy. In short, the barriers to the medical profession are high, and the occupational space within them is generally well protected.

To the degree that physicians regulate themselves, their jurisdiction is their own to populate, but a jurisdiction with no clientele would be no jurisdiction at all. Hence, social acceptance is required for the physician's jurisdiction to have meaning. Patients must trust that granting jurisdiction over their health to the medical community is in their best interests. If this trust is in place, clients grant the medical community authority over medical matters, and a jurisdiction is commonly recognized.

This is not to suggest that the jurisdiction remains stable; recent years have seen it come under threat. Two specific challenges are easy to identify. The first comes from nontraditional sources of medical assistance. For example, the use of "dietary supplements" for the maintenance and restoration of health has exploded despite skepticism regarding their use within the medical community. Likewise, the increasing use of the Internet has made self-diagnosis widespread. Developments such as these represent movement of jurisdictional borders.

A second challenge originates in economics and business practices. The health insurance system providing financial coverage over much of the medical care delivered in the United States imposes requirements on many medical professionals to justify their expenses. These requirements complicate professional medical life, as the practitioner must consider an insurer's reaction to a particular cost. The practitioner's concern for the patient's well-being may conflict with the insurance company's economic obligations. Depending on how that conflict is resolved, this tension between professional ethical judgment and economic reality may threaten the professional's jurisdiction. Similar tensions emerge for the military in the face of bureaucratic regulation and civil control. Budget negotiations for military equipment and personnel, for example, may place professional military judgment at odds with other governmental or political imperatives. Unlike the physician, however, who may have an option to cease accepting certain forms of insurance, the military has no choice but to work for its own government.

Like the medical community, the military possesses a specific sort of expertise and enjoys a jurisdiction spelled out in part by JWT. Samuel Huntington's classic book, *The Soldier and the State,* took the military officer's specific expertise to be the "management of violence."[7] Some military members stand by that definition; it does provide a fairly stark jurisdictional boundary. But others point out that their expertise has little if anything to do with violence. Many military members, especially in the more technically oriented military services such as air forces, remain quite distant from violence over their entire careers.

If the jurisdictional approach is used to describe the military as a profession, it is necessary to come to a shared understanding of just what expertise the military is to possess. In some cases, this is difficult, as the military is composed of many varied fields of expertise. Combat-related specialties, such as infantry or missile launch officer, have no readily identifiable civilian counterparts, and accordingly the jurisdictional boundaries are fairly clear. But this is not so for other military occupations, such as accountant or pilot. In cases like these, it can be difficult to explain just how a uniformed military member's expertise differs from that of a civilian. Accordingly, if the management of violence is taken to characterize military expertise, many military members would be left out. Yet, the military's finance branches seem to require consideration as military professionals even though they have civilian counterparts performing essentially the same functions and possessing nearly identical expertise. Likewise, one may reasonably ask whether the expertise possessed by a pilot of an aerial tanker is materially different from that possessed by pilots at an airline flying essentially the same airframe.

With these difficulties in mind, it would seem that returning to the definition of the military's peculiar expertise as the management of violence would be to exclude many in uniform from identification as professionals. On the other hand, many of the daily tasks performed by uniformed military members are virtually identical to many nonmilitary occupations, so military professionalism must not rely on professional expertise alone.

One way to address this issue is to approach military identity from the perspective of purpose. That is, one can characterize the military identity less by what functions it performs and more by the purpose those functions serve. Doing so complements the identity provided by understanding the military's jurisdiction with an appreciation of the specialized ends that military people are to serve.

Functional Approach to Military Professional Identity. On this avenue of approach, understanding professionalism relies on understanding the enduring societal needs professionals are to meet. For example, communities always require health, and the medical profession has been in place to serve that need over time. Notably, however, the theories and practices of that profession have varied with context, and therefore so has the specific nature of the required expertise. Variations in the jurisdictions of various occupational specialties are to be expected as research and development addresses the needs of the community. Afflictions that once required a visit to the doctor can now be treated using over-the-counter medications.

Like the need for health, security needs endure in all communities, but the sorts of expertise best suited to meeting those needs change. It may be tempting to ground professional identity in certain forms of practice, but such a grounding may prove tenuous. For much of history, good horsemanship was critical to certain sorts of military function. Today, horses are rarely involved in military operations. Accordingly, basing military identity on the sorts of "platforms" a service operates may prove only a temporary solution. Air forces came into being with the airplane, and much of their identity remains tied to that technology. The advent of unmanned cruise missiles and remotely piloted vehicles, as well as evolutions in satellite technology, all in the past 50 years, offer challenges to an airplane-centric identity.

Meeting an enduring need effectively depends on a subset of a community devoting itself to mastering the best techniques for doing so. Should that subset be successful, it may well come to occupy a particular jurisdiction, but the boundaries of that jurisdiction will likely vary even as the need for professional commitment and expertise endure. The very word "profess" may be understood as signifying an individual's identifying himself as devoted to serving an enduring need. On this understanding of professionalism, then, purpose is much more fundamental than jurisdiction.

This functionally oriented line can help capture military members such as the aerial tanker pilot. Although it grants that the expertise required varies little from that demanded of an airline pilot, the purpose of mastering how to fly a tanker differs greatly from the purpose served by mastering how to fly an airliner. The first serves security by transporting and transferring fuel; the second meets a need for transportation but has little or no direct relationship to meeting security needs. Something similar may be said for the military's finance branch as opposed to a civilian accounting firm.

There is another vital ethical aspect to professional military identity. This is the professed willingness to exercise expertise pursuant to the client's orders under potentially lethal circumstances. This willingness to sacrifice characterizes military professionalism further and distinguishes it from most other endeavors.

It is probably healthy to admit that military ethics can identify only some aspects of professional military identity. A profession is weakened less by admitting that there is ambiguity attendant to its identity than it is by asserting a professional identity that is not borne out by reality.

Notes

1. An excellent treatment is available in Thomas E. Ricks, *Making the Corps* (New York: Scribner, 1997).

2. James H. Toner, *Morals Under the Gun: The Cardinal Virtues, Military Ethics, and American Society* (Lexington: The University Press of Kentucky, 2000), 122–124.

3. Thomas Ricks, "The Widening Gap Between the Military and Society," *The Atlantic Monthly* 280, no. 1 (1997): 66–78.

4. Sir John Winthrop Hackett, "The Military in the Service of the State," in *War, Morality and the Military Profession*, ed. Malham M. Wakin (Boulder, CO: Westview Press, 1986), 119.

5. Martin Cook, *The Moral Warrior: Ethics and Service in the U.S. Military* (Albany: State University of New York, 2004), 56.

6. See, for example, Andrew Abbott, *The System of Professions: An Essay on the Division of Expert Labor* (Chicago: University of Chicago Press, 1988).

7. Samuel Huntington, *The Soldier and the State* (Cambridge, MA: The Belknap Press of Harvard University Press, 1957), 11.

Selected Bibliography

Abbott, Andrew. *The System of Professions: An Essay on the Division of Expert Labor*. Chicago: University of Chicago Press, 1988.

Allison, Graham T., and Paul X. Kelley. "Nonlethal Weapons and Capabilities." In *Report of an Independent Task Force sponsored by the Council on Foreign Relations*. New York: Council on Foreign Relations Press, 2004.

Anscombe, G.E.M. "War and Murder." In *The Morality of War*. Edited by Larry May, Eric Rovie, and Steve Viner. Upper Saddle River, NJ: Pearson Education, 2006.

Aristotle. *The Basic Works of Aristotle*. Edited by Richard McKeon. New York: Random House, 1941.

Augustine, St. *The City of God*. Translated by Marcus Dods. New York: The Modern Library, 1950.

Bainton, Roland H. *Christian Attitudes Toward War and Peace: A Historical Survey and Critical Re-evaluation*. New York: Abingdon Press, 1960.

Belkin, Aaron. "Don't Ask, Don't Tell: Is the Gay Ban Based on Military Necessity?" *Parameters*, 33 (2003): 110–113.

Benjamin, Stephan. "Don't Ask, Don't Translate," *New York Times*, June 8, 2007, Op Ed.

Best, Geoffery. *Humanity in Warfare*. New York: Columbia University Press, 1980.

Best, Geoffery. *War and Law since 1945*. New York: Oxford University Press, 1994.

Bourke, Joanna. *An Intimate History of Killing: Face-to-Face Killing in Twentieth-Century Warfare*. n.p.: Basic Books, 1999.

Brown, Dale W. *Biblical Pacifism: A Peace Church Perspective*. Elgin, IL: Brethren Press, 1986.

Browning, Christopher R. *Ordinary Men: Reserve Battalion 101 and the Final Solution in Poland*. New York: Harper Perrenial, 1998.

Cadoux, John C. *The Early Christian Attitude to War*. New York: The Seabury Press, 1982.

Challans, Timothy L. *Awakening Warrior: Revolution in the Ethics of Warfare*. Albany, NY: State University of New York Press, 2007.

Childress, James F. *Moral Responsibility in Conflicts*. Baton Rouge: Louisiana State University Press, 1982.

Christopher, Paul. *The Ethics of War and Peace*. Englewood Cliffs, NJ: Prentice-Hall, 1994.

Clausewitz, Carl von. *On War*. Edited with an Introduction by Anatol Rapoport. Translated by J. J. Graham. New York: Penguin Books, 1982.

Cook, Martin L. *The Moral Warrior: Ethics and Service in the U.S Military*. Albany: State University of New York Press, 2004.

Dombrowski, Daniel A. *Christian Pacifism*. Philadelphia: Temple University Press, 1991.

Dunnigan, James F. *How to Make War: A Comprehensive Guide to Modern Warfare for the Post-Cold War Era*. 3rd ed. New York: William Morrow and Company, 1993.

Dyer, Gwynne. *War: The Lethal Custom*. New York: Carroll & Graf Publishers, 2004.

Falk, Stanley L. *Bataan: The March of Death*. New York: W. W. Norton and Co., 1962.

Fenner, Lorry M., and Marie E. deYoung. *Women in Combat: Civic Duty or Military Liability?* Washington, DC: Georgetown University Press, 2001.

Fotion, Nicholas G. *Military Ethics: Looking Toward the Future*. Stanford, CO: Hoover Institution Press, 1990.

Fotion, Nicholas G., and G. Elfstrom. *Military Ethics: Guidelines for Peace and War*. Boston: Routledge and Kegan Paul, 1986.

Frencke, Linda Bird. *Ground Zero: The Gender Wars in the Military*. New York: Simon and Schuster, 1997.

Gates, Gary J. "Gay Men and Lesbians in the U.S. Military: Estimates from Census 2000." Washington, DC: The Urban Institute, 2004.

Gilbert, Martin. *The Second World War: A Complete History*, rev. ed. New York: Henry Holt, 1989.

Goldhagen, Daniel J. *Hitler's Willing Executioners: Ordinary Germans and the Holocaust*. New York: Alfred A. Knopf, 1996.

Goldman, Nancy L., ed. *Female Soldiers—Combatants or Noncombatants?* Westport, CT: Greenwood Press, 1982.

Grossskruger, Paul L. "Women Leaders in Combat: One Commander's Perspective." In *Women in Combat Compendium*. Edited by Michelle M. Putko and Douglas V. Johnson II. Carlisle, PA: Strategic Studies Institute, U.S. Army War College, 2008.

Grossman, Dave. *On Killing: The Psychological Cost of Learning to Kill in War and Society*. Boston: Little, Brown, 1996.

Grotius, Hugo. *The Law of War and Peace*. Translated by Louise R. Loomis. Roslyn, NY: Walter J. Black, 1949.

Hackett, John Winthrop. "The Military in the Service of the State." In *War, Morality and the Military Profession*. Edited by Malham M. Wakin. Boulder, CO: Westview Press, 1986.

Hanson, Victor Davis. *The Soul of Battle: From Ancient Times to the Present Day, How Three Great Liberators Vanquished Tyranny*. New York: Simon and Schuster, 1999.

Harnell, Margaret C., and Laura Miller. *New Opportunities for Military Women: Effects upon Readiness, Cohesion, and Morale*. Santa Monica, CA: RAND Corporation, 1997.

Hartle, Anthony E. *Moral Issues in Military Decision Making*. Lawrence: University Press of Kansas, 1989.

Hauerwas, Stanley. "Pacifism: Some Philosophical Considerations." In *War, Morality, and the Military Profession*. Edited by Malham M. Wakin. Boulder, CO: Westview Press, 1986.

Herek, Gregory M., Jared B. Jobe, and Ralph M. Carney. *Out in Force: Sexual Orientation and the Military*. Chicago: The University of Chicago Press, 1996.

Hobbes, Thomas. *Leviathan: Parts I and II*. Indianapolis: Bobbs-Merrill 1958.

Holm, Jeanne. *Women in the Military: An Unfinished Revolution*. Novato, CA: Presidio Press, 1982.

Holmes, Arthur F., ed. *War and Christian Ethics*. Grand Rapids, MI: Baker Book House, 1975.

Holmes, Richard. *Acts of War: The Behavior of Men in Battle*. New York: The Free Press, 1985.

Holmes, Robert L. *On War and Morality*. Princeton: Princeton University Press, 1989.

Huntington, Samuel P. *The Soldier and the State*. Cambridge, MA: The Belknap Press of Harvard University Press, 1957.

Ignatieff, Michael. *The Warrior's Honor: Ethnic War and the Modern Conscience*. New York: Henry Holt, 1997.

Johnson, James Turner. *Can Modern War be Just?* New Haven: Yale University Press, 1984.

Johnson, James Turner. *Just War Tradition and the Restraint of War: A Moral and Historical Inquiry*. Princeton, NJ: Princeton University Press, 1981.

Johnson, James Turner. *Morality and Contemporary Warfare*. New Haven: Yale University Press, 1999.

Johnson, James Turner, and John Kelsay, eds. *Cross, Crescent, and Sword: The Justification and Limitation of War in Western and Islamic Tradition*. New York: Greenwood Press, 1990.

Jones, David E. *Women Warriors: A History*. Washington DC: Brassey's, 1997.

Kant, Immanuel. *On History*. Translated by Lewis White Beck, Robert E. Anchor, and Emil L. Fackenheim. Indianapolis: Bobbs-Merrill, 1963.

Keegan, John. *A History of Warfare*. New York: Alfred A Knopf, 1993.

Keegan, John. *The Face of Battle*. New York: Military Heritage Press, 1976.

Keegan, John. *The First World War*. New York: Alfred A. Knopf, 1999.

Keegan, John. *The Second World War*. New York: Penguin Books, 1989.

Kelsay, John and James Turner Johnson, eds. *Just War and Jihad: Historical and Theoretical Perspectives on War and Peace in Western and Islamic Traditions*. New York: Greenwood Press, 1991.

Kennedy, David M. *Freedom from Fear: The American People in Depression and War, 1929–1945*. New York: Oxford University Press, 1999.

Kilner, Peter. "Military Leaders' Obligation to Justify Killing in War." *Military Review*, March-April, (2002): 24–31.

Lackey, Douglas. *The Ethics of War and Peace*. Englewood Cliffs, NJ: Prentice Hall, 1989.

Lorenz, F. M. "Non-Lethal Force: The Slippery Slope to War?" *Parameters* 26, no. 3 (1996): 52–62.

Luban, David. "Just War and Human Rights" In *The Morality of War*. Edited by Larry May, Eric Rovie, and Steve Viner. Upper Saddle River, NJ: Pearson Education, 2006.

MacCoun, Robert J. "Sexual Orientation and Military Cohesion: A Critical Review of the Evidence." In *Out in Force: Sexual Orientation and the Military*. Edited by Gregory M. Herek, Jared B. Jobe, and Ralph M. Carney. Chicago: University of Chicago Press, 1996.

MacIntyre, Alisdair. *After Virtue: A Study in Moral Theory,* 2nd ed. Notre Dame, IN: University of Notre Dame Press, 1984.

Marrin, Albert, ed. *War and the Christian Conscience: From Augustine to Martin Luther King, Jr.* Chicago: Henry Regnery, 1971.

Marshall, S.L.A. *Men Against Fire: The Problem of Battle Command in Future War*. Washington and New York: The Infantry Journal and William Morrow, 1947.

Matthews, Lloyd J., ed. *The Future of the Army Profession*. Boston: McGraw-Hill Primis Custom Publishing, 2002.

May, Larry, Eric Rovie, and Steve Viner, eds. *The Morality of War: Classical and Contemporary Readings*. Upper Saddle River, NJ: Pearson Education, 2006.

McMahan, Jeff. "Innocence, Self-Defense and Killing in War." *Ethics* 114 (2004): 693–733.

Mitchell, Brian. *Weak Link: The Feminization of the American Military*. Washington, DC: Regnery Gateway, 1989.

Mitchell, Brian. *Women in the Military: Flirting with Disaster*. Washington DC: Regnery Publishing, 1998.

Morgenthau, Hans J. *Politics Among Nations*, 4th ed. New York: Alfred A. Knopf, 1967.

Muir, Kate. *Arms and the Woman*. London: Sinclair-Stevenson, 1992.

Murphy, Jeffrie G. "The Killing of the Innocent." In *War, Morality and the Military Profession*. Edited by Malham M. Wakin. Boulder, CO: Westview Press, 1986.

Myers, Charles R. "The Core Values: Framing and Resolving Ethical Issues for the Air Force," *Airpower Journal* 11, no. 1 (1997): 38–53.

Myers, David G. *Psychology: Eighth Edition in Modules*. New York: Worth Publishers 2007.

Narveson, Jan. "Pacifism: A Philosophical Analysis." In *The Morality of War.* Edited by Larry May, Eric Rovie, and Steve Viner, Upper Saddle River, NJ: Pearson Education, 2006.

National Conference of Catholic Bishops, *The Challenge of Peace: God's Promise and Our Response*. Washington, DC: United States Catholic Conference, 1983.

Nelson, T. S. *For Love of Country: Confronting Rape and Sexual Harassment in the U.S. Military*. New York: The Haworth Press, 2002.

New English Bible. Cambridge: The Cambridge University Press, 1970.

Norman, Richard. *Ethics, Killing and War*. Cambridge: Cambridge University Press, 1995.

Orend, Brian. *The Morality of War*. Peterborough, Ontario: Broadview Press, 2006.

Plato. *Republic*. Trans. G.M.A. Grube Rev. C.D.C. Reeve. Indianapolis: Hackett, 1992.

Potter, Ralph B. *War and Moral Discourse*. Richmond, VA: John Knox Press, 1969.

Putko, Michelle M., and Douglas V. Johnson, eds. *Women in Combat Compendium*. Carlisle, PA: Strategic Studies Institute, U.S. Army War College, 2008.

Rachels, James. *The Elements of Moral Philosophy*. New York: Random House, 1986.

Ramsey, Paul. *The Just War: Force and Political Responsibility*. Savage, MD: Littlefield Adams Quality Paperbacks, 1983.

Rawls, John. *A Theory of Justice*. Cambridge, MA: The Belknap Press of Harvard University Press, 1971.

Reichberg, Gregory M., Henrick Syse, and Endre Begby, eds. *The Ethics of War: Classic and Contemporary Readings*. Malden, MA: Blackwell Publishing, 2006.

Ricks, Thomas E. *Making the Corps*. New York: Scribner, 1997.

Ricks, Thomas E. "The Widening Gap Between the Military and Society," *The Atlantic Monthly* 280 (1997): 66–78.

Robinson, Paul, ed. *Just War in Comparative Perspective*. Burlington, VT: Ashgate Publishing, 2003.

Rodin, David. "War and Self-Defense." In *The Morality of War.* Edited by Larry May, Eric Rovie, and Steve Viner, Upper Saddle River, NJ: Pearson Education, 2006.

Sharp, Gene. *The Politics of Nonviolent Action, Part One: Power and Struggle*. Boston: Porter Sargent Publishers, 1973.

Sharp, Gene. *The Politics of Nonviolent Action, Part Two: The Methods of Nonviolent Action*. Boston: Porter Sargent Publishers, 1973.

Sharp, Gene. *The Politics of Nonviolent Action, Part Three: The Dynamics of Nonviolent Action*. Boston: Porter Sargent Publishers, 1973.

Shilts, Randy. *Conduct Unbecoming*. New York: St. Martin's Press, 1993.

Shirer, William. *The Rise and Fall of the Third Reich*. New York: Simon and Shuster, Inc, 1959.

Shue, Henry. *Basic Rights: Subsistence, Affluence, and U.S. Foreign Policy,* 2nd ed. Princeton: Princeton University Press, 1996.

Starke, J. G. *Introduction to International Law,* 10th ed. London: Butterworths, 1989.

Sulzberger, C. L., and the Editors of American Heritage. *The American Heritage Picture History of World War II.* n.p.: American Heritage Publishing, 1966.

Thucydides. *The Landmark Thucydides: A Comprehensive Guide to the Peloponnesian War.* Rev. Ed. Translated by Richard Crawley, Edited by Robert B. Strassler. New York: Free Press, 1996.

Toner, James H. "A Message to Garcia: Leading Soldiers in Moral Mayhem." In *The Future of the Army Profession.* Edited by Lloyd J. Matthews. Boston: McGraw-Hill Primis Custom Publishing, 2002.

Toner, James H. *Morals Under the Gun: The Cardinal Virtues, Military Ethics, and American Society.* Lexington: The University Press of Kentucky, 2000.

U.S. Air Force Academy. *Contrails.* (2008–2009).

U.S. Department of the Army. *The Law of Land Warfare,* Field Manual 27–10. Washington, DC, 1956.

U.S. Department of the Army. *Standards of Medical Fitness,* Army Regulation 40–501. Washington, DC: December, 2007, Rev. September 10, 2008), 102–103 (Department of the Navy) 1:5, 1:8.

U.S. Department of the Army. *Treaties Governing Land Warfare,* Department of the Army Pamphlet 27–1, Washington DC, December, 1956.

U.S. Department of the Navy. *Guidelines Concerning Pregnancy and Parenthood,* OPNAVINST 6000.1c. Washington, DC, June 14, 2007.

U.S. Government Printing Office. "Declarations of a State of War with Japan, Germany, and Italy," 77th Congress 1st Session, President Roosevelt's address to Joint Session, December 8, 1941.

Wakin, Malham M, ed. *War, Morality, and the Military Profession,* 2nd ed. Boulder, CO: Westview Press, 1986.

Waldron, Jeremy, ed. *Theories of Rights.* Oxford: Oxford University Press, 1984.

Walzer, Michael. *Arguing about War.* New Haven: Yale University Press, 2004.

Walzer, Michael. *Just and Unjust Wars.* New York: Basic Books, 1977.

Wasserstrom, Richard. "On the Morality of War: A Preliminary Inquiry." In *War, Morality and the Military Profession.* Edited by Malham M. Wakin. Boulder, CO: Westview Press, 1986.

Webb, James. "Women Can't Fight," *Washingtonian Magazine,* November, 1979. http://www.washingtonian.com/articles/people/2182.html.

White House. *The National Security Strategy of the United States, 2002.* Washington, DC: The White House, 2002.

White House. *The National Security Strategy of the United States, 2006.* Washington, DC: The White House, 2006.

Yoder, John Howard. *The Politics of Jesus.* Grand Rapids, MI: William B. Eerdman's Publishing, 1972.

Yoder, John Howard. *When War Is Unjust: Being Honest in Just War Thinking,* 2nd ed. Maryknoll, NY: Orbis Books, 1996.

Zeigler, Sara L., and Gregory G. Gunderson. *Moving Beyond G. I. Jane: Women and the U.S. Military.* Lanham, MD: University Press of America, 2005.

Zupan, Daniel S. *War, Morality, and Autonomy: An Investigation in Just War Theory.* Burlington, VT: Ashgate Publishing, 2004.

Index

About the Author

BILL RHODES earned his PhD in philosophy at the University of Colorado, Boulder in 1996. He conducts research and development in professional ethics for his company Aerworthy Consulting, LLC., in Franktown, Colorado. He is also Director of the International Society of Military Ethics, a nonprofit organization. A retired military officer, Dr. Rhodes has taught philosophy and professional ethics to military services practitioners for more than 15 years.